A Grand American Enigma

"A Grand American Enigma"

Exploring the Foundations of the Latter-day Saints

Edward Eugene McIsaac

A Grand American Enigma

Exploring the Foundations of the Latter-day Saints

First Printing June, 2023.

Copyright © 2023.

All rights reserved.

Cover photo of Thorvaldsen's Christus taken by Rachael Batie-French

Cover design by McKenzie McIsaac.

ISBN: 979-8-396-85346-1

Library of Congress Cataloging-in-Publication Data is available.

All Scriptural references from various translations have been noted in the body of the narrative.

Printed in the United States of America.

Acknowledgments

I would like to recognize the following people for taking time to read drafts of several chapters of this book and for their helpful suggestions and comments that aided and promoted its evolution. I thank both Larry Eskridge, author and staff member of the Institute for the Study of American Evangelicals at Wheaton College (now retired), and Lynn Wilder, a Christian author and former Brigham Young University professor. I would be remiss if I did not mention my immediate family who, through patient endurance, have given me grace to see this project through to its completion.

The author may be contacted at:

agrandamericanenigma@gmail.com

"Beloved, when I gave all diligence to write unto you of the common salvation, it was needful for me to write unto you, and exhort you that ye should earnestly contend for the faith which was once delivered unto the saints" (*Jude 1:3 KJV*).

Contents:

Introduction   *1*

Chapter Headings

Volume I

1.   *"A Grand American Enigma"*   *24*

2.   *The Historicity of the "Golden Plates"*   *46*

3.   *View of the Hebrews*   *75*

4.   *The Supersession of Mormonism*   *119*

5.   *"Upon This Rock I Will Build My Church"*   *147*

6.   *"The Keys of the Kingdom"*   *165*

7.   *God's Blanket Denouncement*   *178*

8.   *Was there a Great Apostasy?*   *193*

9.   *"The Spirit of Man is the Candle of the Lord"*   *238*

10. *A "Homely, Wild, Vulgar Fanaticism"*   *252*

NOTES   *273*

Volume II

11. *A Clash of Doctrines*

12. *The Citadel of Mormonism*

13. *"Zion Shall Not Be Moved out of Her Place"*

14. *The Fifth Gospel: Another Testament*

15. *The Book of Abraham*

16. *"Heaven is My Throne and the Earth is My Footstool"*

17. *The Vision of the Redemption of the Dead*

18. *The Veil Between the Living and the Dead*

19. *Mediums and Familiar Spirits*

20. *The Whole Doctrine of Christianity*

Volume III

21. *A Greater Than Solomon Is Here*

22. *First Vision—A Personal Theophany*

23. *An Incredible Convergence of "Heavenly Emissaries"*

24. *Spiritual Wifery—Joseph Smith's Plural Marriage Revelation*

25. *The Law of Eternal Progression*

26. *Disreputable Witnesses*

27. *A Question of Authority*

28. *"A Purely American Gnosis"*

29. *Philosophical Meanderings and Theological Odysseys*

30. *The Doctrine of Divine Sonship*

Volume IV

31. *"Puny God"*

32. *"In the Beginning"*

33. *The Ultimate Origin of All Things*

34. *The Pumpkinification of the Divine*

35. *The Basis of the Universe*

36. *"Ye Are From Beneath; I Am From Above"*

37. *The Superior Ministrations of Christ*

38. *The Conference of the Melchizedek Priesthood*

39. *Salvation by Grace Alone*

40. *Archaeological Evidence for the Book of Mormon*

1

Introduction

With any religious institution, there is an inseverable connection between the historical roots of its founding and the ideological belief system of its devotees, history inevitably determining the contextual framework for the present. History is the potter's clay and matrix that ultimately brandishes the wearer's cloth. The contemporary zeitgeist of the Church of Jesus Christ of Latter-day Saints (also known simply as "Latter-day Saints" abbreviated LDS), whose congregants are colloquially and historically known as Mormons, cannot be fully understood without embracing "What's past is prologue."[1] Pandit Jawaharlal Nehru (1889-1964), Prime minister of the Republic of India, well said: *"You don't change the course of history by turning the faces of portraits to the wall."* C. S. Lewis' criticism of what he called " 'Chronological Snobbery,' the uncritical acceptance of the intellectual climate common to our own age and the assumption that whatever has gone out of date is on that account discredited" seems to be a truism that reflects Mormonism's current state of affairs.[2] It is the objective of this narrative to pull back the curtain, and unmask the principle players whose script and dais lie in obscurity behind the edifice now before us.

In the early nineteenth century of antebellum America, Mormonism arose as a specter on the stage of religious absolutism, demanding recognition as "the only true and living Church upon the face of the whole earth," while shamelessly unhinging the "entire gospel framework" of the doctrinal creeds and "Councils of Antiquity," reconfiguring Christian orthodoxy and the very nature of the Godhead. Joseph Smith (1805-1844), Mormonism's founding Prophet and first President, contravened the mores of conventional wisdom and clearly defined Biblical mandates by reinterpreting and profusely adding to, what orthodox Christians believe is, the already complete and unamenable corpus of the Scriptural canon. In addition to the *Bible* (The LDS Church uses the Authorized *King James Version* as its official *Bible* for historical continuity with the so-called "restoration"), the Latter-day Saints have canonized the *Book of Mormon*, the *Pearl of Great Price* and the *Doctrine and Covenants*. Joseph Smith shamelessly, and devil-may-care, exploited and redefined the norms of commonly held beliefs, implicitly demanding that his followers commit themselves to a totally new paradigm of who God is and how it is that God saves. Smith boldly asserted his calling and preeminence as *the* chosen arbiter (appointed by Moroni, an "angelic" messenger) heralding in the so-called "Restoration" of the Kingdom of God, establishing the ideal theocratic society (a "theocratic democracy," or as some have suggested, a theocratic despotism) in what the Mormon Church has defined as "The Last Dispensation."

Mormon apologists Fiona and Terryl Givens conclude the "Restoration" of the Church of Jesus Christ of Latter-day Saints called for "a wholesale rehabilitation of religious vocabulary," suggesting that Joseph Smith went about unmooring the familiarity of well-established terms within the Christian vernacular, recasting and redefining "*Salvation, heaven, the Fall, sin, repentance, forgiveness, justice, atonement, grace, obedience, worthiness, and judgment,*" reframing each concept "in the context of a different story, with a different beginning and a different plot." Fiona and Terryl offer: "If you change the beginning, you change the ending— and everything in between." Ergo, Joseph Smith's reinterpretation of the *Genesis* account of creation as found in his "translation" of the *Book of Abraham* (in what Mormons call the *Pearl of Great Price*). In *All Things New*, Fiona and Terryl quote from Edward Beecher's *The Concord of Ages* where he states: " 'If there is in fact a malignant power intent on making a fixed and steady opposition to the progress and the cause of God' he would 'pervert and disgrace' the story of our true origins." Indeed! To rewrite the story of man's *Genesis* as Joseph Smith did in his spurious rendition of the so-called *Book of Abraham* (which includes his vision of the cosmos and its creation) qualifies as a flagrant "fixed and steady opposition" intended to upend the mores of traditional Christianity. (See the chapter titled *The Book of Abraham* Volume II.) Fiona and Terryl Givens admit "the Saints espouse a different story with a different beginning and end . . ." Fiona and Terryl Givens contend: "One can live in blithe indifference to, or in ignorance of, one's historical foundations and still be profoundly shaped by them in ways large and small."[3]

The Mormon religion (America's largest home-grown religion), as are all religions, is predicated upon unique historical events that have molded and configured its narrative. Events such as Joseph Smith's "First Vision" and the historicity of the *Book of Mormon* (both topics which are covered in depth in the chapters and volumes to follow) have become foundational elements and pillars of the Mormon faith. The obfuscated tapestry of Mormon history is notoriously polemical, if not sordid in part, particularly when reflecting on its scandalous practice of polygamy (mollified by the alternate terms "Spiritual Wifery" and "Celestial Marriage") for nearly half a century, and its shameful and unconscionable stance concerning Blacks (for Mormons, a stigmatized race because of the so-called "curse of Cain"—Black being a "mark" of inferiority). Polygamy was first introduced into the Biblical narrative through Lamach of Cain's lineage who was the "archetypal bad guy of the prediluvian world" (see *Genesis 4:16-24*). (For more on the topic of polygamy, see the chapter titled "*Spiritual Wifery—Joseph Smith's Plural Marriage Revelation,*" Volume III.)

Brigham Young (1801-1877), who became the second president of the Church of Jesus Christ of Latter-day Saints from 1847 until his death in 1877, pronounced, "*Shall I tell you the law of God in regard to the African race? If the white man who belongs to the chosen seed mixes his blood with the seed of Cain, the penalty, under the law of God, is death on the spot. This will always be so*"[4] In a Latter-day Saint church publication in 1868, the *Juvenile Instructor* (a monthly periodical first published in 1866) featured an article titled, "From Caucasian to Negro" where the Negro was characterized as:

> [T]he lowest in intelligence and the most barbarous of all the children of men. The race whose intellect is the least developed, whose advancement has been the slowest who appear to be the least capable of improvement of all people. The hand of the Lord appears to be heavy upon them, dwarfing them by the

side of their fellow men in every thing good and great.

In 1947, the First Presidency of the Church of Jesus Christ of Latter-day Saints (also called the Quorum of the Presidency of the Church or simply the Presidency) consisting of President George Albert Smith, and his First Counselor J. Reuben Clark, and his Second Counselor David O. McKay, issued a letter to Dr. Lowry Nelson, a prominent Mormon who criticized Church policy in this matter, stating:

> From the days of the Prophet Joseph [Smith] even until now, it has been the doctrine of the Church, never questioned by any of the Church leaders, that the Negroes are not entitled to the full blessings of the Gospel.
>
> Furthermore, your ideas, as we understand them, appear to contemplate the intermarriage of the Negro and White races, a concept which has heretofore been most repugnant to most normal-minded people from the ancient patriarchs till now. God's rule for Israel, his Chosen People, has been endogamous [marrying only within the limits of a local community, clan, or tribe]. Modern Israel has been similarly directed.
>
> We are not unmindful of the fact that there is a growing tendency, particularly among some educators, as it manifests itself in this area, toward the breaking down of race barriers in the matter of intermarriage between whites and blacks, but it does not have the sanction of the Church and is contrary to Church doctrine.[5]

John J. Stewart (1925-2014), a prolific author and Associate Professor of Journalism at the Utah State University of Logan, Utah, wrote in his book *Mormonism and the Negro*: "Extending brotherly Christian love to the Negro . . . does not and should not include intermarriage, for we would bring upon our children the curse of Cain . . ."[6] This indefensible policy of the Latter-day Saints strictly opposed interracial marriages with Whites and vehemently resisted their eligibility to hold the priesthood office from 1849 to 1978, a span of 129 years. An 1868 *Juvenile Instructor* article points to the *Pearl of Great Price* and the *Book of Abraham* as the "source of racial attitudes in church doctrine." This Mormon theology was attributed to the belief that the line of Ham—one of Noah's three sons—was ineligible to hold the "Priesthood" because Ham's wife (according to the Book of Abraham, her name was Egyptus) was of Cain's lineage (see *Abraham* 1:23-25).

It was not until September 24, 1890, that the Church reluctantly issued the "Mormon Manifesto," found appended to the *Doctrine and Covenants* (*D&C*), titled "Official Declaration 1" in which LDS President Wilford Woodruff declared that all Latter-day Saints are to uphold the anti-polygamy laws of the nation. The majority of the Latter-day Saint polygamists, however, continued to cohabit with their plural wives in violation of the Edmunds Act—also known as the Edmunds Anti-Polygamy Act of 1882—a United States federal statute signed into law on March 23, 1882 by President Chester A. Arthur, declaring polygamy a felony in federal territories. "Official Declaration 1" was added, with reticence, to the canon of LDS Scripture (*Doctrine and Covenants*) in 1908, 18 years after the "revelation" to rescind the practice, while *D&C* Section 132 (commanding the practice of polygamy)—the last of Joseph Smith's formal written revelations penned in July of 1843—remains unchanged to this day since its first inclusion in 1876.

"Official Declaration 2," also appended to the *D&C*, is a so-called "revelation" that came to Church President Spencer W. Kimball, and was also affirmed to "other" Church leaders in the Salt Lake Temple on June 1, 1978, in which "all restrictions with regard to race that once applied to the priesthood" were removed. This "revelation" was sustained before an assembly of the Church on September 30, 1978. Each of these dramatic changes in Church policy (polygamy and racial discrimination) were instituted by so-called "revelations," albeit under the duress and exigency of political pressures that mandated a transformation. In both "Declarations," the Church failed to repudiate its deplorable policies; neither did the Church offer an apology nor admit culpability for their past offenses, believing its corporate practices were initially commanded by God and later rescinded.

In an article published in the *New York Times* on August 18, 2012 titled "Why Race Is still a Problem for Mormons," John G. Turner, historian of American religion, and professor of religious studies at George Mason University and the award-winning author of *Brigham Young: Pioneer Prophet*, exclaims: "The revelation may have lifted the ban, but it neither repudiated it nor apologized for it." Turner further states that, "a fuller confrontation with the past would serve the church's interests" as "African-Americans, both members and prospective converts, find the history distinctly unsettling."

Joanna Brooks, an award-winning scholar of American religion, race gender and culture, and author of *Mormonism and White Supremacy* notes:

> [T]he problem of anti-Black racism [in the LDS Church] as a system that degraded the faith and its adherents has not been systematically addressed.
>
> To this day, church-attending Mormons report that they continue to hear from their fellow congregants in Sunday meetings that African Americans were the accursed descendants of Cain whose spirits due to their lack of spiritual mettle in a premortal existence were destined to come to earth with a 'curse' of Black skin.

Joanna Brooks further states that, "In place of critical self-examination, the LDS Church has used multi-culturalism, rhetorical evasion, and duplicity to manage the legacy of Mormon anti-Black racism without taking responsibility for it."[7]

On January 30, 2015, Dallin Oaks (who since 2018 has been the First Counselor in the First Presidency) told the *Salt Lake Tribune* that "the history of the Church is not to seek apologies or to give them" and that "we look forward and not backward." Oaks "doubles down," again stating that the Church does not "seek apologies, and we don't give them." Dallin Oaks emphasized the Church's position a few days later during video chat on "Trib Talk" (a digital forum for dialogue and debate about the day's news) insisting that the word "apology" does not appear in LDS scriptures. In a composition titled "Mormon leaders and the fear of apologizing" (October 14, 2022),

Jana Riess, a senior columnist for *Religion News Service* (*RNS*), wrote, "I think the inability to apologize is damning to us spiritually as a church. I mean 'damning' in the Latter-day Saint sense of the word, that it impedes our progress." Patrick Hardy, a sociology Ph.D. student at the University of Iowa, and an active member of the LDS Church, wrote an article for the *Salt Lake Tribune* on May 4, 2023 addressing the institution's lack of accountability suggesting: "[W]hen the church declines to acknowledge faults, give genuine public apologies, and make necessary policy changes in the wake of justified criticisms, it damages the trust of its members and validates its opponents."

In 1981, Boyd K. Packer (1924-2015), who served as president of the Quorum of the Twelve Apostles of the Church of Jesus Christ of the Latter-day Saints from 2008 until his death, gave an address to Church educators called "The Mantle [the Prophetic Mantle] is Far, Far Greater Than the Intellect," which was presented around four "cautions." Addressing the second "caution," Packer stated:

> There is a temptation for the writer or teacher of Church history to want to tell everything whether it is worthy or faith promoting or not. Some things that are true are not very useful [useful, that is, in the sense that it does not serve the interest of the Church].

Packer's "caution" is what classical historians would define as an "Identity Narrative" or "Sacred Story" versus a factual blow-by-blow "Historical" account. The Mormon Church's practice of scrubbing and white-washing their ignominious past, foments a false paradigm as they continue to evade historical transparency.

D. Michael Quinn (1944-2021), an American historian who has focused on the history of the Church of Jesus Christ of Latter-day Saints, and was a professor at Brigham Young University from 1976 until he resigned in 1988, responded to Packer's address comparing it to "the Roman Catholic doctrine of papal infallibility," suggesting that the honest depiction of flawed human beings (i.e., the prophets as they are depicted in the *Bible*) is "an absolute refutation of the kind of history" Packer was promoting. Quinn also criticized senior Apostle Ezra Taft Benson (1899-1994), the thirteenth president of

The Church of Jesus Christ of Latter-day Saints (LDS), who had made similar comments to Packer's insinuating that a history full "of benignly angelic church leaders apparently advocated by Elders Benson and Packer would border on idolatry."[8]

Quinn, who called the use of deception by LDS church leaders, "theocratic ethics,"[9] further asserted that Apostle Boyd K. Packer has created,

> "an enemy that doesn't exist" for it is impossible for any good historian, Mormon or otherwise, to write about Mormonism without discussing the prophetic claims of its leaders . . . to ignore the limitations of the prophets, Quinn feels, would be as false as to ignore their visions, revelations and testimonies.[10]

It was suggested to Dr. Leonard Arrington (1917-1999), a one-time Church historian (appointed in 1972), by Elder Howard W. Hunter (1907-1995), advisor to the Historical Department and the previous Church Historian, that what the Church needed was a professionally trained historian to bring to light "new histories." Elder Hunter believed that the Church had reached a level of maturity where information that had previously been suppressed could now be brought to light, setting a new standard for Mormon historical scholarship and an expectation of transparency. Arrington took Hunter's charge to heart, and soon became the head of the History Division of the Church Historian's Office. Arrington would be the first academically trained historian to hold the post previously occupied by high-ranking LDS officials. Arrington surrounded himself with a coterie of young, professional historians (at its peak fourteen historians and three secretaries) and forged ahead with his assignment. His courageous effort did not sit well, however, with the Church's oligarchy who were apprehensive about what damage a candid and open approach to the Church's history would do to the faith of the Latter-day Saints. Arrington's work (which he once referred to as the days of "Camelot," and by others as "Arrington's Spring") would be stymied by the Church's bureaucracy and ecclesiastical censorship, and after less than a decade the History Division was summarily dismantled while Arrington and his remaining staff were reassigned to the Joseph Fielding Smith institute of Church History at Brigham Young University.

In a featured story published in the *Salt Lake Tribune*, titled "Leonard Arrington's vast journals shows battles the Mormon historian had with the church's past" (May 9, 2018), religion writer, Bob Mins reports: "Arrington's scholarly approach, along with the opening up of . . . long-restricted document archives, was just too freewheeling—to the point of sacrificing official church history's primary 'faith promoting' role on the altar of academic candor and inquiry." Just two years into Arrington's tenure as Church Historian, Belva Ashton, the wife of *Deseret News* publisher Wendell Ashton, told Arrington that "his dream of writing objective church history [the unvarnished truth] from the inside was a fool's errand." Belva stated: "Your writing can never be as objective and straightforward and honest as that of someone who doesn't have to consider the wishes of the Church."[11]

In 1976, shortly after James B. "Jim" Allen (born June 14, 1927), an official Assistant Church Historian (one of two hired by Arrington), and Glen M. Leonard (Senior Historical Associate) published *The Story of the Latter-day Saints*, they met with abrasive criticism from members of the Quorum of the Twelve Apostles (the Prophet and his regents). Ezra Taft Benson reprimanded Arrington, arguing that the book was "faith-damaging" and offensive to the narrow scope of their staunch ecclesiastical-driven sensibilities. Although Arrington boldly defended Allen and Leonard's book, under duress, he agreed to allow Apostolic oversight of future publications. Despite the book's popularity (it was a quick sell-out), *The Story of The Latter-day Saints* was shelved by Deseret Book publishers for years before a second printing was approved in 1986. A growing mistrust of Arrington's Historical Division by the old-school bureaucratic Quorum led to the cancellation of a 16-volume comprehensive history scheduled to coincide with the church's sesquicentennial in 1980.

James B. Allen recollects a talk given by G. Homer Durham (1911-1985) who had recently been promoted (called to serve on April 2, 1977) as a General Authority to the First Quorum of the Seventy. In his "first meeting with the entire division on May 3, 1977, [Durham] sent shock waves through the already nervous members of the History Division." Durham gave a solemn warning: "You have to be careful. You have to write your history in the image of Brother [Ezra Taft] Benson." Durham was intimating that Brother Benson, who was next in line to be President of the Church, along with Mark E. Petersen, and others of the Quorum were concerned about what might be revealed by the prospective publications of the Historical Department. (Through the Quorum's oversight, only nine of sixteen intended volumes were ever published by Arrington's stable of writers, Benson and Petersen opposing history as Arrington's cadre interpreted it.) A year later, on May 4, 1978, "Boyd K. Packer, now advisor to the History Department, addressed all department employees at length, among other things, telling them 'We are required to tell the truth but we are not required to tell the whole truth.' "[12]

Delbert Leon Stapley (1896-1978), a member of the Quorum of the Twelve, "then relayed the sentiment of some within the Twelve that 'We should not put anything in any of our histories that reflects badly on the Church.' " To wit, Arrington replied:

> If our picture is entirely rosy [too triumphalist or celebratory] nobody, even members of the Church, will have confidence in what we write because members of the Church know that there are warts and blemishes [*The Crooked Timber of Humanity*—see Isaiah Berlin who quotes from Immanuel Kant] and unless we acknowledge some of these they will not have confidence that we are writing the whole truth and nothing but the truth.[13]

On November 11, 1980, in the final two years of Arrington's tenure as the overseer of the Church's History Division, Arrington acknowledged the "evidence that some church officers [namely within the Quorum] do not want the church to promulgate historical truth." Arrington further stated: "If they do not want historical truth, what do these officials want? They favor the purveying of traditional truth which is different from historical truth, scientific truth or philosophical truth." The shift from faith promoting historiography to scholarly and professional research and analysis put Arrington on a collision course with the Mormon hierarchy's ecclesiastical standards. "Arrington's final, frustrating years as church historian were a kind of cold-war freezing of once-open archives and liberated inquiry into the Mormon past," and in 1982, "with his ecclesiastical foes on the ascendancy, Arrington was effectively demoted when his Church History Division was transferred from Salt Lake City to church-owned Brigham Young University in Provo [renaming it the Joseph Fielding Smith Institute for Church History]."[14] Elder Hugh Pinnock (1934-2000), a General Authority of the Church of Jesus Christ of Latter-day Saints from 1977 until his death, offered: "Rather than fire [Arrington] they simply transferred him and his staff to BYU." Arrington's own candid assessment as to why he was removed from the office of Church Historian was the Division's "decision to write history instead of propaganda."[15]

In a column circulated in *Sunstone* magazine (sponsoring forums of Mormon thought and experience) on April, 1985 titled "Church Historian: Evolution of a Calling," Peggy Fletcher Stack (born July 1, 1951), a Pulitzer Prize winning American journalist, reports:

> On January 25, 1982, Leonard Arrington received a letter from the First Presidency extending him an "honorable release" from his ecclesiastical and bureaucratic positions "with sincere appreciation." On February 8, 1982, Elder G. Homer Durham was set apart as "Church Historian," in a private session.

In the collective opinion of the Quorum, there were incongruities between their expectations and Arrington's objective historical analysis, and to relinquish this position to an academically trained historian was just too risky! Thus, the office of Church Historian had come full-circle, and was once again commandeered by a high-ranking LDS official.

In *Dialogue: A Journal of Mormon Thought* (sponsored by Arrington from its inception), an independent quarterly established to express Mormon culture and to examine the relevance of religion to secular life, Clara Viator Dobay (1937-2020), who completed her master's degree in history from the University of Houston in 1970, and earned a Ph.D. in American History in 1980, decried: "The history of the Latter-day Saints has always posed formidable problems for objective scholarship." Dobay noted that "Arrington's division had fallen victim to the antipathy orthodox Mormons felt toward naturalistic versions of their religion's past."[16] Dobay averred, "minutes of the meetings of general authorities, diaries of members of the First Presidency, and church financial records remained sequestered" while "valuable journals and letters of such nineteenth-century Mormons as William C. Clayton, John Taylor, George Q. Cannon, and Francis M. Lyman, selectively available in the 1970s, disappeared from scrutiny."[17] For the LDS Church, there continues to be an agonizingly slow process of peeling away layers of secrecy. A transparent history would have to wait, surreptitiously kept under lock and key in the First Presidency's Vault. Arrington took issue with the Church's Orwellian culture of suppression stating:

> It is unfortunate for the cause of Mormon history that the Church Historian's Library, which is in possession of virtually all of the diaries of leading Mormons, has not seen fit to publish these diaries or to permit qualified historians to use them without restriction.[18]

In an essay written by Peggy Fletcher Stack published in the *Salt Lake Tribune* on May 11, 2017 titled " 'Trust gap' hounds the Mormon Church, research shows," Stack addresses the "Lack of transparency" that has pushed some believers away. Stack states that church members "feel deceived by Mormon authorities, whom they blame for keeping [controversial historical] details from them, and wonder what else these men might be hiding." (Peggy Fletcher Stack studied religious history at California's Berkeley Graduate Theological Union after which she received a fellowship to work on Arrington's elite staff when he headed the short-lived Latter-day Saints Church History Division.)

In an article published in the *Utah Statesman* on November 2, 2001 titled, "LDS Church and Utah State University fight over rightful ownership of the Arrington files" (see also "USU and Church are at odds over historical papers" in the *Deseret News*, October 25, 2001), we read that the Mormon Church attempted to sequester, take control over and privatize Arrington's Records Collection that his family donated to Utah State University upon his death in 1999. The *Utah Statesman* reports: "The church started to pursue this matter legally soon after the collection [which comprised roughly 600 boxes of materials] was made available to the public at the Merrill [-Cazier] Library Special Collections department on Oct. 11." The 600 boxes were equivalent to a staggering 219 linear feet. Archivists measure collections in linear feet as if the documents, which are filed in folders inside the boxes, were laid flat and stacked up. According to *The Herald Journal*, November 25, 2001, the Church originally requested the return of upwards of one-fifth of Arrington's collection. In the end, less than one-half of one percent of the collection was returned.

The pervasive culture of secrecy that has been so endemic to the Mormon Church is distinctly manifest in its esoteric "Temple Endowment Ceremonies." In the ambiguous history of the "Endowment Ceremony" (the pinnacle of spiritual experience for sincere Mormons), Latter-day Saints were instructed that they were under "the greatest obligation of secrecy" when initiated into the fraternity of clandestine rituals—miming slitting their throats, disemboweling themselves, and ripping open their chests—pantomiming their own death if they were to betray the furtive ritual's strict confidentiality. (The Mormon Temple Endowment Ceremony was revised in 1990, simplified from its nineteenth-century form, eliminating the "bloody oaths" which were sanctimoniously performed for 148 years.) Today, Mormons are simply obligated to take a solemn oath to "never reveal" the so-called "sacred rituals" associated with these secret Temple Ceremonies and Ordinances that involve symbolic "washings" and "anointings," "signs" and "tokens," "gestures" and "passwords," and vows of non-disclosure of their sacred priesthood, allowing them entrance into Mormonism's exclusive "Celestial Kingdom." The Endowment Ceremony was revised on January 16, 2005, January 1, 2019, and again in early February of 2023.

Mormons are reticent when pressed for disclosure suggesting that their "Temple Ceremonies" are so "sacred" that they cannot be openly discussed. Prior to 1990, the phrase "obligation to secrecy" was mentioned five times in relationship to the instructions given relative to the initiate's endowment. "Secret" means: "done, made, or conducted without the knowledge of others"; "kept from the knowledge of any but the initiated or privileged" ("secret," *Dictionary.com*).

The deliberations of the Council of Fifty (officially named by "revelation," "The Kingdom of God and his Laws, with the Keys and power thereof, and judgment in the hands of his servants, 'Ahman Christ' ") were shrouded in secrecy for 172 years. (For more on the Council of Fifty see the chapter titled "*A Greater Than Solomon Is Here*," Volume III.) In the Council's minutes on March 11, 1843, we read what became a permanent resolution of the Council:

> [A]fter the order of God, every member of it to be bound to eternal secrecy as to what passed here, not to have the privilege of telling anything which might be talked of to any person even to our wives, and the man who broke the rule "should lose his cursed head."[19]

The LDS Church scrupulously guarded the "Council of Fifty" minutes, which were kept under restricted access (locked away in the archives) in the custody of the First Presidency, until the *Joseph Smith Papers: Council of Fifty, Minutes* was published in September 2016 (the first and only published volume). The "Council of Fifty" (there were roughly fifty members) was a secretive organization chaired by Joseph Smith whose purpose it was to lay the groundwork for a theocracy that was to be the beginning of the literal Kingdom of God on earth with Joseph (a Yankee Prophet) having himself crowned as the Messianic King of Israel and, by extrapolation, "King of the World." "Joseph Smith ordained the council to be the governing body of the world, with himself as chairman, Prophet, and King over the Council and the world . . ."[20] J. Keith Melville (1921-1995), a political science professor at Brigham Young University, reveals: "This kingdom, a politico-religious organization of world-wide proportions as conceived by the Mormons, was ultimately to assume sovereignty over all the kingdoms of the world."[21] To nineteenth-century Americans who had severed their ties with the long-arm of the King of England and "fended off Federalist attempts to make the Presidency something like a monarchy," this appointment did not sit well. Nor did it sit well with Mainstream Christianity whose only King was Jesus Christ.[22]

Though the "minutes" of the "Council of Fifty" is a portrait of a face that has only recently been turned away from the wall for the historian's scrutiny, there is much that remains masked by the Church's carefully meted out curation of its revisionist history, while deliberately censoring "sensitive" information that would negatively affect the faith of the Saints. Historical revisionism, simply stated, is a falsification and/or distortion of the historical record. This method of sanitizing, and thereby misrepresenting the transparent historical narrative, is called hagiography (an adulatory and idealized representation of chronicled events). Boyd Packer insensitively and incredulously stated:

> I have a hard time with historians because they idolize the truth. The truth is not uplifting. It destroys. I could tell most of the secretaries in the Church office building that they are ugly and fat. That would be the truth, but it would hurt and destroy them. Historians should tell only that part of the truth that is inspiring and uplifting.[23]

Richard Lyman Bushman, dean of Mormon historians (born June 20, 1931), an American historian and Gouverneur Morris Professor of History emeritus at Columbia University, who served as president of the Mormon History Association, bemoaned:

> [I]t may be easier for Latter-day Saint scholars who don't live in [Utah,] the Beehive State to write about the church.
>
> "The trouble is, if you live in Utah, you write aware of general authorities looking over your shoulder [like Boyd Packer]. You can't do that. You can't write to please the general authorities. You've got to write what you think is true. It's just very hard to do in Utah, because there's such a presence."[24]

In 1958, Bruce R. McConkie (1915-1985), a general authority of the Church of Jesus Christ of Latter-day Saints for 38 years, and, at the time of its publication, a member of the First Council of the Seventy (starting in 1946), wrote the encyclopedic compendium, *Mormon Doctrine*. *Mormon Doctrine* (originally subtitled *A Compendium of the Gospel*) was published by Bookcraft, a major publisher of books and products for members of the LDS Church. McConkie, the son-in-law of Joseph Fielding Smith (1876-1972), who served as the tenth president of the Church of Jesus Christ of Latter-day Saints from 1970 (at the age of 93) until his death in 1972, described his book as "the first major attempt to digest, explain, and analyze all of the important doctrines of the kingdom" and "the first extensive compendium of the whole gospel—the first attempt to publish an encyclopedic commentary covering the whole field of revealed religion [namely the Mormon religion]."[25] In 1966, a second edition with its "approved" revisions under the guidance of Spencer W. Kimball (1895-1985), the twelfth president of The Church of Jesus Christ of Latter-day Saints, was published, and again in 1978 was further revised after the "revelation" allowing Blacks to hold the Priesthood.

Though McConkie's *Mormon Doctrine* was quietly and forcefully taken out of print in 2010, it remains a Latter-day classic and all-time bestseller. During its publication run of 52 years (and 40 printings), *Mormon Doctrine* sold hundreds of thousands of copies, and at the time it was taken off the market it was still experiencing modest sales. The work, however, is now no longer officially recognized by the Church, and all references to *Mormon Doctrine* have been expunged from the Gospel Principles manual used by the Priesthood and Relief Society classes, though many entries in the Church's *Bible Dictionary* still use references taken from McConkie's compendium.

In 1992, McConkie became a member of the Quorum of the Twelve Apostles of the Church of Jesus Christ of Latter-day Saints until his death. In the same way that Thomas Henry Huxley (1825-1895), an English biologist and anthropologist specializing in comparative anatomy, was called "Darwin's Bulldog" for his pugnacious defense of the theory of evolution through natural selection, so likewise, Bruce R. McConkie rose to the occasion as a zealous perennial defender and expositor of the doctrinal tenets of Mormonism. McConkie once said, "I determined that perhaps a sketch of a bulldog would be the most appropriate symbol for me, as I somewhat resemble this animal as it represents my personality very well."[26] McConkie was a prolific writer and, besides *Mormon Doctrine* (856 pages), authored *The Doctrinal New Testament*

Commentary (a three- volume set), the six-volume *Messiah* series, and *A New Witness for the Articles of Faith*. It is widely rumored that McConkie authored the *Book of Mormon*'s introduction as well as the book's chapter headings while contributing to other supplemental materials including footnotes and cross references, all of which were added to the *Book of Mormon* in 1981. McConkie's ineradicable contributions have left their cultural, doctrinal, and historic mark on the LDS Church. McConkie cannot be lightly dismissed nor his portrait turned to the wall!

Sandra Tanner (born January 14, 1941), a great-great granddaughter of Brigham Young and a prolific Mormon researcher and archivist who has spent a lifetime comparing Mormonism to Christian Orthodoxy, said:

> I believe the main reason McConkie's *Mormon Doctrine* was taken out of print was due to its candid discussion of LDS doctrine that the Church is now trying to hide. Such teachings as God once being a man, his wife-Heavenly mother, and Jesus being the literal, physical Son of God are just a few of the doctrines that are being minimized in current manuals. If the LDS Church felt *Mormon Doctrine* presented a faulty compilation of their doctrines, why haven't they issued an authorized compendium of their beliefs? Mormons often say to me, "That's not official doctrine" as though there was some place to look up the official teachings. Where is the official systematic theology of Mormonism?[27]

In a report issued in the *San Francisco Chronicle* (dated Sunday, April 13, 1997), religion writer, Don Lattin, interviewed Mormon President Gordon B. Hinckley and asked:

> Don Lattin: There are some significant differences in your beliefs [when compared to orthodox Christianity]. For instance, don't Mormons believe that God was once a man?

> Gordon B. Hinckley: I wouldn't say that. There is a couplet coined, "As man is, God once was. As God is, man may become." Now that's more of a couplet

than anything else. That gets into some pretty deep theology that we don't know very much about.

Clearly, Hinckley's response was disingenuous and was not straightforward! The fact is, the doctrine that "God was once a man" is foundational to the Mormon religion and was forever memorialized in Joseph Smith's King Follett Discourse delivered at a General Conference on April 7, 1844:

> I will go back to the beginning before the world was, to show what kind of being God is. What sort of a being was God in the beginning? Open your ears and hear, all ye ends of the earth, for I am going to prove it to you by the Bible, and to tell you the designs of God in relation to the human race, and why He interferes with the affairs of man.
>
> *God himself was once a man as we are now, and is an exalted man, and sits enthroned in yonder heavens! That is the great secret.*

Apparently, Gordon B. Hinckley wanted to keep Joseph Smith's revelation a secret!

In a critical analysis presented on August 22, 2011 by the Institute for Religious Research (IRR.org), a Christian apologetics and counter-cult organization based in Cedar Springs, Michigan (formerly known as Gospel Truths Ministries), Joel B. Groat and Luke P. Wilson wrote:

> President Gordon B. Hinckley seemed to dodge and dissemble in an August 4, 1997 *Time* cover story [titled "Kingdom come" (p. 56)] when veteran religion writer Richard N. Ostling [co-author of *Mormon America: The Power and the Promise*] asked him about the distinctive Mormon teaching that humans can become gods, and that God the Father was once a man. [*Time* magazine serves a large audience with a total circulation which averages over 3.2 million annually and a readership which is estimated to be 25 million.]

On whether the LDS Church holds that, "God the Father was once a man, he sounded uncertain, 'I don't know that we teach it, I don't know that we emphasize it . . . I understand the philosophical background behind it, but I don't know a lot about it,' " Hinckley told *Time*.

Richard N. Ostling: Just another related question that comes up is the statements in the King Follett discourse by the Prophet [Joseph Smith, Jr.].

Hinckley: Yeah.

Ostling: . . . about that, God the Father was once a man as we were. This is something that Christian writers are always addressing. *Is this the teaching of the church today, that God the Father was once a man like we are?*

Hinckley: I don't know that we teach it. I don't know that we emphasize it. I haven't heard it discussed for a long time in public discourse. I don't know. I don't know all the circumstances under which that statement was made. I understand the philosophical background behind it. But I don't know a lot about it and I don't know that others know a lot about it.

Groat and Wilson contend, "What Joseph Smith declared proudly and unambiguously [in the King Follett Sermon]—that God the Father was once a man—President Hinckley apparently now wished to conceal from the public." In the *Improvement Era*, an official magazine of the Church of Jesus Christ of Latter-day Saints published between 1897 and 1970, under the heading "The Origin of Man" by the First Presidency of the Church (Volume XIII, November 1907, pp. 75-81), we read:

The Church of Jesus Christ of Latter-day Saints, basing its belief on divine revelation, ancient and modern, proclaims man to be the direct and lineal offspring of Deity. God Himself is an exalted man, perfected, enthroned, and supreme. . . .

Man is the child of God, formed in the divine image and endowed with divine attributes, and even as the infant son of an earthly father and mother is capable in due time of becoming a man, so the undeveloped offspring of celestial parentage is capable, by experience through ages and aeons, of evolving into a God.

Joseph Smith called the belief that God is an "exalted man" the "first principle of the Gospel."[28] Robert L. Millet (born December 30, 1947), a professor of Ancient Scripture and emeritus Dean of Religious Education at Brigham Young University (BYU) in Provo, Utah, admits that *the teaching of the church today, [is] that God the Father was once a man like we are*:

The tougher issue for many Christians to deal with is the accompanying doctrine set forth in the King Follett Sermon and the Lorenzo Snow couplet [mentioned above]—namely, that God was once a man. Latter-day scriptures state unequivocally that God is a man, a Man of Holiness (Moses 6:57) [found in the Latter-day Saints' *Pearl of Great Price*] who possesses a body of flesh and bones (D&C 130:22) [*Doctrine and Covenants*, abbreviated *D&C*, is another "book" of Mormon "Scripture"]. These concepts are clearly a part of the doctrinal restoration [of the Church of Jesus Christ of Latter-day Saints]. We teach that man is not of a lower order or different species than God. This, of course, makes many of our Christian friends extremely nervous (if not angry), for it appears to them that we are lowering God in the scheme of things and thus attempting to bridge the Creator/creature chasm.[29]

Andrew C. Skinner (born 1951), dean of religious education at Brigham Young University, Provo, states that President Gordon B. Hinckley unequivocally taught: "The whole design of the gospel is to lead us onward and upward to greater achievement, even, eventually to godhood. This great possibility was enunciated by the Prophet Joseph Smith in the King Follett sermon and emphasized by President Lorenzo Snow. . . . Our enemies have criticized us for believing in this."[30] Remember, Hinckley said, "I don't know that we teach it." Skinner calls Lorenzo Snow's couplet "the official belief of the LDS Church."[31]

In both interviews mentioned above, one must ask why Hinckley was deflecting and dismissing what is patently obvious to almost everyone who knows anything about Mormonism. Joanna Brooks contends that the Church's controversial issues are carefully managed "with a combination of avoidance, denial, selective truth-telling, determined silence, and opportunistic redirection."[32] On a recent trip to Salt Lake City, Utah (December 1, 2017), Tim Keesee, the founder and executive director of Frontline Missions International (an evangelical Christian organization) appraised the religion of the Latter-day Saints as "a cosmic pyramid scheme whereby faithful Mormons can become gods themselves. And even have their own planet!"[33] (For a more exhaustive look at the doctrine promoted by the Mormon Church suggesting "God was once a man," see the chapter titled "*Puny God*," Volume IV.)

Richard Bushman stated that, to a large extent, "the context in which [Joseph Smith] is placed profoundly affects how people see [him]," in part because it requires the Prophet to "assume the character of the history selected for him."[34] Davis Bitton (1930-2007), coauthor with Leonard Arrington of *The Mormon Experience: A History of the Latter-day Saints*, admitted that, "all history is affected to one degree or another by the faith position of the historian."[35] In the UCLA History Initiative 3 Historical Analysis and Interpretation, we read that "historians may differ on the facts they incorporate in the development of their narratives and disagree as well on how those facts are interpreted." The study of historical interpretations and how they change over time is called historiography. Sometimes the interpretation of history can be ideologically driven, biasing the narrative. "If you dig deep enough, you can find alternate interpretations for almost any historical event."[36] So likewise, if history is superficially "cherry picked" to support an ideological bias, the historian has sacrificed objectivity for personal loyalties, and, in the case of Joseph Smith, religious fanaticism, reducing history to the level of fiction. Voltaire (1694-1778), a French enlightenment writer, historian and philosopher, pointed out that "history is a patch of tricks we play upon the dead."

Under an entry in the *Salt Lake City Messenger* titled "Book of Abraham Translation or Invention?", Sandra Tanner addresses the rising tide of disaffections:

> When Marlin K. Jensen, retired General Authority and historian of the Church of Jesus Christ of Latter-day Saints, was asked in November of 2011 if the LDS leaders were aware that people are leaving the Mormon Church in droves after learning of troubling aspects of church history, he responded:
>
> > The fifteen men [the First Presidency (which includes the President and his two Counselors) and Quorum of Twelve, often designated as the "Q15"] really do know, and they really care. And they realize that maybe since Kirtland, we never have had a period of, I'll call it apostasy, like we're having right now; largely over these issues.[37]

During a July 12, 2016 fireside, Richard Bushman responded to a participant's question regarding whether the traditional understanding of Church history is accurate, stating, "I think that . . . the Church . . . has to reconstruct its narrative. The dominant narrative is not true; it can't be maintained." The Apostle Peter warned, "In their greed these teachers will exploit you with fabricated stories [with stories they have made up]" (*2 Peter 2:3 NIV*). In a May 2006 interview, Jon Butler, dean of the Graduate School of Arts and Sciences at Yale University and a professor of American History, conceded:

> Mormonism's relationship to intellectuals has become difficult because of the interest in Mormon history. The interest in Mormon history has uncovered and revealed complexities, peculiarities, oddities, difficulties inside the history of early Mormonism that has become difficult for contemporary church leaders to accept.[38]

Terryl L. Givens, a practicing Mormon who received his bachelor's degree in comparative literature from Brigham Young

University, and is a professor of literature and religion at the University of Richmond, where he holds the James A. Bostwick Chair in English, acknowledges:

> At the present, therefore, while Mormons wait for an increasingly persuasive Book of Mormon apologetics—or the sheer magnitude of their burgeoning numbers—to attract more serious attention to their scripture, the Book of Mormon wars that rage most furiously are taking place *within* the Mormon scholarly community. For under that controversial rubric of the "new Mormon history," the Book of Mormon has drawn a fresh generation of interpretation and approaches.[39]

B. H. Roberts (1857-1933), who was a member of the Mormon Church's First Council of the Seventy, and Mormon General Authority, asked:

> Shall we boldly acknowledge the difficulties in the case, confess that the evidences and conclusions of the authorities are against us, but notwithstanding all that, we take our position on the Book of Mormon and place its revealed truths against the declarations of men, however learned, and wait the vindication of the revealed truth? Is there any other course than this? And yet the difficulties to this position are grave. Truly we may ask who will believe our report?[40]

Mark Twain rightly stated: "The glory which is built upon a lie soon becomes a most unpleasant incumbrance. . . . How easy it is to make people believe a lie, and [how] hard it is to undo it again!"[41]

Mormon historicists have not been realistic in their approach to the "given" of their history when tracing the causation of events, nor have they been honest in their conclusions when examining the complete fabric defining the church's historical existence.

1

"A Grand American Enigma"

For the students of religion, the Prophet Joseph Smith today remains a grand American enigma— too potent a force to be dismissed uncommented, and yet too complex for facile categorization (Lance S. Owens, author of "Joseph Smith and Kabbalah: The Occult of Connection").[1]

Fanatic, imposter, charlatan, he may have been, but these hard names furnish no solution to the problem he presents to us. Fanatics and imposters are living and dying every day, and their memory is buried with them; but the wonderful influence which this founder of a religion exerted and still exerts throws [Joseph Smith] into relief before us, not as a rogue to be criminated, but as a phenomenon to be explained (Josiah Quincy IV, son of former president John Quincy Adams).[2]

[The Church of Jesus Christ of Latter-day Saints] is an enigma to the world. . . . Philosophy cannot comprehend it; it is beyond the reach of natural philosophy. . . . it is . . . beyond the ken of human judgment, beyond the reach of human intelligence (John Taylor, who served as the third President of the LDS Church).[3]

In the Gospel of *Matthew*, chapter 13, Jesus told His disciples a number of parables which He compared to the kingdom of heaven. In conclusion, Jesus related one final parable in which He said:

> Again, the kingdom of heaven is like unto a net, that was cast into the sea, and gathered [fish] of every kind: Which, when it was full, they drew to shore, and sat down, and gathered the good into vessels, but cast the bad away. So shall it be at the end of the world: the angels shall come forth, and sever the wicked from among the just. And shall cast them into the furnace of fire: there shall be wailing and gnashing of teeth.[4]

Jesus asked, "Have ye understood all these things?" They said, "Yea, Lord." Then Jesus said to them:

> Therefore every scribe *which is* instructed unto the kingdom of heaven is like unto a man *that is* an householder, which bringeth forth out of his treasure *things* new and old.[5]

Of the many volumes that have been written on the enigmatic, yet fascinating life of Joseph Smith, the celebrated architect of the Church of Jesus Christ of Latter-day Saints (comprising less than 2 percent of the U.S. population, and only 0.2 percent of this planet's 8 billion people), and the controversial, often-nettlesome leitmotif of the so-called "Restored Church," it is this author's conviction that the reader will find this book a provocative narrative (a casting of the net if you will) and an engaging, as well as informative exegesis of "things new and old."

Although the Galilean's net, as used in the passage mentioned above, is a metaphor related to the Kingdom of God, it is also symbolic of the physical, psychological and spiritual entanglements of the Enemy's snare. It is Jesus' desire to set us free from the entrapments of this world. The Apostle Paul wrote: "Stand fast therefore in the liberty by which Christ has made us free, and do not be entangled again with a yoke of bondage (*Galatians 5:1 NKJV*).

The *Cambridge English Dictionary* defines entanglement as "a situation or relationship that you are involved in and that is difficult to escape from." The exploitation of false religion is the most subversive and diabolical of all entanglements, jeopardizing one's eternal soul.

François-Marie Arouet, known by his *nom de plume* Voltaire, said, "If you wish to converse with me, define your terms."[6] While addressing the "heart" of Mormonism (a purely American born religion originating in Jacksonian America), and its stormy, mercurial, and yet meteoric rise to prominence, I assure my audience that I will endeavor not to "carp and cavil upon the insignificant," but will focus, rather, on the Saints' salient and preponderant snowcapped granite pinnacles "of the Wasatch by Monte Christo, Baldy, Observatory, the mighty Cottonwoods, Clayton, Timpanogos, Nebo—its loftiest [cathedral of] peaks [some towering at nearly 12,000 feet; metaphorically representing the pillars of this thesis]—not by its maze of [superfluous] rolling elevations or hillocky spurs, rocky ravines, or trifling canyons [of which there are many]."[7] Further, my prayer to the Lord has been that I communicate with a clarion voice, and to "Put me where I can feel the pillars that support the temple, so that I may lean against them" (*Judges 16:26 NIV*) as I explore the labyrinth of Mormonism.

The Wasatch Front with Salt Lake City in the foreground. The tallest building on the far left is the Church of Jesus Christ of Latter-day Saints' International Headquarters.

In the words of Bruce R. McConkie (1915-1985), a member of the Quorum of the Twelve and authority on Mormon doctrine, "I will not stoop to petty wranglings about semantics but shall stay with matters of substance."[8] To use urban vernacular: I will attempt "to unpack" the "meat and potatoes," the practical details, and the "nuts and bolts" of Mormonism. I will look under the hood and discover what "ignites the spark that runs the very engine of Mormonism,"[9] and ferret out the truth. In an article titled "Study portrays Mormons as outsiders looking in" (January 31, 2012), Daniel Burke, who writes for *Religion News Service* (*RNS*), wrote, "In some ways, Mormonism is the ultimate American religion. Born in America, it was unveiled by an American prophet who believed the Constitution was divinely inspired and the Garden of Eden bloomed in Independence, Mo."

Benjamin E. Park, who received his bachelor's degree in both English and history from Brigham Young University in 2009 and went on to study at the University of Edinburgh and completed a doctorate at the University of Cambridge in 2014, admits, however, "To the extent that modern Mormonism is accepted in contemporary America is largely due to Mormons' ability to keep quiet about their distinctive beliefs and practices."[10] McKay Coppins, staff writer for *The Atlantic*, describes Mormons as "avatars [embodiments] of a Norman Rockwellian ideal"[11] for which we will examine whether

Mormons have reimagined and are merely imitating true Christianity (intentionally blurring the distinction between their beliefs and conventional Biblical Christianity, camouflaging their eccentric doctrines) while masquerading as children of light. Are the polished and carefully scripted Madison Avenue, Reader's Digest images of Mormonism (via a chameleon-like marketing venue) but a façade and misrepresentation of an institution whose theological axioms (when meticulously scrutinized) are at variance with orthodox Christianity? It is precisely the "distinction of doctrines" that distinguishes Mormonism from the "Gospel Culture" of Mainstream Christianity that is the crux of this thesis.

In an article posted by *The Centre for the Study of World Christianity* (*CSWC*) a research centre based in New College, the School of Divinity at the University of Edinburgh, titled "Mormonism and the Study of World Christianity" posted on April 3, 2018 by Jeffery Cannon (a scholar of world Christianity and a research associate at Brigham Young University), we read that "from the standpoint of the creeds that have defined Western orthodoxy, Mormons are at the very least unorthodox." The doctrinally complex and monopolistic religious structure of the Latter-day Saints is considered by most Protestant Americans as alien and threatening (lying well-outside of the fraternity of orthodox Christianity), not comporting to traditional American values and beliefs. In 2011, a National Survey of 1,000 Mormons across the country was conducted by the Pew Research Center's Forum on Religion & Public Life. The results were the first of its kind ever published by a non-LDS research organization. Two thirds (68%) of those interviewed said the American people as a whole do not see the Church of Jesus Christ of Latter-day Saints as a part of mainstream America. Gregory Smith, a senior researcher at Pew Forum said, "Clearly this is a population that sees itself as outsiders looking in."

In 2010 the LDS Church initiated "I'm a Mormon," a multi-million- dollar P.R. marketing campaign (which included television infomercials, billboards, and ads on buses and the internet produced by Boncom—Bonneville Communications) seeking to bolster their image while integrating Mormonism into the common fold of the Christian community of faith. The "I'm a Mormon" campaign continued to 2018 when the newly ordained successor (January 14, 2018) and President of the Church Russel M. Nelson (born in 1924) said the use of nicknames such as *Mormon* (as in "I'm a Mormon") was "a major victory for Satan." The *Salt Lake Tribune* (October 7, 2018) headlined: "Members 'offend' Jesus and please the devil when they use the term 'Mormon,' President Nelson says." As a result of President Nelson's refusal to give the once familiar label "Mormon," his imprimatur, the outreach campaign abruptly came to an end. Shortly after President Russel Nelson's edict against the "Mormon" moniker, the growth rate for the Mormon Church plummeted, reaching a 100-year low in the United States. The 2020 data showed that for the third straight year Salt Lake County saw a decline in the number of Latter-day Saints. It fell by 5,734 people, even as the county population grew by 36,600. Jana Riess reveals in her book, *The Next Mormons: How Millennials Are Changing the LDS Church* (p. 4): that "the number of young adults who are leaving Mormonism appears to be rising sharply." Riess further states:

> [T]he church's conservatism on social issues has become an obstacle to their continued participation . . . Over the past decade both the Pew Research Center and the General Social Survey (GSS) have noted a quietly rising tide of disaffiliation from the LDS Church in the United States.

Because of declining numbers, the Mormon Church withheld membership data related to the growth rate in Utah in 2021 (for the first time in 40+ years) to Utah's government. The church did, however, release some worldwide numbers in April of 2020, showing an overall membership growth in 2020 of 98,627, or just 0.6%; significantly lower than the 3-4% annual growth rates the Church enjoyed in the 1970s and 80s. This statistic shows that the Church's conversion rate fell well behind the annual increase of the world's burgeoning population which stood at 1.1%.

While Latter-day Saints reject both Catholic and Protestant Churches' authority to baptize, the top three religious institutions in America (among a long list of others) likewise dismiss the legitimacy of the baptismal ceremony conducted under the auspices of the Church of Jesus Christ of Latter-day Saints decrying that

Mormonism lies well outside of the pale of Christian ecumenical communion. In an article published in *Deseret News*, an official organ of the LDS Church, May 13, 2000, titled "Methodists say LDS Church is outside Christian Tradition," we read that the United Methodist Church, the nation's third largest religious body with approximately 7 million members, issued a statement at their 2000 National Conference declaring that the Jesus Christ of Latter-day Saints "by self-declaration, does not fit within the bounds of the historic apostolic tradition of the Christian faith." The nine-page declaration stated the LDS Church has "some radically differing doctrines on such matters of belief as the nature and being of God; the nature, origin, and purpose of Jesus Christ; and the nature and way of salvation." The Methodist Church further stated the LDS Church believes in a "gendered, married and procreating god" with "a body of flesh and bones," and has a theology that "more closely resembles a tritheistic or possibly, a polytheistic faith" than monotheism—worship of the one God.

In the official newspaper of the Holy See, *L'Osservatore Romano*, August 1, 2001, a publication of the Catholic Church (the largest religious body in the United States with 70 million members and 1.3 billion members worldwide), under the heading: "The Question of the Validity of Baptism Conferred in the Church of Jesus Christ of Latter-day Saints," Friar Luis Ladaria Ferrer (born April 19, 1944), a Spanish Jesuit of the Society of Jesus, Secretary to the Congregation for the Doctrine of Faith (appointed Cardinal in 2018), and a member of the Catholic Church's International Theological Commission, concluded that "the words Father, Son and Holy Spirit, have for the Mormons a meaning totally different from the Christian meaning." Ladaria, after reading Joseph Smith's King Follett Sermon (notable for its assertion that God was once a man), concluded that Mormonism's cosmology was unquestionably heretical. As to the "validity" of the Church of Jesus Christ of Latter-day Saints' baptismal ceremonies and whether they could be accepted among American Catholic bishops (when Mormons are converted to Catholicism) the overwhelming consensus was the repudiation and disqualification of baptisms performed by those who embraced such heretical positions.

In an article published in *Deseret News*, June 6, 1998, titled "Do the LDS, Baptists believe in the same Jesus Christ," we read that in 1997, the North American Mission Board of the Southern Baptist Church (the second-largest religious body in the United States, and the largest Protestant Christian denomination in America with approximately 14 million members) issued a training video titled "The Mormon Puzzle," along with a companion book *Mormonism Unmasked*, to inform its members that the Church of Jesus Christ of Latter-day Saints have surreptitiously "cultivated a media image that leads people to believe they are Christians, when in fact they are not." Carrie A. Moore, Religion Editor, reports that Tom Elliff, president of the Southern Baptist Convention, warned, "The Christ that the Mormons speak about is not, in our minds, identified with the Christ identified solely in the scriptures."

In an official publication posted in the *Presbyterian Banner* February 12, 1879, we read:

> Latter-day Saints and the historic churches view the canon of scriptures and interpret shared scriptures in radically different ways. They use the same words with dissimilar meanings. When the Church of Jesus Christ of Latter-day Saints speaks of the Trinity, Christ's death and resurrection, and salvation, the theology and practices related to these set it apart from the Orthodox, Roman Catholic, and Protestant churches.

Under the heading: "Frequently Asked Questions (FAQ's)— Denominations," published by the Lutheran Church, it states:

> The Lutheran Church—Missouri Synod, together with the vast majority of Christian denominations in the United States, does not regard the Mormon church as a Christian church. That is because the official writings of Mormonism deny fundamental teachings of orthodox Christianity.

The Lutheran Church further states that the teachings of the Mormon Church are "destructive to the Gospel of Jesus Christ" and undermine "the very heart of the scriptural Gospel itself" and are "indicative of the fact that Mormon teaching is not Christian."

In the *Encyclopedia of Religion and Society,* under "Mormonism," it confirms:

> [M]ainstream Protestantism, especially the more evangelical and fundamentalist varieties, has generally been unwilling to consider Mormons as part of the Christian family despite the continuing claims to being the one, true, authentic church of Jesus Christ, restored to usher in a new dispensation of the fullness of the Gospel.

As an Evangelical Christian, it is my hope that upon reading this treatise my audience will see with greater clarity the dichotomy separating orthodox Christianity from the Church of Jesus Christ of Latter-day Saints. I pray also that this will not be seen as a pejorative narrative or "Poking the Bear," but will be received, rather, as a genuine effort on my part to expose the contradistinctions.

B. H. Roberts, "widely regarded as the foremost historian and theologian of the Mormon Church"[12] offered a queue of cogent and compelling questions focusing on the red marrow of Mormon dogma that I will address and venture to resolve. Roberts asks:

> Is [the *Book of Mormon*] sober history inspired written and true, representing things that actually happened? Or is it a wonder-tale of an immature mind, unconscious of what a test he is laying on human credibility when asking men to accept his narrative as solemn history.[13]

> Did the world stand in need of revelation from God in the early decades of the nineteenth century of the Christian era? Did Joseph Smith receive such a revelation? Was the Prophet's story of the origin of the *Book of Mormon* true? Does the book bear evidence of divine origin? Had a New Dispensation of divine authority been committed to Joseph Smith by personages formerly holding that authority and divine commission? Or are there insuperable difficulties to such an unfolding of truth, or the granting of such a magnificent series of dispensations all entering into and forming one great

dispensation to be known as the Dispensation of the Fulness [*sic*] of times?[14]

G. K. Chesterton (1874-1936), an English writer, poet, philosopher, dramatist, journalist, orator, lay theologian, biographer, and literary and art critic, said, "We talk much about 'respecting' this or that person's religion; but the way to respect a religion is to treat it as a religion: to ask what are its tenets and what are their consequences."[15] The "position statement" for H.I.S. (He Is Savior) Ministries International (a ministry dedicated to helping Mormons who have questions about their belief system being Christian or not), December 31, 2015, under the heading, "Why Investigate?" reads, in part: "[I]n order to have a reasonable faith (one rooted in historical truth and supported by rational inquiry) a defense of truth requires 'full disclosure' of what can be known about a given religion." It is by "rational inquiry" into the foundations of the LDS religion that I have endeavored to present a "full disclosure" of the historical and theological underpinnings of Mormonism. The Apostle Paul (a wise master-builder) warned:

> For other foundation can no man lay than that is laid, which is Jesus Christ [the Cornerstone upon which the Church is reared]. Now if any man build upon this foundation gold, silver, precious stones [the fundamental doctrines of the Christian religion], wood, hay, stubble [worthless and unsubstantial vapid and trivial doctrines]; every man's work shall be made manifest: for it shall be revealed by fire; and the fire shall try every man's work of what sort it is (*1 Corinthians 3:11-13 KJV*).

The Church of Jesus Christ of Latter-day Saints teaches that their institution represents the embodiment of the "fulness [*sic*] of the everlasting Gospel"—the whole doctrine of redemption—that was first established by Christ and his disciples but was corrupted and forestalled during the time of the so-called "Great Apostasy" that endured for 1700 years. The Latter-day Saints claim that the "restoration" of Christ's Church began in earnest in 1830 with the organization of their Church in Fayette, New York on April 6, and that through their newly formed body of believers (Although about thirty people were present, only six—Joseph Smith, Oliver

Cowdery, Hyrum Smith, Peter Whitmer, Jr., Samuel H. Smith, and David Whitmer—became the first legal members of the Church) a resurgence of the sacred truths, for which they were solely entrusted, were given rebirth. Joseph Smith was God's supposed chosen vessel to bring about the "restoration" of "the only true and living Church upon the face of the whole earth" (*Doctrine and Covenants* 1:30) and to reinstate the ordinances of salvation, priesthood keys, and presiding priesthood authority, all of which the Latter-day Saints teach were lost soon after the death of the first-century Apostles. (*Doctrine and Covenants*, abbreviated *D&C*, is another "book" of Mormon "Scripture" that contains supposed revelations from Joseph Smith and a few other Latter-day Saint prophets.) It is from this platform that the Latter-day Saints have made their mark on this nation and the world at large, challenging and contravening both orthodox Christianity and the Biblical canon which they deem to have been corrupted.

As a note of curiosity, in my research I have observed that the vast majority of Mormon historians and authors habitually employ the archaic form "fulness" (single l) over the modern "fullness (double l)." The reason for using this peculiar spelling is not clear to me, other than the archaic form "fulness" appears in both the *King James Version* of the *Bible* and the *Book of Mormon*. Another reason for this anomaly, perhaps, is that it lends emphasis (and draws attention) to the Saint's unusual paradigm concerning "fullness" that separates Mormonism from all other religious sects. The implication being that all other creeds fall short of what the Church of Jesus Christ of Latter-day Saints perceive as God's specific criteria concerning the true meaning of "fullness." A "fulness" that uniquely quantifies Mormonism's concept of salvation, eternal life, and, more specifically, one's modus operandi through the process of "exaltation," that qualifies its strictly disciplined adherents to enter into the most sacred dominion of the "Celestial Kingdom" (Mormonism's third and highest level of heaven).

Thomas Ford (1800-1850), the eighth governor of Illinois, who was a contemporary of Joseph Smith and was responsible for his incarceration at Carthage, wrote in his autobiographical *History of Illinois*, published in 1854:

The Mormons were the greatest zealots, the most confident in their faith, and filled with a wilder, fiercer, and more enterprising enthusiasm, than any sect on the continent of America; their religion gave promise of more temporal and spiritual advantages for less labor, and with less personal sacrifice of passion, lust, prejudice, malice, hatred, and ill will, than any other perhaps in the whole world. Their missionaries abroad, to the number of two or three thousand [as of the end of 2016, there were 70,946 full-time LDS missionaries serving in 421 church missions throughout the world], were most earnest and indefatigable in their efforts to make converts; compassing sea and land to make one proselyte. When abroad, they first preached doctrines somewhat like those of the Campbellites . . . and when they had made a favorable impression, they began in far-off allusions to open up their mysteries, and to reveal to their disciples that a perfect 'fulness of the gospel' must be expected. This 'fulness of the gospel' was looked for by the dreamy and wondering disciple, as an indefinite something not yet comprehended, but which was essential to complete happiness and salvation. He was then told that God required him to remove to the place of gathering, where alone this sublime 'fulness of the gospel' could be fully revealed, and completely enjoyed. When he arrived at the place of gathering, he was fortified in the new faith by being withdrawn from all other influences; and by seeing and hearing nothing but Mormons and Mormonism; and by association with those only who never doubted any of the Mormon dogmas. Now the 'fulness of the gospel' could be safely made known. If it required him to submit to the most intolerable despotism; if it tolerated and encouraged the lusts of the flesh and a plurality of wives; if it claimed all the world for the saints; universal dominion for the Mormon leaders; if it sanctioned murder, robbery, perjury, and larceny, at the command of their priests, no one could now doubt but that this was the 'fulness of the gospel', the liberty of the saints, with which Christ had made them free.[16]

In the theological mindset of Mormonism, "fulness" can be nothing short of achieving personal godhood through the process of "transhumanism" (a form of pietistic self-glorification)—evolving beyond mans' current physical and mental limitations. Joseph F. Smith, Sr. (1838-1918), who served as the sixth president of The Church of Jesus Christ of Latter-day Saints (LDS) from 1901 to 1918, and was the son of Hyrum Smith who was the older brother of the Prophet Joseph Smith, taught, "Those who have been born unto God through obedience to the Gospel may by valiant devotion to righteousness obtain exaltation and even reach the status of Godhood."[17] When Mormons speak of "Godhood," they infer a Godhood that is on the same level that Jesus their so-called first-born spirit brother, elder brother, fore-runner, and exemplar (I am using Mormon terminology) attained when his own personal "fulness" and exaltation came into fruition.

Concerning mans' ostensible exaltation to "Godhood," Joseph F. Smith, Sr. stated: "Even Christ himself was not perfect at first . . ." (This contradicts the staid position of orthodox Christianity that Christ was fully God from the beginning.) Smith expounds on the LDS position that Jesus "received not a fulness [sic] at first, but he received grace for grace until he received fulness [sic]." This statement is clearly stated in *Doctrine and Covenants* 93:11-13. Smith then compares our own progression to that of Christ's: "Is not this to be so with the children of men?" Smith asks, "If Jesus, the Son of God, and the Father of the heavens and the earth in which we dwell, received not a fulness [sic] at the first" (here Joseph F. Smith is suggesting that the Father "was not perfect at first"), "but increased in faith, knowledge, understanding and grace until he received a fullness" (this is an expression of the Mormon doctrine of "eternal progression"), "is it not possible for all men who are born of women" to ultimately achieve godhood receiving a "fulness [sic], as he [Jesus] has received a fulness [sic]," and became coequal with Christ in the "presence of the Father?"[18] Alex Beam, author of *American Crucifixion*, calls the doctrine of eternal progression, "the

Mormons' supremely optimistic belief in the perfectibility of men and women living on earth."[19]

The Latter-day Saints teach that we were co-eternal with God Himself, and were given birth (procreated by a Father and Mother God) and organized as spirit entities in a pre-existent state of being before we were born into this mortal world. They teach that we will continue on eternally, passing through other stages of development (eternal progression), ultimately transforming into deities, and as gods, we will be given our own planets giving birth to other spirit entities who will follow the same course *ad infinitum.*

Joseph F. Smith, Sr. gave further exposition stating, "The object of our earthly existence is that we may have a fulness [*sic*] of joy, and that we may become the sons and daughters of God, in the fullest sense of the word . . ." Smith infers that "we" have the potential of literally becoming gods in our own right governing our own kingdoms. Smith further states, "being heirs of God and joint heirs with Jesus Christ" (see *Romans 8:14-17*), we will be elevated to a position of "kings and priests unto God" inheriting "glory, dominion, exaltation" to godhood, as well as inheriting "thrones and every power and attribute possessed by our Heavenly Father." Here again, "Heavenly Father" has progressed and "developed" into his exalted position having once been a mere man.

Smith emphasizes, "This is the object of our being on this earth," no less than to "be as gods" (see *Genesis 3:5 KJV*). Smith states, "In order to attain unto this exalted position it is necessary that we go through this mortal experience"—what Mormons call a probationary period—through which they may prove themselves "worthy."[20]

Spencer W. Kimball taught that "God created man to live in mortality and endowed him with the potential to perpetuate the race [of both men and gods], to subdue the earth, to perfect himself and to become as God, omniscient and omnipotent." Note that Kimball does not mention "omnipresent" as Mormonism teaches that God is confined to a body of flesh and bone. Kimball further enunciated that we are "gods in embryo with the seeds of godhood neatly tucked away in him, and with the power to become a god eventually."[21]

Francis J. Beckwith (born November 3, 1960), an American philosopher, professor, scholar, speaker, writer, and lecturer, and is currently Professor of Philosophy & Church-State Studies, Affiliate Professor of Political Science and Associate Director of the Graduate Program in Philosophy, at Baylor University, addresses the peculiar teachings endemic to the Latter-day Saints:

> Although there is certainly disagreement among Mormon scholars concerning some precise points of doctrine, it is safe to say the LDS church currently teaches that God is, in effect, (1) a contingent being, who was at one time not God (not necessary and not eternally God); (2) limited in *knowledge* (not truly omniscient), power (not omnipotent), and being (not omnipresent or immutable); (3) one of many gods; (4) a corporeal (bodily) being, who physically dwells at a particular spatiotemporal location and is therefore not omnipresent like the biblical God (respecting His intrinsic divine nature—we are not considering the Incarnation of the Son of God here); and (5) a being who is subject to the laws and principles of a universe He did not create.
>
> The Mormon concept of God can best be grasped by understanding the overall Mormon worldview and how the deity fits into it. Mormonism teaches that God the Father is a resurrected, "exalted" human being named Elohim who was at one time not God. Rather, he was once a mortal man on another planet who, through obedience to the precepts of his God, eventually attained exaltation, or godhood, himself through "eternal progression." The Mormon God, located in time and space, has a body of flesh and bone and thus is neither spirit nor omnipresent.[22]

If the truth were told (as is my full intention), it is only in Jesus that we find fullness and the satisfaction of our spirit's longing. Jesus said that only He can give us the water of life that will forever quench our thirst. "[B]ut whoever drinks the water I give them will never thirst. Indeed, the water I give them will become in them a spring of water welling up to eternal life."[23]

The "fullness" of God and of Christ is available to every believer as a gift from above through our Creator's unmerited favor and love, and is spoken of in the Gospel of *John* in the past tense, as if "the fullness of Christ" has already been delivered (and it has) to every Christian as our prerogative and rightful inheritance as believers. "And of his fulness have all we received, and grace for grace" (*John 1:16 KJV*). In *Colossians 2:9-10 KJV*, we read, "For in him dwelleth all the fulness of the Godhead bodily. And ye are complete [filled to the fullest measure] in him, which is the head of all principality and power . . ." In *2 Peter 1:3 NIV*, we read, "His divine power has given us everything we need for a godly life through our knowledge of him who called us by his own glory and goodness."

Mormonism, broadly speaking, would have us (Christians as defined outside of the context of Mormonism) reexamine both our position in Christ subsequent to our surrender to Him, and our understanding of what is meant by the fullness of Christ and "our inheritance in the Saints" so that they (the hierarchy of Mormonism) may supplement what they deem as our woefully insufficient paradigm of Christianity, with their so-called extra-biblical "restorative doctrines." To accomplish this the Mormon Church must disparage orthodox Christianity's timeless truths (for which they have become well adept as you shall see) and its fundamental tenets and beliefs, thereby creating a contrived vacuum in which to stuff their arbitrarily conjectured doctrines and fabricated truths— i.e., their so-called "restored gospel."

Richard Lyman Bushman writes: " 'Fulness' [*sic*] was the critical word in Joseph's exaltation revelations. The word implied that no blessing, power, or glory of God would be withheld from worthy humans [what is meant by "worthy humans" is another subject altogether that will be addressed later]."[24] " 'Fulness' [*sic*] meaning the fulness [*sic*] of God's glory."[25] Bruce R. McConkie adds, "fulness [*sic*] of the everlasting gospel" means:

> [T]hat we have all that is needed to gain the fulness
> [*sic*] of salvation. We have truth, doctrine, and

principles, every rite, power, and ordinance—all that is needed—to gain exaltation in the highest heaven of the celestial world.[26]

Elder Marcus B. Nash (born March 26, 1957) of the Seventy (in the Mormon Church there are currently eight quorums of the Seventy, who are often referred to simply as "Seventies") instructs:

> When the Lord speaks generally of "the" new and everlasting covenant He is speaking of the fulness [*sic*] of the gospel of Jesus Christ, which embraces all ordinances and covenants necessary for the salvation and exaltation of mankind.[27]

Again, Joseph Fielding Smith, Jr. (1876-1972, son of Joseph F. Smith, Sr.), who served as the tenth president of the Church of Jesus Christ of Latter-day Saints from 1970 (at the age of 93) until his death in 1972, observed that the new and everlasting covenant "is the sum total of all gospel covenants and obligations."[28] Joseph Smith averred: "[A]ll those who have this law [of the everlasting covenant] revealed unto them must obey the same." Joseph Smith vouchsafes that the Lord—speaking in the first person—announced:

> For behold! I reveal unto you *a new and an everlasting covenant*; and if ye abide not that covenant **then ye are damned**; for no one can reject this covenant and be permitted to enter into my glory . . . he that receiveth a fulness [*sic*] thereof, must and shall abide the law, or **he shall be damned**, saith the Lord God.[29]

Rex E. Lee (1935-1996), who was an American Lawyer, law clerk for former U.S. Supreme Court Justice Byron White, and the United States Solicitor General during the Reagan administration and was an alumnus and the tenth president of Brigham Young University (BYU), Provo, enjoins: "The authenticity of Mormonism stands or falls with the book from which the Church derives its nickname." Lee further states:

> [T]he only real way to reach a bottom line yes or no with respect to the restoration issue is to start with the bottom line itself: Did Joseph Smith really have

the experiences that he said he had? Is the Book of Mormon really the work of a series of [American Jewish] prophets to whom God revealed his word in ancient times? Have our Heavenly Father and his Son Jesus Christ restored all things, including [Mormon] apostles and prophets?[30]

NOTE: The "Restoration" has been referred to by Mormons as "the gospel in its pristine purity," "the testimony of the ancients," "the ancient gospel brought back again," "the pure gospel of Jesus," "the pure and undefiled religion," "the true order of heaven," "the ancient order of His kingdom," "the original plan of salvation," "the re-establishment of the Church as of old," "the primitive Church," "the primitive Christian faith restored," "the gospel of Paul and the primitive saints," "the dispensation of the fulness [sic] of times," among other similar descriptions.

Rollin Lynde Hartt (1869-1946), a journalist and Congregational minister, observed, "Massing his proof, [the Mormon] declares his peerless religion the one immutable, eternal faith, lost in the early age and restored in the latter days."[31] Truman G. Madsen (1926-2009), who was an emeritus professor of religion and philosophy at Brigham Young University, Provo, asserted that, **"Mormonism has no claim to be a viable religion in the present unless it has been a viable religion in the past**."[32]

Mormonism is not a reformation—as in the "Protestant Reformation" (although it is the LDS Church's intention to reform both Protestants and Catholics)—but is, rather, a so-called restoration of practices and beliefs that were supposedly lost and discontinued in ages past. In the Explanatory Introduction to the *Doctrine and Covenants* it announces "the **re-establishment** of the Church of Jesus Christ on earth . . ."[33] In the Church of Jesus Christ of Latter-day Saints' April General Conference (1998), President Gordon B. Hinckley said: "Let us never forget that this is a restoration of that which was instituted by the Savior of the world. It is not a reformation of perceived false practice and doctrine that may have developed through the centuries."

Eric Shuster, author of *Catholic Roots, Mormon Harvest* (Eric Shuster, is a former Catholic, and is now a Mormon convert), along with his co-author Charles Sale, explain in their book, *The Biblical Roots of Mormonism*:

> There is a widespread misunderstanding that the Prophet Joseph Smith founded The Church of Jesus Christ of Latter-day Saints. He did not. He was the prophet of the restoration of Christ's church, not its founder.[34]

Lorenzo Snow (1814-1901), an American religious leader who served as the fifth president of the Church of Jesus Christ of Latter-day Saints (LDS Church) from 1898 until his death and was the last President to come from Joseph Smith's generation, affirmed:

> Mormonism, a nickname for the real religion of the Latter-day Saints, **does not profess to be a new thing**, except to this generation. It proclaims itself as the original plan of salvation, instituted in the heavens before the world was, and revealed from God to man in different ages. . . . Mormonism, in short, is the primitive Christian faith restored, the ancient gospel brought back again—this time to usher in the last dispensation, introduce the millennium, and wind up the work of redemption as pertaining to this planet.[35]

Joseph F. Smith addressed the "restored gospel":

> Joseph the Prophet . . . became the means, in God's providence, to restore the **old truths** of the everlasting gospel of Jesus Christ, the plan of salvation, which is older than the human race. It is true, also, that his teachings were new to the people of his day because they had apostatized from the truth—but the principles of the gospel are the oldest truths in existence. They were new to Joseph's generation, as they are in part to ours, because men had gone astray, been cast adrift, shifted hither and thither by every new wind of doctrine which cunning men—so called progressives—had advanced. This made the Prophet Joseph a restorer, not a destroyer, of old truths.[36]

Joseph Fielding McConkie, Jr. (1941-2013), son of Bruce R. McConkie, professor emeritus of Ancient Scripture at Brigham Young University, Provo, offered his analysis of the restoration stating: "Though it is generally understood that we are a restored church, what has not been understood is that it was the Old Testament church that Joseph Smith restored." McConkie explains that Joseph Smith "received keys at the hands of Adam, who the LDS Church teach is now Michael the archangel, and from the angel 'Raphael,' presumably Enoch, 'Noah,' who Joseph Smith identified as Gabriel, 'an Elias' [according to Mormonism there was more than one Elias] from Abraham's dispensation (perhaps Abraham himself or Melchizedek), Moses, Elijah, John the Baptist, and Peter, James, and John."

McConkie asserts that "Of that number only the Baptist and Peter, James, and John are associated with the New Testament." McConkie clarifies that according to LDS revelation, "John's authority traces from Aaron (see D&C 84:27)." But when one asks what it was that Peter, James and John restored, McConkie asserts that it was, "of course . . . the Melchizedek or the Old Testament Priesthood." McConkie concludes: "**It is a little difficult to argue that ours**" (the *Church of Jesus Christ of Latter-day Saints*) "**is a New Testament church if every key, power, authority, doctrine, or covenant that we possess has its roots in the Old Testament.**"[37]

Will Bagley (born 1950), an historian specializing in the history of the Western United States and the American Old West, stated, "The Saints believed they were literally the Children of Israel, the chosen people of God's new covenant, making early Mormonism very much an Old Testament religion."[38]

Bruce R. McConkie conjectures:

> *If* the Book of Mormon is true, then Joseph Smith was called of God to usher in the dispensation of the fulness [*sic*] of times and to set up again on earth the Church and kingdom of God [when Mormon authorities talk about the "kingdom of God" they mean the LDS Church exclusively]. . . . *If* he received the plates from an angel; *if* he translated them by the

gift and power of God; *if* he received revelations from the Almighty . . . who can say that he was not a prophet?[39]

The plain fact is that salvation itself is at stake in this matter. *If* the Book of Mormon is true—*if* it is a volume of holy scripture, *if* it contains the mind and will and voice of the Lord to all men, *if* it is a divine witness of the prophetic call of Joseph Smith—then to accept it is to be saved, and to reject it and walk contrary to its teachings is to be damned. . . .

[T]hose who reject the book outright or who simply fail to learn its message and believe its teachings never so much as begin to travel that course along the straight and narrow path that leads to eternal life.[40]

McConkie pointedly asks (*as we must all ask*), "Was Joseph Smith called of God? . . . [and] Is the Book of Mormon the mind and will and voice of God to all men?"[41] McConkie further states:

Either the Book of Mormon is true, or it is false; either it came from God, or it was spawned in the infernal realms. It declares plainly that all men must accept it as pure scripture or they will lose their souls. It is not and cannot be simply another treatise on religion; it either came from heaven or from hell. And it is time for all those who seek salvation to find out for themselves whether it is of the Lord or of Lucifer.[42]

Hugh Nibley (1910-2005), an American scholar and an apologist of The Church of Jesus Christ of Latter-day Saints who was a professor at Brigham Young University, Provo for nearly 50 years, proposed, "Joseph Smith was either telling the truth or he was a criminal—not just a fool."[43] Nibley further stated:

Joseph Smith was either the fantastic, preposterous, implausible genie his enemies describe—perpetrating the most monstrous crimes ever conceived by man . . .—or else he was telling the truth. There is no middle way . . .[44]

2

The Historicity of the "Golden Plates"

For most modern readers, the plates are beyond belief, a phantasm, yet the Mormon sources accept them as fact (Richard Lyman Bushman, author of *Joseph Smith: Rough Stone Rolling*).[1]

Were there really gold plates and ministering angels, or was there just Joseph Smith seated at a table with his face in a hat dictating to a scribe a fictional account of the inhabitants of the Americas? (Brigham D. Madsen, professor emeritus of history at the University of Utah, Salt Lake City).[2]

Brigham D. Madsen conveys:

Many members of the Mormon Church teeter on the edge of the precipice of the Book of Mormon historicity. They hang on to their beliefs and loyalty despite harassments and sometimes ludicrous pronouncements from church leaders until suddenly they discover what many suspected all along—"All that he [Joseph Smith] did as a religious teacher is not only useless, but mischievous beyond human comprehending."[3]

Mormon Apostle Dallin H. Oaks (born August 12, 1932), who since 2018 has been the First Counselor in the First Presidency of The Church of Jesus Christ of Latter-day Saints, addressed the problematic origin and historicity of the *Book of Mormon*, stating:

> Some who term themselves believing Latter-day Saints are advocating that Latter-day Saints should "abandon claims that [the *Book of Mormon*] is a historical record of the ancient peoples of the Americas" [quoting Anthony A. Hutchinson who has an M. A. in classics from Brigham Young University]. They are promoting the feasibility of reading and using the Book of Mormon as nothing more than a pious fiction with some valuable contents. These practitioners of so-called "higher criticism" raise the question of whether the Book of Mormon, which our prophets have put forward as preeminent scripture of this dispensation, is fact or fable—history or just a story.[4]

The authoritative LDS position appears to be that the *Book of Mormon* is either historical or worthless. There is no middle ground.

The *Book of Mormon* (as of 2020 more than 180 million copies had been printed in over a hundred languages) was purportedly translated from the "Golden Plates" that the angel Moroni instructed Joseph Smith to find buried in a hill called Cumorah (a glacial drumlin located about three miles from Smith's home in Palmyra, New York, a canal town west of Port Byron 23.3 miles from Rochester) where they were interred four hundred years after Christ's resurrection. This most uncommon script was named after the prophet Mormon (a Nephite military commander) who, by Joseph Smith's account, wrote most of the book inscribed on golden plates; after which they were entrusted to his son Moroni who appended the final annotations before it was laid to rest. The Hill Cumorah, located in Manchester, New York, is also known as Mormon Hill, Gold Bible Hill, and Inspiration Point.

Hill Cumorah in Manchester, New York.

The Golden Plates that were allegedly dug up by Joseph Smith in September of 1827, are described by Smith as follows:

These records were engraven [*sic*] on plates which had the appearance of gold, each plate was six inches wide and eight inches long and not quite so thick as a common tin. They were filled with engravings, in Egyptian characters and bound together in a volume, as the leaves of a book with three rings running through the whole. The volume was something near six inches in thickness, a part of which was sealed. The characters on the unsealed part were small, and beautifully engraved ["with hieroglyphics, in grooves of which was a 'black, hard stain' that contrasted against the golden page"[5]]. The whole book exhibited many marks of antiquity in its construction and much skill in the art of engraving. With the records was found a curious instrument which the ancients called "Urim and Thummim," which consisted of two transparent stones set in the

rim of a bow fastened to a breast plate. Through the
medium of the Urim and Thummim I [Joseph Smith]
translated the record by the gift and power of God.[6]

In order for the plates (the gold leaf) to have been etched,
engraved, or embossed on both sides, they would, necessarily, have
been thick enough to prevent the text from appearing through the
backside thereby obscuring the narrative. To accommodate 500
pages of transcript, and the so-called untranslated "sealed" portion
of the book (constituting upwards of 2/3 of its volume), the "Golden
Tablets" would have been unwieldy and excessively heavy, let alone
incapable of ascribing to the given dimensions—"six inches wide
and eight inches long . . . near six inches in thickness." McConkie
notes: "Orson Pratt says two-thirds of the volume was sealed
(*Journal of Discourses*, vol. 3, p. 347), George Q. Cannon that only
one-third was sealed. (George Q. Cannon, *Life of Joseph Smith*, new
ed., p. 45.)"[7]

Gold weighs 1,204 pounds per cubic foot. Given the dimensions
as mentioned above, the "Golden Tablets" amounted to one-sixth of
a cubic foot weighing just over 200 pounds making it nearly
impossible for one person to pack around with ease. To somewhat
remedy this difficulty, Mormon Apostle John Widtsoe (1872-1952)
allowed a 10 percent air gap between the gold plates (thus
diminishing its mass-per-volume and number of inscribed pages)
thereby reducing the weight to one hundred and seventeen pounds
(still a bit cumbersome).[8] Ried Putnam, a Mormon blacksmith and
metallurgist, cited by Mormon apologists, further reduced this
estimate suggesting that there may have been a 50% air gap thus
mitigating its mass-per-volume placing the weight at around 100
pounds. Putnam again further reduced this weight to somewhere
between 50 and 80 pounds by suggesting that the plates were
composed of a copper/gold ratio of 66% copper and 33% 8-12 Karat
gold of a Central American alloy called tumbaga (a name given by
the Spaniards). This estimate corroborates with the testimonies of
William Smith and Martin Harris (who both hefted the so-called
plates), giving weights ranging between 40 and 60 pounds.[9]

Joseph Smith's mother, Lucy Mack Smith (as reported by
Andrew H. Hedges in *Ensign*, January 2001 under the heading
"Take Heed Continually": Protecting the Gold Plates), testified that

when her son retrieved the "Golden Tablets" which were about three miles from his home:

> "As he was jumping over a log [with the "Golden Plates" tucked under his arm], a man sprang up from behind and gave him a heavy blow with a gun. Joseph turned around and knocked him to the ground, and then ran at the top of his speed. About half a mile further, he was attacked again in precisely the same way. He soon brought this one down also and ran on again, but before he got home, he was accosted the third time with a severe stroke with a gun." Joseph struck this third and final attacker with such force that he dislocated his own thumb. He continued running, "being closely pursued until he came near his father's house," at which time his assailants, "for fear of being detected," broke off the chase. Reaching a fence corner, he "threw himself down . . . to recover his breath," then rose and continued running until he reached the house.

In Lucy's playbook, she pictures her athletic son Joseph running interference, straight-arming his opponents with a 15-ounce pigskin tucked under his left arm, which was clearly not the case! Even given the weight of 50lbs (equivalent to a sack of Redi-Mix concrete) tucked under his arm while fleeing from three would-be thieves navigating for three miles with broken-field running ("at the top of his speed") through a forest strewn with deadfall over which he would leap and bound ("being closely pursued"), presents a picture that is hardly believable given the encumbrance of the weight of the "Golden Plates" and the fact that Joseph Smith had a noticeable limp from four surgeries for osteomyelitis of his left tibia when he was seven years old.

The Church of Jesus Christ of Latter-day Saints, the Mormons, affirms that Joseph Smith, their venerated iconoclast millennialist prophet, and gilded icon, who is honored and heralded by millions of adoring "Saints," was directed by the angel Moroni (once an Ephraimite Jew, and the last of the Nephite prophets, living in the Americas—circa 420 AD) to the Hill Cumorah in Manchester, New York; where he recovered (plied out of the ground in 1827) the

Golden Tablets (inscribed with "Reformed Egyptian" text—a script unheard of by modern linguists) that he miraculously translated, via the Urim and Thummim stones (which he concealed upon his person), and published as the *Book of Mormon*, so named after its last redactor and scribe.

Fifty pounds of the gold alloy tumbaga (the approximate weight of the "Golden Tablets") would be worth approximately $687,000 given the price of gold and copper per ounce in 2022. On Wednesday, September 20, 2017, the Community of Christ sold a printer's manuscript of the *Book of Mormon* to the Church of Jesus Christ of Latter-day Saints for $35 million dollars, setting a new record for what is believed to be the most expensive manuscript ever sold for actual dollars paid, discounting inflation. *The Joseph Smith Papers, Revelations and Translations, Vol. 5: Original Manuscript of the Book of Mormon*, published by The Church Historian's Press, was released Tuesday, January 25, 2022.

A facsimile of the "Golden Tablets."

Richard Lyman Bushman addresses what those outside of the pall of Mormonism might perceive as the "extravagant nature of the Latter-day Saint religion" and the "miraculous events" that "strain one's credulity." Bushman rightly asks: "How can anyone . . . believe that God sent angels [sent the angel Moroni] to speak to [Joseph Smith] and require[ed] such unlikely acts as the translation of an ancient history with the aid of a Urim and Thummim?"[10]

NOTE: Joseph Smith's mother Lucy Mack Smith tells us that "Joseph kept the Urim and Thummim constantly about his person, by the use of which he could in a moment tell whether the plates were in any danger."[11] Sally Denton, author of *American Massacre: The Tragedy at Mountain Meadows, September 1857*, notes, "If by carelessness Smith lost control of the hallowed book, Moroni warned, he would be 'cut off' as the chosen revelator."[12] Joseph Smith testified, "I obtained them [the plates], and the Urim and Thummim with them by means of which, I translated the plates; and thus came the book of Mormon."[13]

The first mention of the Urim (OOR-reem) and thummim (THOOM-meem) is found in *Exodus 28:30*:

> And thou shalt put in the breastplate of judgment [perhaps in a bag or pouch] the Urim [Hebrew: אוּרִים *uriym, Strong's Concordance* #H224 which literally means "lights"] and the Thummim [Hebrew תֻּמִּים *tummiym, Strong's Concordance* #H8550 which literally means "perfections" or emblem of truth]; and they shall be upon Aaron's heart, when he goeth in before the LORD: and Aaron shall bear the judgment of the children of Israel upon his heart before the LORD continually (*KJV*).

Of the seven places where they are specifically mentioned in Scripture—*Exodus 28:30, Leviticus 8:8, Numbers 27:21, Deuteronomy 33:8, 1 Samuel 28:6, Ezra 2:63* and *Nehemiah 7:65*—there is no physical description (their appearance or the material from which they were made) of just what the Urim and Thummim were. Some scholars suggest they were stones (one white, one black) used as a "lot oracle" when inquiry was made of the Lord, giving divine guidance in matters of importance eliciting "yes" or "no" answers. Flavius Josephus (37-100 AD), a first-century Romano-Jewish historian and the earliest systematic commentator on the *Bible* (*Old Testament*) and one of the foremost historians of the beginning of the Christian era, implied in his writings that the Urim and Thummim fell out of use two hundred years prior to his writings (see *Antiquities of the Jews*, Book 3, Chapter 8, Section 9). There is no hint that the Urim and Thummim were ever used as "interpreters" as was suggested by Joseph Smith, nor were they fashioned as quixotic spectacles. Lucy Mack Smith described the interpreters (the scrying instrument) as "two three cornered diamonds" that were framed in silver and "connected with each other in much the same way, as old-fashioned spectacles" as is pictured below.[14]

Martin Harris (1783-1875), one of the most complicated figures associated with the early history of the LDS Church, who was a wealthy farmer, the first of Joseph Smith's scribes, and one of the earliest converts to the Latter Day Saint movement, and also served as one of "Three Witnesses" who testified that they had seen the "Golden Plates" from which Joseph Smith said the Book of Mormon had been translated, was recorded as having said that Joseph Smith had been directed "not to let any mortal being examine them, under no less penalty than instant death."[15]

A facsimile of the Urim and Thummim; also known as the "Nephite interpreters."

Martin Harris was pressured by Joseph Smith to financially support the first printing of the *Book of Mormon* in 1830—to the tune of $3,000 for five-thousand copies (equivalent to $97,178 in 2022)—for which he was never reimbursed. In a "revelation" given by Joseph Smith, the Lord told Martin:

> I command thee that thou shalt not covet thine own property, but impart it freely to the printing of the Book of Mormon, which contains the truth and the word of God. . . . Impart a portion of thy property, yea, even part of thy lands, and all save the support of thy family. Pay the debt thou hast contracted with the printer. Release thyself from bondage (*Doctrine and Covenants* 19:26, & 34–35).

Harris, one of the most socially and politically prominent members of the community, sold 151 acres of his property that, in the end, "cost him his political office, his social position and ultimately helped lead to the dissolution of his marriage."[16] A year later, in 1831, Martin Harris (the so-called "Great Benefactor") was further fleeced through Joseph Smith's specious "revelation" concerning the establishment of Zion in Jackson County, Missouri and the Law of Consecration (the United Order): "It is wisdom in me [saith the Lord], that my servant Martin Harris should be an example unto the Church, in laying his moneys before the bishop of the church [Edward Partridge]" for the purchase of lands in Independence (*D&C* 58:35). Still digging deeper into Harris's pockets, in 1834 we read: "And let my servant [Martin Harris] devote his moneys for the proclaiming of my words, according as my servant [Joseph Smith, Jun.] shall direct" (*D&C* 104:26).

Though Joseph Smith supposedly had the Urim and Thummim artifact secreted away in his possession (starting in 1827), his preferred method of translating the plates was with a so-called talismanic "seer stone" (also called a "peep stone") that he found while digging a well for Willard Chase (when he was 17 years of age) sometime around 1822. Betsy Gaines Quammen, a historian and conservationist who holds a doctorate in Environmental History from Montana State University, notes that despite having the "Urim and a thummim necessary for decoding what [Joseph Smith] declared was a type of reformed Egyptian writing . . ." Joseph "went back to a process he knew so well, plunging his face into the opening of his hat and staring into the darkness toward his own seer stone perched in its crown."[17] Terryl and Fiona Givens note that "Joseph found a seerstone more congenial to his purposes than the Urim and Thummim."[18] Don Bradley, author and independent historian specializing in the early history of the Latter-day Saints Restoration, surmises that, "an observer unacquainted with Joseph's translation process may think he seemed more interested in what was at the bottom of his hat than what was on the plates . . ." calling this transcription process "odd and counterintuitive."[19]

Alexander L Baugh (born 1957), professor of Church History and Doctrine at Brigham Young University, notes that "Between 1822 and 1827, [Joseph Smith] successfully obtained an unspecified number of visions by means of the seer stone."[20] William L. Davis, in his book *Visions in a Seer Stone*, notes:

> Along with locating lost objects and a variety of buried treasures [for which Joseph Smith had a penchant], seer stones possessed several other purported powers, such as detecting witchcraft; identifying thieves and stolen property; revealing secrets and hidden knowledge; facilitating communication with angels, spirits, and demons; and revealing anything about the past, present, and future—a particular advantage if one were hoping to obtain information about the history of otherwise mysterious and unknown American civilizations.[21]

David Whitmer (1805-1888) revealed:

> Joseph Smith would put the seer stone into a hat, and put his face in the hat, drawing it closely around his face to exclude the light; and in the darkness the spiritual light would shine. A piece of something resembling parchment would appear, and on that appeared the writing. One character at a time would appear [in "Reformed Egyptian"], and under it was the interpretation in English. Brother Joseph would read off the English to Oliver Cowdery, who was his principle scribe, and when it was written down and repeated to Brother Joseph to see if it was correct, then it would disappear, and another character with

the interpretation would appear. Thus the Book of Mormon was translated . . .[22]

Whitmer further stated, "I, as well as all of my father's [Peter Whitmer Sr.'s] family, Smith's wife [Emma], Oliver Cowdery and Martin Harris, were present during the translation. . . . He [Joseph Smith] did not use the plates in translation."[23]

Grant H. Palmer (1940-2017), who was the director of the Church Educational System (CES) of the Church of Jesus Christ of Latter-day Saints and was best known for his controversial book, *An Insider's View of Mormon Origins*, which ultimately led to his being "disfellowshipped" in 2004, wrote that Whitmer further stated:

> "[T]he plates were not before Joseph, while he translated, but seem to have been removed by the custodian angel [Moroni]." Isaac Hale [Joseph Smith's father-in-law] said that while Joseph was translating, the plates were "hid in the woods." Martin Harris and Joseph Smith Sr., respectively, added that the plates were covered "in the box" and hid "in the mountains" while they were being translated.[24]

Richard Bushman reveals:

> Neither Joseph nor Oliver explained how translation worked, but Joseph did not pretend to look at the "reformed Egyptian" words, the language on the plates, according to the book's own description. The plates lay covered on the table while Joseph's head was in a hat looking at the seerstone, which by this time had replaced the interpreters [the Urim and Thummim].[25]

I pray those who read this text will see just how odd, ludicrous and unbelievable this must appear to the skeptic whose spiritual and rational bearing demand that he dismisses Joseph Smith's interpretative prowess as sheer nonsense! Joseph Smith's contrived "rabbit in the hat" (pulling the *Book of Mormon* out of his hat) magician's shenanigans should readily be seen, by a well-reasoned mature and informed audience, as an outright blatant imposture.

Joseph Smith with his face buried in his hat looking at the seerstone (in lieu of the Urim and Thummim) while translating the *Book of Mormon*.

Emma Hale Smith, who was her husband's (Joseph Smith's) first scribe, said to her son, Joseph Smith III, "In writing for your father I frequently wrote day after day, often sitting at the table close by him, he sitting with his face buried in his hat, with the stone in it, and dictating hour after hour with nothing between us."[26] Emma does not mention the Urim and Thummim. Royal Skousen (born August 5, 1945), a professor of linguistics and English at Brigham Young University, writes, "Joseph Smith dictated for long periods of time without reference to . . . the plates themselves . . . In fact, according to Emma Smith, the plates were wrapped up and not directly used."[27]

Emma Smith

Oliver Cowdery (1806-1850), Joseph Smith's principle scribe and an early convert to the Latter-day Saint movement is purported to have mused:

> I have sometimes had seasons of skepticism in which I did seriously wonder whether the Prophet and I were men in our sober senses when [Joseph Smith] would be translating from the plates through the 'Urim and Thummim' [the seerstone was often called by the same name] and the plates not in sight at all.[28]

McConkie notes that, "The Prophet also had a *seer stone* which was separate and distinct from the Urim and Thummim, and which (speaking loosely) has been called by some a Urim and Thummim."[29] These accounts beg the question, "*Why, if the plates and the Urim and Thummim were preserved for well over a millennia, were they not implemented in the translation process?*" It appears the "Golden Plates" (though in Joseph Smith's immediate possession) were never directly facilitated in the translation of the reformed Egyptian text. The sacred document (which would have been of inestimable worth) was but a veiled trophy (wrapped in a linen cloth) that remained inexplicably concealed throughout the curious transcription process. Joseph Smith's bizarre modus operandi lends itself to a new nomenclature for the idiom "to talk through one's hat." "To talk through one's hat," is understood as to make unsupported claims, or profess to be knowledgeable about a subject about which one knows nothing.

Grant H. Palmer critically assesses this conundrum stating: "That Joseph Smith literally translated ancient documents is problematic." Palmer notes that Smith "mistranslated portions of the Bible" including known scribal errors and mistranslations (for example, *Isaiah 5:2* found in *2 Nephi* 15:2 reads "And he **fenced it** and gathered out the stones thereof . . ." should read "And he **dug it up**, and gathered out the stones thereof."), "as well as the Book of Joseph, the Book of Abraham" which were in reality burial rites similar to the *Egyptian Book of the Dead*, "the Kinderhook plates" now proven to be a forgery, "and a Greek psalter" that Joseph mistakenly identified as containing Egyptian hieroglyphics. Palmer concludes, "There is no evidence that he ever translated a document as we would understand that phrase."

Palmer draws our attention to the fact that, "although these records" (the "Golden Plates") "were said to have been preserved for generations by Nephite prophets, Joseph Smith never used them in dictating the Book of Mormon." Palmer obviates, "If we accept the idea that he dug up a real, physical record, then we must account for the fact that he never used it in the translation process."[30]

Joseph Smith declared, "But through the kind providence of our Father a portion of his word [the *Book of Mormon*] which he delivered to his ancient saints, has fallen into our hands."[31] Andrew H. Hedges (born 1966), who is a co-editor of the Joseph Smith Papers, and from 1995 until 2009 was an associate professor of Church History and Doctrine at Brigham Young University (BYU), Provo, writes, "Joseph stood 'on the west side of the hill [Cumorah, "convenient to the village of Manchester, Ontario county, New York"]' toward its north end, 'not far from the top.' There he obtained his first view of the plates [plates that Moroni had buried fourteen hundred years earlier]."[32]

Joseph Smith

At the conclusion of four unsuccessful attempts in as many years (beginning in 1823), Joseph was finally allowed, in 1827, to retrieve the *Book of Mormon*, and the High Priest's breastplate upon which were fastened the Urim and Thummim. (The angel Moroni on all previous endeavors had restrained Joseph Smith.) Joseph Smith reported, "I have taken the severest chastisement that I have ever had in my life. As I passed by the hill of Cumorah, where the plates are, the angel met me, and said that I had not engaged enough in the work of the Lord . . ."[33] Joseph Smith testified:

[I] made three attempts to [take the "Golden Plates"] but was forbidden by the messenger. I cried unto the Lord in agony of my soul, [asking] why I could not obtain them, and the angel said unto me that I had not kept the commandments of the Lord . . . for . . . I had been tempted . . . [by] the adversary and sought the plates to obtain riches and kept not the commandment that I should have an eye single to the glory of God. Therefore, I was chastened.[34]

Martin Harris (here I must remind you that Harris was one of the so-called reliable "Three Witnesses" of the *Book of Mormon*) offered a story that to most would appear incredulous:

I will tell you a wonderful thing that happened after Joseph had found the plates. Three of us [Porter Rockwell and another who is not identified] took some tools to go to the hill [Cumorah—also called Ramah as the Jaredites called it] and hunt for some more boxes or gold or something, and indeed we found a stone box. We got quite excited about it, and we were ready to take it up, but behold, by some unseen power it slipped back into the hill. We stood there and looked at it, and one of us took a crow bar and tried to drive it through the lid to hold it, but it glanced and broke one corner of the box.[35]

Porter Rockwell (1813-1878), a Mormon Danite, nicknamed The Destroying Angel of Mormondom, tells what appears to be a confabulation of his side of this story as recounted by Brigham Young:

I will tell you a story which will be marvelous [unbelievable] to most of you. It was told to me by Porter, whom I would believe just as quickly as any man that lives. When he tells a thing he understands he will tell it just as he knows it; he is a man that does not lie. He said that on this particular night, when they were engaged hunting for this old treasure, they dug around the end of a chest for some twenty inches. The chest was about three feet square. One man, who was determined to have the contents of that chest, took his pick and struck into the lid of it, and split through into the chest. The blow took off a piece of the lid, which a certain lady kept in her possession until she died. The chest of money went to the bank. Porter describes it so; he says this is just as true as the heavens are. I have heard others tell the same story. I relate this because it is marvelous to you. But to those who understand these things, it is not marvelous.[36]

After coming into Joseph Smith's possession, the so-called "Golden Tablets" whose gold-leaf sheets were engraved on both sides and bound with three D-shaped rings were subsequently concealed in a menagerie of odd places:

- The plates were initially placed in a pillow case and wrapped in Joseph's outer cloak (a farmer's smock) and stuffed in the hollow of a birch log (others sources state the plates were deposited in a hollow black oak tree) three miles southeast of the Smith family farm where they were concealed for about ten days, while the magic spectacles remained with Joseph.

- Afterwards, the "Golden Plates" were kept safe in his brother Hyrum's wooden chest under lock and key. (The chest had initially belonged to his brother Alvin who was now deceased.)

- Once, the plates were wrapped in a cloth and hidden under Joseph's sisters Katherine and Sophronia's bedcovers.

- Then, to elude intruders, the "Golden Bible" was covered in a linen frock and hidden under the hearthstone of his father's farmhouse fireplace.

- Once more, as a ruse to betray would-be thieves, the chest (now empty) was secluded under the floorboards of the Smith's cooper shop (where the chest was found and broken into);

- While its treasured contents, which were summarily removed beforehand, were buried and left unnoticed under a pile of flax in the cooper's loft.

- From June of 1828 until September 22, the "Golden Plates" were abruptly taken back into Moroni's possession because of Joseph Smith's indiscretion and violation of trust.

- It is reported that the plates were then placed in Father Alvah Beman's (Beaman's) —a friend of Joseph Smith's—Ontario glass box (a wooden box that once held glass plates).

- According to Emma Smith, the "Golden Plates" were kept in a box and lay under her bed for months.

- Lucy Mack Smith documents that the "Golden Plates" were secreted away in a "nailed up box" and placed in the bottom of a forty-gallon cask of beans to conceal their transport to Harmony, Pennsylvania.

- They were subsequently placed in Emma's red morocco trunk (Emma, Joseph Smith's wife, confessed that she never once laid eyes on the plates—a condition of Joseph Smith's custodianship).

- When the plates were not in her red morocco trunk, they lay wrapped in a linen tablecloth. Sally Denton observes, "Emma dared not disturb the plates that were wrapped in linen, for Joseph had warned her of instant death if her eyes fell upon them."[37]

- While refusing to show the plates to Emma's father, Isaac Hale, who doubted their authenticity, Joseph Smith responded in kind by hiding them in the nearby woods.

- Later, the "Golden Bible" was whisked away by Moroni, an angelic messenger, in Harmony, Susquehanna County Pennsylvania, and delivered one hundred and thirty-five miles distant to Peter

Whitmer Sr.'s garden near his home in Fayette Township, Seneca County, New York.

- The plates were then concealed in the Whitmer's family barn until they were reinterred (sometime after the so-called translation was completed in 1829) in the Hill Cumorah never to be seen again. "When thou hast read the words which I [Moroni] have commanded thee, and obtained the witnesses which I have promised unto thee, then shalt thou seal up the book again, and hide it up unto me . . ."[38]

I find it hard to imagine the *"Great Isaiah Scroll"* of Qumran (designated 1QIsa[a], discovered in 1947), recognized as the oldest copy of the *Book of Isaiah*—written across 17 sheets of parchment in Biblical Hebrew—housed in the Shrine of the Book in the Israel Museum—or the very delicately etched silver scrolls written in Hebrew (known as the *Kelef Hinnom* amulets, discovered in 1979) containing the priestly benediction of *Numbers 6* from the late seventh-century BC—housed in the Israel Museum in Jerusalem—being withheld from the world and treated with the same measure of nonchalance and disrespect. The Dead Sea Scrolls continue to be handled with the utmost reverence and have been made available for both religious and scholarly rumination (unlike the so-called "Golden Tablets" which were perpetually hidden and veiled in secrecy).

Although the plates were kept in Joseph Smith's possession for nearly two years, we read in *Doctrine and Covenants* 25:1-4:

Emma Smith . . . thou art an elect lady, whom I have called. Murmur not [It may be assumed that she was murmuring] because of the things [the "Golden Plates"] which thou hast not seen, for they are withheld from thee and from the world . . .

Brigham Young relates the following concerning the "Golden Plates" reinternment in the Hill Cumorah:

When Joseph got the plates, the angel [Moroni] instructed him to carry them back to the Hill Cumorah, which he did. Oliver [Cowdery] says that when Joseph and Oliver went there, the hill opened [apparently of its own volition], and they walked into a cave, in which there was a large and spacious room. He says he did not think, at the time, whether they had the light of the sun or artificial light; but that it was just as light as day. They laid the plates on a table; it was a large table that stood in the room. Under this table there was a pile of plates as much as two feet high, and there were altogether in this room more plates than probably many wagon loads; they were piled up in the corners and along the walls.[39]

David Whitmer, on the other hand, testified:

The same heavenly visitant [the angel Moroni] appeared [at Peter Whitmer's farm] and reclaimed the gold tablets of the ancient people [for which Joseph Smith had been given temporary stewardship], informing Smith that he would replace them with other records [those which had been sealed and/or withheld] of the lost tribes . . .[40]

In another interview with P. Wilhelm Poulson, David Whitmer gave the following account of the cave:

[Poulson]: Where are the plates now?

[Whitmer]: In a cave, **where the angel has hidden them up** till the time arrives when the plates, which are sealed, shall be translated. God will yet raise up a mighty one, who shall do his work till it is finished and Jesus comes again.

[Poulson]: Where is that cave?

[Whitmer]: In the State of New York.

[Poulson]: In the Hill of Comorah [sic]?

[Whitmer]: No, but not far away from that place.[41]

According to David Whitmer, it was the "heavenly visitant" who reinterred the "gold tablets," not Joseph Smith, Joseph Sr., Oliver Cowdery, and others. Also, the tablets were not taken back to the Hill Cumorah, but to a cave "not far away from that place."

66

So what are we to believe? Perhaps both contradictory tales are outlandish fabrications! Psychologists tell us that the inability to consistently keep one's stories straight is a "cue to deception."

An 1841 engraving of the Hill Cumorah.

In *Psalm 85:11*, written by the sons of Korah to the Chief Musician, we read, "Truth shall spring out of the earth; and righteousness shall look down from heaven" (*KJV*). Mormons will often quote *Psalm 85:11* as a "proof-text" and prophetic voice from the *Old Testament* (to lend Biblical legitimacy to Joseph Smith's story) announcing, as it were, the coming forth of the *Book of Mormon* springing "out of the earth"—i.e., the Hill Cumorah. Joseph Smith, in chronicling the history of the Church, affirmed, "Now, what do we hear in the gospel which we have received? . . . a voice of truth out of the earth . . . Glad tidings from Cumorah! . . . the book to be revealed."[42]

In lieu of the many cryptic expressions found in the text of the *Bible*, one should remember that the Psalmists (as well as the Prophets) often employed poetic license and metaphor—departing from the convention of "rules of language" and "literal meanings"— to affect and capture the audience's imagination. For example, a passage in *Isaiah 55:12 KJV* reads: "[T]he mountains and the hills shall break forth before you into singing, and all the trees of the field shall clap *their* hands." Mountains do not literally sing, nor do trees literally "clap their hands."

Is *Psalm 85:11* describing the coming forth of the *Book of Mormon,* or is the author simply speaking of the "universality of

God's righteousness and covenantal fidelity?"[43] Is the author personifying earth and heaven, as the earth springs up and heaven bows down, to find commonality in the idyllic agency of God's favor?

Another passage of Scripture quoted by Mormons, in support of their contention that there is Biblical precedence bolstering the authenticity of the *Book of Mormon*, is *Isaiah 29:4* (also found in *2 Nephi* 26:16):

> And thou shalt be brought down, and shalt speak out of the ground, and thy speech shall be low out of the dust, and thy voice shall be, as one that hath a familiar spirit, out of the ground, and thy speech shall whisper out of the dust (*KJV*).

In an article titled, "Out of the Dust: An Examination of Necromancy as a Literary Construct in the Book of Mormon," Amanda Colleen Brown, a graduate from Brigham Young University with a degree in ancient Near Eastern Studies, and holds an MA in Bible and the Ancient Near East from The Hebrew University at Jerusalem, observes: "Almost from the outset of Mormonism's doctrinal history, Isaiah 29:4 was associated with the coming forth of the Book of Mormon."[44] To suggest that the *Book of Mormon* can be ferreted out of this passage, however, is to conflate what is clearly not apparent to the vast majority of Biblical commentators! McConkie, a perennial defender of Mormonism, contends:

> But a record would be preserved [the *Book of Mormon* retrieved from the Hill Cumorah], and through it the great things revealed to their prophets [residing in the Americas from around 600 BC to 400 AD] would be known again. "And thou shalt speak out of the ground, and thy speech shall be low out of the dust, and thy voice shall be, as one that hath a familiar spirit, out of the ground, and thy speech shall whisper out of the dust." The spirit and tone and tenor of the message shall be *familiar*. A like account, one dealing with the same truths, the same

laws, and the same ordinances, [as] is found in the Bible.[45]

McConkie suggests the "familiar spirit" is but a "*like account . . . found in the Bible*," whereas the correct rendering of a "familiar spirit" is that of a demonic entity! In European folklore and folk-belief of the Medieval and Early Modern periods, **familiar spirits** (sometimes referred to simply as "**familiars**" or "**animal guides**") were believed to be supernatural entities that would assist witches and cunning folk in their practice of magic.[46]

A late 16th-century English illustration of a witch feeding her familiars.

Merriam-Webster defines a Familiar Spirit "as a spirit or demon that serves or prompts an individual" or "the spirit of a dead person invoked by a medium to advise or prophesy." *Leviticus 19:31; 20:6, 27;* and *Deuteronomy 18:9-14* refer to "mediums and familiar spirits" and strictly forbids being involved with them, as they are "an abomination to the Lord":

> When thou art come into the land which the LORD thy God giveth thee, thou shalt not learn to do after the abominations of those nations. There

shall not be found among you *any one* that . . . useth divination . . . or a consulter with familiar spirits (*Deuteronomy 18:9-11 KJV*).

A man also or woman that hath a familiar spirit, or that is a wizard, shall surely be put to death: they shall stone them with stones: their blood *shall be* upon them (*Leviticus 20:27 KJV*).

The *Encyclopedia Britannica* defines a Medium as "a person reputedly able to make contact with the world of spirits [where] . . . disembodied voices are said to speak, either directly or through the medium." McConkie writes, "Today also there are mediums and wizards who chirp and mutter as they arrange for their devotees to hear from the dead."[47] "And when they shall say unto you, Seek unto them that have familiar spirits, and unto wizards that peep, and that mutter: should not a people seek unto their God? for the living to the dead?" (*Isaiah 8:19 KJV*).

In the *Encyclopedia of Mormonism* under the heading "Voice From the Dust," William Sheffield, an American attorney and retired judge in the state of California, who once said "that Joseph Smith's story was more Disney than Disney,"[48] notes:

> For Latter-day Saints, the phrase "voice from the dust" speaks of the coming-forth of the Book of Mormon (cf. 2 Ne. 25:18;26:16), which was translated from metal plates buried in the ground for fourteen centuries. As early as Joseph Smith, LDS leaders have consistently indicated that this phrase applies to the Book of Mormon (*PJS*, p. 307; [Hinckley, Gordon B. *Faith, The Essence of True Religion*. Salt Lake City, 1989, p. 10]). This distinctive phrase and others like it usually appear in a context that speaks of the need for repentance and of an accompanying voice of warning that will "whisper out of the dust" (Isa. 29:4).
>
> Latter-day Saints believe prophets foresaw that in the latter days a book, a companion to the Bible, would come forth as another testament of Jesus Christ (Ezek. 37:15-19; 2 Ne. 29:1-14). This other

testament is the Book of Mormon. The Lord foretold the coming-forth of such a record to Enoch: "And righteousness will I send down out of heaven; and truth will I send forth out of the earth, to bear testimony of mine Only Begotten" (Moses 7:62; cf. Ps. 85:11; *TPJS*, p. 98). According to the Book of Mormon, Joseph of Egypt also prophesied that one of his descendants would write words from the Lord that "shall cry from the dust; yea, even repentance unto their brethren, even after many generations have gone by them" (2 Ne. 3:18-20; cf. 33:13; Morm. 8:16, 23, 26; Moro. 10:27).

In the *Jamieson-Fausset-Brown Commentary: A Commentary, Critical and Explanatory, On the Old and New Testaments,* on *Isaiah 29:4*, they note:

Jerusalem shall be as a captive, humbled to the dust. Her voice shall come from the earth as that of the spirit-charmers or necromancers (Isaiah 8:19), faint and shrill, as the voice of the dead was supposed to be. Ventriloquism was doubtless the trick caused to make the voice appear to come from the earth (Isaiah 19:3). An appropriate retribution that Jerusalem, which consulted necromancers, should be made like them!

Having reviewed the definition of "familiar spirits," and the brief commentary on *Isaiah 29:4*, McConkie's quote mentioned above confounds the imagination! In so many words, McConkie admits that the *Book of Mormon* is but a compilation of mutterings of "Familiar Spirits" that is an imitation ("a like account") of the *Bible,* conjured by a pretended converser with the dead! That would make the *Book of Mormon* a compendium of "seducing spirits, and doctrines of devils!"[49]

At his October 2007 General Conference address entitled "Scriptural Witnesses," Apostle Russell M. Nelson (now the presiding President of the LDS Church) forcefully asserted that the *Bible* predicted the coming forth of the *Book of Mormon*:

How do scriptures of the Restoration clarify the Bible? Many examples exist. I will cite but a few, beginning with the Old Testament. Isaiah wrote, "Thou shalt . . . speak out of the ground and thy speech shall be low out of the dust, and thy voice shall be, as one that hath a familiar spirit out of the ground, and thy speech shall whisper out of the dust." *Could any words be more descriptive of the Book of Mormon, coming as it did "out of the ground" to "whisper out of the dust" to people of our day?* (Italics added).

Joseph Fielding Smith, Jr. concurs that, "One of the most important predictions regarding the Book of Mormon is that found in the 29th chapter of Isaiah."[50] Smith adds:

Approximately 725 B.C. the Prophet Isaiah wrote a marvelous prophecy concerning the Book of Mormon. Isaiah tells of a record that would come forth from the ground which would be a history of a destroyed nation. . . .

An analytical study of Isaiah chapter 29, leaves room for no other interpretation than that offered for the Book of Mormon.[51]

Charles R. Harrell, associate professor in Brigham Young University's School of Technology in Provo, Utah, has taken issue with the traditional LDS eisegetical interpretation of this passage in *Isaiah 29:4*, arguing that the phrase, "as if one that hath a familiar spirit" is "an archaic way of referring to a necromancer or medium who communicates with the dead."[52] The *eisegetical* interpretation of this passage, for which the Mormon Church has shown a preference, reflects a subjective preconceived bias supporting an *a priori* agenda—reading into the text, imposing and importing an interpretation—rather than seeing the Scripture through the lens of its original *exegetical* context.

The weight of the argument indicates that the so-called "whisper out of the dust" was but the muttering incantation of the underworld from whence the *Book of Mormon* (according to the LDS General Authorities) finds its derivation! Amanda C. Brown draws our attention to the fact: "Once again, the Hebrew words that are translated here [in the *Isaiah 29:4* pericope] as 'one that hath a familiar spirit' (NRSV 'voice of a ghost'), along with words such as 'dust' and 'out of the ground,' are indicative of necromancy." Amanda Brown concludes: "The definition of necromancy carries greater literary weight than normally understood by Latter-day Saints . . ."[53]

Marvin W. Cowan, a former member of the Church of Jesus Christ of Latter-day Saints and author of *Mormon Claims Answered*, notes:

> Mormons also apply Isa. 29:1-4 to the *B[ook] of M[ormon]*. Apostle LeGrand Richards says of v. 4, "Now, obviously, the only way a dead people could speak 'out of the ground' or 'low out of the dust' would be by the written word, and this people did through the *B. of M.* Truly it has a *familiar spirit* for it contains the words of the prophets of the God of Israel" (p. 69).[54] There are 15 Old Testament references to "familiar spirits" and *all* of them deal with *witchcraft*! (See Lev. 20:6,27; Deut. 18:10-12 etc.). If the LDS believe the *B. of M.* has a *"familiar spirit*," they are identifying it with witchcraft![55]

Fiona and Terryl Givens concede the Latter-day Saints "believe in a porous membrane joining heaven and earth, which allows us to affect the welfare of the dead and our own." The Givens' further state: "Joseph's dominant preoccupation throughout his life and ministry was to connect the disparate realms of the living and the dead . . ."[56] The *Bible* calls this practice "necromancy" for which God sternly forbids, calling it an abomination in His sight (see *Deuteronomy 18:9-12*). Necromancy is the occult practice of conjuring the dead ("familiar spirits") for divination; sometimes referred to as "death magic," or "black magic." Mediums are practitioners (or pretenders) of dark magic who ostensibly communicate with the dead. The *Bible* references those who practice this art (which is strictly forbidden and condemned by God's codified laws) as necromancers, spiritists, sorcerers, wizards, witches, or diviners (depending on the context and translation).

The Lord sternly warned: "Give no regard to mediums and familiar spirits; do not seek after them to be defiled by them: I am the LORD your God" (*Leviticus 19:31 NKJV*). Not only are those who practice necromancy defiled, but are found guilty of a capital offence by stoning—an insidiously gruesome, agonizingly slow, and painfully punitive form of punishment; the severity of the punishment suggesting the severity of the offence. The Lord commanded: "A man or a woman who is a medium, or who has familiar spirits [practices necromancy] shall surely be put to death; they shall stone them with stones. Their blood *shall be* upon them" (*Leviticus 20:27 NKJV*). (For more on Joseph Smith's association with necromancy see the chapters titled "*Mediums and Familiar Spirits*" Volume II, and "*An Incredible Convergence of "Heavenly" Emissaries*," Volume III.)

The Church of Jesus Christ of Latter-day Saints, under the guise of the "Restoration," was built upon the foundation of the wholesale marketing of these forbidden occult practices. On April 6, 1853, in a speech delivered on the North-East Corner Stone of the Temple at Great Salt Lake City, after the Stone was laid, Parley Pratt (1807-1857), the Mormon Church's first so-called apostolic theologian, announced that in the early 1800s, "an obscure boy [Joseph Smith] and his few associates, in the western wilds of New York, commenced to hold converse with the dead." Pratt stated that in Joseph Smith "a medium of communication with the invisible world had been found, whereby the living could hear from the dead. . . ." Pratt further pontificated that one of the leading or fundamental truths of "Mormon philosophy" is "*That the living may hear from the dead. . . .* We have laid these Corner Stones, for the express purpose that the living might hear from the dead . . . [where] the world of spirits may commune together . . . [and] sit in grand Council, and hold a Congress, or court on earth . . . [where] Conversations and correspondence with . . . [familiar] spirits, shall be had only in the sanctuary of His Holy Temple [which was] prepared for that purpose." Parley P. Pratt opined that the temple-going Mormons would be "acting as mediums through which the living can hear from the dead."[57]

Pratt asked:

Who instructed [Joseph Smith] in the mysteries of the Kingdom, and in all things pertaining to Priesthood, law, philosophy, sacred architecture, ordinances, sealings, anointings, baptisms for the dead, and in the mysteries of the first, second, and third heavens, many of which are unlawful to utter? . . . [They were] spirits from the eternal worlds. . . . Who revealed to [Joseph Smith] the plan of redemption, and of exaltation for the dead . . .? Those from the dead![58]

3

"View of the Hebrews"

These partially civilized people became extinct. What account can be given of this, but that the savages extirpated them, after long and dismal wars? And nothing appears more probable than that they were the better part of the Israelites who came to this continent, who for a long time retained their knowledge of the mechanic and civil arts; while the greater part of their brethren became savage and wild.—No other hypothesis occurs to mind, which appears by any means so probable (Ethan Smith's *View of the Hebrews*).[1]

Robert L. Millet wrote:

Now, in regard to the historicity of the [*Book of Mormon*], it seems to me that only three possibilities exist: Joseph Smith told the truth, did not know the truth, or told a lie. If Joseph Smith merely thought there were Nephites [the tribes of the Nephites who were "white and delightsome" (*2 Nephi* 30:6), and the wicked Lamanites who were dark-skinned "filthy and loathsome" (*Mormon* 5:15)—former inhabitants of the American continent who were of Hebraic origin—are two of the main motifs found in the narrative of the *Book of Mormon*] and supposed that such persons as Nephi and Jacob and Mormon and Moroni [all prominent Nephite prophets (they were the "good guys") in the *Book of Mormon*] wrote things that they did not, then he was deluded or remarkably imaginative. He is to be pitied, not revered. If, on the other hand, the Prophet was solely responsible for the perpetuation of the Book of Mormon story—if he created the notion of a Moroni, of the golden plates and Urim and Thummim [a Hebrew term meaning "Lights and Perfection"; an instrument used to translate languages], and of a thousand-year-old story of a people [Ephraimite Jews] who inhabited ancient America, knowing full well that such things never existed—then he was a deceiver pure and simple. He and the work he set in motion are to be feared, not followed. No matter the intensity of his labor, his own personal magnetism, or the literary value of his embellished epic, the work is a hoax and the word of the New York farm boy is not to be trusted in matters of spiritual certainty any more than Hawthorne or Dostoyevski [*sic*]. . . .

[T]o create the doctrine (or to place it in the mouths of Lehi or Benjamin or Abinadi) [again, all notable Nephites represented in the *Book of Mormon*] is unacceptable. The latter is tantamount to deceit and misrepresentation; it is, as we have said, to claim that the doctrines and principles are of ancient date (which the record itself declares) when, in fact, they are a fabrication (albeit an "inspired" fabrication) of a nineteenth-century man.[2]

Both Hawthorne (1804-1864) and Dostoevsky (1821-1881) incorporated religious imagery and moral themes as major motifs that defined their fictional characters capacity for good and for evil. An early LDS publication declared:

Besides, so much depends on an answer to the question, Is the story of [the *Book of Mormon*'s] origin true or not: for, on the one hand, if it is not true, then the entire structure of Mormonism is built on a false foundation; and, on the other hand, if it is true, it becomes the strongest physical evidence for the authenticity of Joseph Smith's teachings.[3]

Sterling McMurrin (1914-1996), a liberal Mormon theologian and Philosophy professor at the University of Utah, addressed the inseparable connection between Mormonism's historical roots and their faith, stating:

> [The Church of Jesus Christ of Latter-day Saints] insist that the truth of their religion, the authority of their priesthood, and the divine foundations of their Church depend entirely on the factual truth of certain of their historical claims. The truth of two of those claims is held to be absolutely crucial. If Joseph Smith's vision of the Father and the Son was not in fact an objective, veridical experience, and if the Book of Mormon was not brought forth, as Joseph Smith insisted, by the hand of God, in very fact an account of God's involvement with ancient Americans descended from the people of ancient Judah then the Church and its priesthood and Mormonism as a religion are abject frauds. This is the position in which the Church has, by its own official pronouncements, voluntarily placed itself. It has tied its faith to its own history and to the authenticity of its distinctive scripture, the Book of Mormon.[4]

McMurrin further asks, "Did [the *Book of Mormon*] have the origin claimed for it—gold plates, an angel, a miraculous translation, and all else?"[5]

Grant H. Palmer wrote:

> On 4-5 January 1922, B. H. Roberts, senior president of the church's seven presidents of the seventy, presented to ranking church leaders what he called "Book of Mormon difficulties" . . . Elder Roberts said: "In a church which claimed continuous revelation, a crisis had arisen where revelation was necessary." He hoped his brethren would bring "the inspiration of the Lord" to solve these problems.

However, after his presentations, his colleagues reaffirmed their testimonies of the Book of Mormon and offered no solutions.[6]

Brigham D. Madsen (1914-2010), who was a professor emeritus of history at the University of Utah, Salt Lake City notes that B. H. Roberts wrote a "400 type written page thesis" that he presented to President Heber J. Grant (1856-1945), the seventh President of the Church of Jesus Christ of Latter-day Saints, in which:

> He swings to a psychological explanation of the Book of Mormon and shows that the plates were not objective but subjective with Joseph Smith, that his exceptional imagination qualified him psychologically for the experience which he had in presenting to the world the Book of Mormon and that the plates with the Urim and Thummim were not objective.[7]

Madsen further states that B. H. Roberts:

> [P]resents an intense and probing evaluation of the possibility that Ethan Smith's *View of the Hebrews* furnished a partial framework for Joseph Smith's written composition, that the Mormon prophet had the intellectual capacity and imagination necessary to conceive and write the Book of Mormon, and that internal contradictions and other defects added further evidence that it might not be of divine origin.[8]

B. H. Roberts boldly proposed:

> [I]f the origin of the Book of Mormon could be proved to be other than that set forth by Joseph Smith; if the book itself could be proved to be other than it claims to be, . . . then the Church of Jesus Christ of Latter-day Saints, and its message and doctrines, which, in some respects, may be said to have arisen out of the Book of Mormon, must fall; for if that book is other than it claims to be; if its origin is other than that ascribed to it by Joseph

Smith, then Joseph Smith says that which is untrue; he is a false prophet of false prophets; and all he taught and all his claims to inspiration and divine authority, are not only vain but wicked, and all that he did as a religious teacher is not only useless, but mischievous beyond human comprehending.[9]

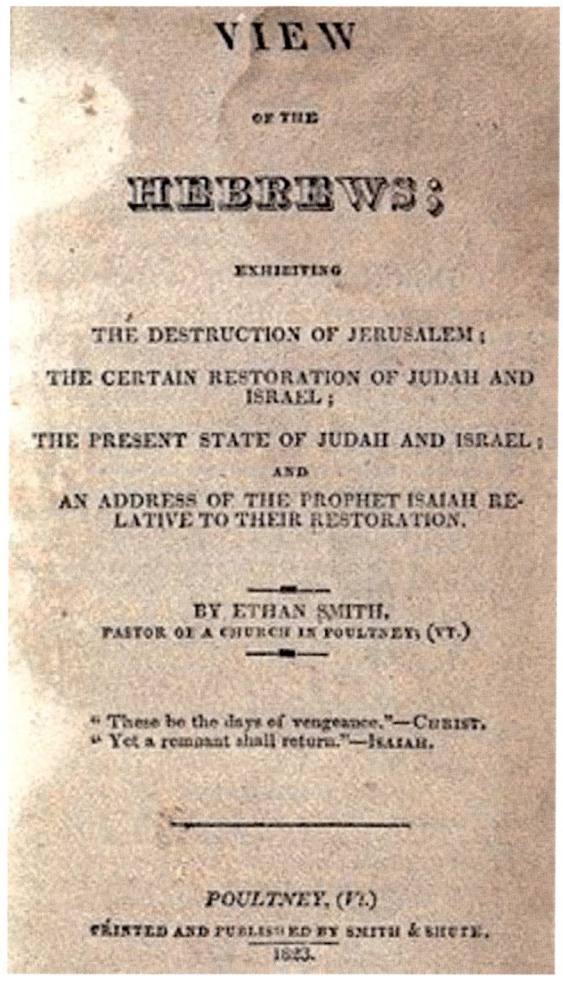

Title page of Ethan Smith's *View of the Hebrews* published in 1823.

Joel B. Groat, Director for Institute for Religious Research (IRR), presents the following in an article titled, "A Mormon General Authority's Doubts About the Authenticity of the Book of Mormon":

> Incredible as it may seem to many Latter-day Saints, Brigham H. Roberts (1857-1933), an LDS General Authority widely considered Mormonism's greatest apologist and historian, expressed the grave doubt that the Book of Mormon is a translation of ancient scripture. Elder Roberts reached this conclusion after his research uncovered extensive evidence that Joseph Smith borrowed the basic plot and many details from other books. This evidence—long suppressed because it is considered harmful to the Mormon Church—is presented in detail in three essays by Roberts, now published as *Studies of the Book of Mormon* (Salt Lake City: Signature Books, 1992).
>
> More than fifty years after his death, Roberts is still well known through his many writings. They include the—Introduction and Notes—to Joseph Smith's seven volume *History of the Church*, the six volume *A Comprehensive History of the Church of Jesus Christ of Latter-day Saints, Outlines of Ecclesiastical History*, and *New Witnesses for God* (3 vols). However, in 1922 Roberts became aware of troubling evidence that Joseph Smith borrowed much of the plot and other details of the Book of Mormon from other books readily available to him, in particular Josiah Priest's *Wonders of Nature and Providence*, and Ethan Smith's *View of the Hebrews*. For instance, it is often thought the Book of Mormon claim that the American Indians are descendants of Hebrew immigrants is a novel idea that young Joseph Smith could not have invented. But Roberts discovered from Priest's book, published in 1824, six years before the first edition of the Book of Mormon (1830), that it was the almost

universal opinion of the ministers of New England and the Middle States, that the Indians were the descendants of the Hebrews (*Studies*, p. 153).

In Ethan Smith's *View of the Hebrews*, first published in 1823, seven years before the Book of Mormon (and in a second edition in 1825), Roberts discovered a virtual ground plan for the Book of Mormon. In section two of *Studies of the Book of Mormon*, entitled, "A Book of Mormon Study," Roberts takes nearly 100 pages to describe the specific parallels between Ethan Smith's, *View of the Hebrews* and the Book of Mormon.

Did Ethan Smith's *View of the Hebrews* furnish structural material for Joseph Smith's Book of Mormon? Roberts was forced to admit that the evidence pointed in this direction:

> It has been pointed out in these pages that there are many things in the former book [Ethan Smith's *View of the Hebrews*] that might well have suggested many major things in the other [the *Book of Mormon*]. Not a few things merely, one or two or half a dozen, but many; and it is this fact of many things of similarity and the cumulative force of them that makes them so serious a menace to Joseph Smith's story of the Book of Mormon's origin . . . the material in Ethan Smith's book is of a character and quantity to make a ground plan for the book of Mormon.

Sterling McMurrin relates:

> [I]n a "Book of Mormon Study," [B. H. Roberts] found that much of the substance of the Book of Mormon was quite common in the thought and literature of Joseph Smith's time and place, that a literary analysis does not support the authenticity of

the book, and that Smith had the talent and creative imagination to have been its author.[10]

Long before Joseph Smith came into possession of the so-called "Golden Tablets," Joseph Smith's mother, Lucy Mack Smith testified:

> During our evening conversations, Joseph would occasionally give us some of the most amusing recitals that could be imagined. He would describe the ancient inhabitants of this continent, their dress, mode of travel, and the animals upon which they rode; their cities, their buildings, with every particular; their mode of warfare; and also their religious worship. This he would do with as much ease, seemingly, as if he had spent his whole life among them.[11]

In an article titled "Archaeological Trends and the Book of Mormon Origins," John E. Clark (born 1952), professor of anthropology at Brigham Young University, and director of the New World Archaeology Foundation, writes that critics "argue, [Joseph Smith] wrote the [*Book of Mormon*] from his galloping imagination, aided and abetted by scraps of truth and speculation rifled from others." In 1945, Fawn Brodie (1915-1981) wrote: "Thus where the *View of the Hebrews* was just bad scholarship, the *Book of Mormon* was highly original and imaginative fiction."[12]

B. H. Roberts concedes, "that it could be urged that [Joseph Smith's] family doubtless had this book [*View of the Hebrews*] in their possession."[13] Roberts asks, "Did Ethan Smith's *View of the Hebrews*, published eight and five years before Joseph Smith's Book of Mormon, Supply the Structural Outline and some of the Subject Matter of the Alleged Nephite Record?"[14]

Again, B. H. Roberts admits:

> Contact with [*View of the Hebrews*], and knowledge of its contents, by the Smiths, is in every way a great probability. And even if that were not so, as to this particular book—if the Smiths never owned the book, never read it, or saw it, still its contents—the

materials of which it was composed—would be, under all the circumstances, matter of "common knowledge" throughout the whole region where the Smiths lived from the birth of Joseph Smith in 1805, to the publication of the Book of Mormon in 1829-30.

I say this with great confidence because Ethan Smith's book is constructed of material that was largely of community knowledge and discussion before collected and published in Ethan Smith's book.[15]

Thomas Stuart Ferguson (1915-1983), who dedicated his life to finding archaeological evidence for the *Book of Mormon*, notes:

Since Oliver Cowdery was born in 1806 and was in Poultney from 3 years of age until he was 19 years of age—16 years in all. And these years encompassed the publication of *View of the Hebrews*, in 1822 [1823] and 1825. His three little half sisters, born in Poultney were all baptized in Ethan Smith's church. Thus the family had a close tie with Ethan Smith.[16]

Jon Krakauer (born April 12, 1954), author of *Under the Banner of Heaven*, observes:

The Book of Mormon explained the origins of these ancient tumuli in a way that dovetailed neatly with both Christian scripture and a theory then in wide circulation, which posited that the American Indians were descended from the lost tribes of Israel.[17]

Terryl L. Givens articulates:

Ethan Smith's was but one in a long line of tracts and treatises that placed the American Indian into the history of the tribes of Israel. This connection was suggested as early as the sixteenth century by the Dominican friar Diego Duran and saw print by 1607 in Gregorio Garcia's *Origin of the Indians of the New World*. The first English publication on the subject was probably Thomas Thorowgood's *Jews in*

America, or Probabilities That the Americans are of that Race (1650), which influenced the Puritan John Eliot. More influential was James Adair's later *History of the American Indians* (London, 1775). Elias Boudinot (*A Star in the West*, 1816) and Josiah Priest (*The Wonders of Nature and Providence*, 1825) argued the same point to large readerships.[18]

In his book, *Lewis & Clark among the Indians*, James P. Ronda recounts that Benjamin Rush (1746-1813), a signer of the Declaration of Independence and a civic leader in Philadelphia, where he was a physician, politician, social reformer, humanitarian, and educator, "gave Lewis a detailed list of ethnographic queries":

> Like so many other European and American scientists, Rush was fascinated by Indian religions. Moreover, he believed, as did many of his contemporaries, that studies of Indian languages and religious ceremonies might prove or disprove a very old and persistent notion about the origin of native people. A widespread academic theory held that Indians might constitute one of the lost tribes of the children of Israel. If the Mandans were misplaced Welshmen, as so many thought, why not see if there were any Jewish Indians in the West.[19]

In an article published by the Native American Heritage Project: "Documenting the Ancestors, concerning the Mandan," posted April 29, 2012, we read the following:

> In 1796 the Mandan were visited by the Welsh explorer John Evans, who was hoping to find proof that their language contained Welsh words. Evans had arrived in St. Louis two years prior, and after being imprisoned for a year, was hired by Spanish authorities to lead an expedition to chart the upper Missouri. Evans spent the winter of 1796–97 with the Mandan but found no evidence of any Welsh influence. In July 1797 he wrote to Dr. Samuel Jones, "Thus having explored and charted the Missurie [*sic*] for 1,800 miles and by my Communications with the

Indians this side of the Pacific Ocean from 35 to 49 degrees of Latitude, I am able to inform you that there is no such People as the Welsh Indians."

Just as the theory of the Mandan/Welsh connection has proven to be incredible for which there is no substantive proof, so the Native American/Jewish connection has proven, through incontrovertible DNA evidence, to be false. Grant H. Palmer reveals:

During the last ten years, scientists from various research organizations, including biologists from Brigham Young University, have tested the DNA of over 7,000 American Indians. These tests cover about 130 tribes scattered throughout North, Central, and South America. This research has revealed that in excess of 99 percent of the ancestors of living Native American women arrived on the American continent from Asia over 12,000 years ago. About 90 percent of the men have Y-chromosome DNA from the same place of origin. Lesser DNA lineages originate in Africa or Europe, most likely Spain, but not from the Middle East.

The LDS position that Israelites "are the principal ancestors of the American Indians" is no longer probable even if a possibility still exists for the yet uncharted 1-2 percent of Indian DNA.[20]

Paul C. Gutjahr, Ruth N. Halls Professor of English at Indiana University, observes:

At the turn of the twenty-first century, certain scientifically minded members of the Church turned to DNA research to help prove that there exists a genetic link between the Middle East and Native Americans. Just as Thomas Ferguson and his New World Archaeological Foundation began to pursue archaeological research in the 1950s to prove the historical reliability of the Book of Mormon [see my chapter on "Archaeological Evidence for the Book of Mormon"], more recent Mormon academics have turned their attention to genetics with a similar hope.

Through analyzing DNA groupings found in both the Middle East and the Americas, they sought evidence that at least some portion of the Native American population descended from Middle Eastern ancestors.

A significant player in such research was BYU microbiologist Scott Woodward, who in 2000, with the help of philanthropist Ira Fulton and James Sorenson, launched a multimillion-dollar study to gather genetic information to link past and present human beings. Like the New World Archaeological Foundation before it, Woodword's Molecular Genealogy Research Group (MGRG), completed a great deal of valuable work, but produced little to defend the *Book of Mormon* as either an ancient or a historically accurate text. In the case of DNA research, the work of the MGRG offered no compelling counterevidence to debunk the reigning theory that Native Americans are descended from Asiatic gene pools, not Middle Eastern ones. In the words of anthropologist Thomas Murphy, "While DNA shows that ultimately all human populations are closely related, to date no intimate genetic link has been found between ancient Israelites and indigenous Americans, much less within the time frame suggested by the Book of Mormon."[21]

DNA tediously collected from ancient paleo-human remains, as well as from a broad spectrum of modern Native American tribes, unequivocally connects their common ancestry to the mongoloid race found in Asia. In the 1990s, Luigi Luca Cavalli-Sforza (1922-2018), a renowned Italian born population geneticist and professor emeritus at Stanford University with the collaboration of others developed procedures for defining "Genetic Geography" using specific genetic markers to indicate the ethnicity and cultural background of individual people. The resultant data developed by Cavalli-Sforza and other geneticists tell us that the Native Americans have very distinctive genetic (DNA) markers, some of whose similarity (i.e., ancestral predecessors) among old world populations, have been associated with the ethnic groups living in the Atlay Mountains area of southern Siberia lying at the intersection of what is today Russia, Mongolia, China and Kazakhstan, not of Jewish Middle Eastern ancestry. The evidence from the DNA analysis accords with a large body of archaeological, anthropological, and linguistic conclusions that Native American peoples' ancestors migrated from Asia, not Israel, at the latest 16,500–13,000 years ago, long before the Jaredites, Nephites and Lamanites populated the Americas. In short, it appears that the mainstream scientific consensus concerning the origin of the Native American population is clearly at odds with the claims put forth in the *Book of Mormon*.

Starting with the American Revolution (between 1765 and 1783), toward the end of the eighteenth century and into the nineteenth century, religion in America saw an evangelical thrust and an "Awakening" bringing Presbyterians, Baptists and Methodists to the forefront, becoming the largest Protestant denominations in America. The numbers of congregants registered with the Methodist church grew from 58,000 in 1790 to 258,000 in 1820, and 1,661,000 in 1860 growing by a factor of 28.6 times while the population in the United States grew by a factor of 8 times, becoming one of the dominant forces of evangelicalism in American religion.[22] The Second Great Awakening (circa 1795-1835), which spread religion through revivals and emotional preaching, exercised a profound impact on church attendance in America and is credited with the founding of numerous colleges and seminaries. (Princeton, Rutgers, Brown, and Dartmouth universities were all established as a direct result of the Great Awakening.)

It was during the fervor of the Second Great Awakening that new religious movements emerged—such as Adventism, Dispensationalism, and the Latter-day Saint movement. The third phase (circa 1825-1835) of the Second Great Awakening, spurred on by the preaching of Presbyterian revivalist Charles Finney (1792-1875), was centered in western New York State. The extent of the fire of revival reached such a fevered pitch of spiritual fervor that the western and central regions of New York were later referred to as the "Burned-over District" (a name given by Finney).

"Burned-over District" of New York.

New York became the crucible of a number of religious movements. It was during this phase of the Second Great Awakening that Joseph Smith of Palmyra, New York started the Mormon movement in 1830; William Miller of Low Hampton, New York the Millerites in 1834; the Fox Sisters of Hydesville, New York the American movement of Spiritualism in 1848; the Shakers established their communal farm in central New York in 1826; the Oneida Society established a community in central New York in 1848; Washington Gladden founded the Social Gospel in Owego, New York in 1832; and the Amana Colony was first settled near Buffalo, New York in 1844.

Alex Beam, in his book *American Crucifixion*, wrote:

> Joseph was hardly the first prophet of America's Second Great Awakening—the tide of religious fervor that washed across the country at the start of the nineteenth century—to traffic in millenarian predictions, and he wasn't the last. But he was the most successful.[23]

Betsy Gaines Quammen writes:

> New York State's "Burned-over District" marinated in a stew of wild revivalism cults, and extremists

preparing adherents for end-times . . . millennialism was rampant, as were utopian societies promoting everything from sexual libertinism (Oneidans) to abstinence (Shakers). . . .

Growing up Joseph picked through hot embers of the Second Great Awakening, pursuing both buried riches and new versions of Christianity.

. . . [I]f there was ever a place that might inspire someone [i.e., Joseph Smith] to imagine his own version of a religion or fancy herself a mystic [i.e., Ann Lee, the founder, and later, leader of the American Shakers], the Burned-over District was it with plenty of muses from which to draw encouragement.[24]

Benjamin E. Park, assistant professor at Sam Houston State University, notes:

Communitarian groups like the Shakers, followers of a British protest sect and led by a female prophet, organized closed societies designed to separate themselves from the ills of modernity. They were followed by other radical movements—both religious and secular—that hoped to establish utopias within the new nation. Nearly every "reading man," complained Ralph Waldo Emerson in 1840, had "a draft of a new community in his waistcoat pocket."[25]

Park further states:

During the same decade when Joseph Smith was introducing his Abrahamic order, John Humphrey Noyes, a Yale-educated theologian with Christian perfectionists tendencies, was envisioning a new social order that freed men and women from the strict confines of marriage. He was also accused of adultery, and in response created his own commune in Oneida, New York, filled with believers who were all linked together through a complex marriage system. The scheme allowed sexual relations as an acceptable form of both spiritual and social practice.[26]

W. D. Davies (1911-2001), who was a Welsh Congregationalist minister, theologian, author and professor of religion in England and the United States, suggested that, "Mormonism arose in a place and time when many utopian, populist, socialistic ideas were in the air."[27] David Roberts, author of *Devil's Gate*, proposes that when Joseph Smith received the *Book of Mormon*, "There was no more propitious time or place in American history for the concoction of new religions." Roberts adds:

> Nowhere was that zeal for new faith more rabid than on the semi-frontier of western New York state. The region centering on Palmyra acquired among circuit-riders a sobriquet as "the burnt-over district." In biographer Fawn Brodie's gloss: "One revival after another was sweeping through the area, leaving behind a people scattered and peeled, for religious enthusiasm was literally being burnt out of them."[28]

At the turn of the century, Rollin Lynde Hartt, a contributing writer for *The Atlantic*, observed:

> [O]riginally, the power of Mormonism was unquestionably the power of doctrine. It entered American life at a period of intense illiberality. The air was full of schism. The sects teemed with recalcitrants. The time was ripe for the establishment of a church so broadly comprehensive as to welcome the malcontents of all Christendom.[29]

Jon Krakauer echoes:

> Mormonism appeared in the right place, at the right time, to exploit a ripe niche that had opened in the nation's ever-shifting spiritual ecology. Many Americans were dissatisfied with the calcified religions of the Old World. Joseph preached a fresh message that was exactly what a great number of people were eager to hear. He took measure of the

public's collective yearning and intuitively shaped his ideas to fit the precise dimensions of that inchoate desire.[30]

Richard Lyman Bushman adds:

Joseph Smith's experiences can be compared to reports from the other visionaries of his time, just as he can be linked to other 19th century culture—universalism, rational skepticism, republicanism, progress, revivalism, magic, communitarianism, health reform, Zionism, and a host of others.[31]

Alex Beam writes:

Sixteen-year-old Elias Smith (no relation to Joseph) met "the Lamb upon Mt. Sion" in the woods near his Woodstock, Vermont, home. John Thompson, a teacher at Palmyra Academy, saw Christ descend from the sky "in a glare of brightness exceeding tenfold the brilliancy of the meridian Sun." Pamphleteer Asa Wild of Amsterdam, New York, spoke with "the awful and glorious majesty of the Great Jehovah" and learned "that every denomination of professing Christians had become extremely corrupt," news akin to the divine message received by Joseph Smith.[32]

It was during this same period that Ralph Waldo Emerson (1803-1882), an essayist, lecturer, philosopher, and poet, led the American transcendentalist movement of the mid-19th century.

The question that is often asked is: *Did Joseph Smith fabricate the Book of Mormon from his contemporary culture?* Alexander Campbell (1788-1866), a Scots-Irish immigrant who became an ordained minister in the United States and joined his father Thomas Campbell as a leader of a reform effort that is historically known as the Restoration Movement, and by some as the "Stone-Campbell Movement," observed that the *Book of Mormon* reproduced,

. . . every error and almost every truth discussed in New York for the last ten years. [It] decides all the great controversies—infant baptism, ordination, the trinity, regeneration, repentance, justification, the fall of man, the atonement, transubstantiation, fasting, penance, church government, religious experience, the call of the ministry, the general resurrection, eternal punishment, who may baptize, and even the question of free masonry, republican government, and the rights of man.[33]

Blake Ostler (born 1955), an American philosopher, theologian, and lawyer who has written numerous articles on the topics of Mormon theology, philosophy, and thought, concedes:

Many Book of Mormon doctrines are best explained by the nineteenth-century theological milieu. . . . it is likely that Joseph Smith expanded the Book of Mormon . . . some doctrines in the book's pre-Christian sections are simply too developed and too characteristic of the nineteenth-century to explain as pre-existic ideas. The presence of the KJV [*King James Version* of the *Bible*] in the book is, it seems to me, indisputable. . . .[34]

Ross Anderson, the founding pastor of Wasatch Evangelical Free Church in Roy, Utah, notes:

The Book of Mormon reflects nineteenth-century American theology and political themes. It offers guidance on democracy, the practice of capitalism, and various Protestant controversies. Some scholars see parallels between the Book of Mormon's secret societies—the Gadianton robbers—and contemporary concerns about Freemasonry. Many see the warning in 1 Nephi 13 about a "great abominable church" as a close parallel to anti-Catholic propaganda in the 1830s. Sermons by Nephite prophets echo the form and language of nineteenth-century evangelists. The conversion experiences described in the Book of Mormon are similar to spiritual awakenings commonly reported in the American revival movement of the early 1800s.[35]

Anderson asks, "Why are the contents of an ancient work so closely tied to the concerns of one American generation?"[36] Mormon Church Historians, Leonard J. Arrington (1917-1999), and Davis Bitton (1930-2007), concurred, suggesting:

> [T]he text of the Book of Mormon represents a rewording of Smith's private concerns and the larger issues swirling about western New York. Certainly the origin of the American Indian, anti-Masonism, anti-Catholicism, and questions of authority, predestination, and baptism loomed large in the minds of Smith's neighbors, and such concerns can be mirrored in the text of the Book of Mormon. Such parallels suggest to some scholars that the book originated in the fertile mind of a questioning youth in nineteenth-century western New York, not in ancient America.[37]

Again, Arrington and Bitton further intimated:

> [T]here is no inclination by non-Mormon scholars to accept the [*Book of Mormon*'s] claim to be an ancient document written by prophets on the American continent between 600 B.C. and A.D. 421. The book is viewed by non-Mormons as a product of nineteenth-century America, whether actually written by Smith or simply taken over by him.
>
> . . . the [*Book of Mormon*] substantially concern[s] itself with current issues. Granting this, the book could then be read, at least in part, as specifically designed to answer to the needs of its contemporary readers.[38]

Brent A. Gardner (born 1951), an American researcher, writer and speaker on the *Book of Mormon*, concedes that the *Book of Mormon* "has a history that is demonstrably related to the nineteenth century American Northeast with "obvious nineteenth-century elements of language and imitative style." Gardner notes that Mark D. Thomas (born 1949), director of field studies in the Marriott School of Management at Brigham Young University, in his book, *Digging in Cumorah: Reclaiming Book of Mormon Narratives*, mentions the nineteenth-century sounding phrases found in the *Book of Mormon* contemporary to Joseph Smith that were used by evangelicals to describe the conversion experience:

> In addition to biblical phrases evangelicals had their own conventional phrases or formulas for describing conversion: "redeeming love," "to taste redeeming love," "to hear the shouts of redeeming love," and "to sing the song of redeeming love," a phrase that also appears in the Book of Mormon (Alma 5:26).

Brent A. Gardner observes:

> Both the specificity of the phrase and the theological context in which it appears, locate this phrase in Joseph Smith's cultural background. Although not proof, it is strong evidence suggesting that the phrase "to sing the song of redeeming love," as found in Alma 5:26, comes from a nineteenth-century production culture.[39]

William L. Davis, an independent scholar, draws our attention to the fact that the *Book of Mormon* is "dominated by a patchwork of nonbiblical wording and nineteenth-century religious phraseology" and these same "nonbiblical terms" appear to be sequestered "from Smith's nineteenth-century religious milieu."[40] Davis relates that "King Benjamin's sermon topics," found in the *Book of Mosiah* (circa 130-120 BC), "consist of generic fundamental Christian doctrines and controversies . . . [whose] fundamental principles could . . . appear, with little modification, in any revival or camp meeting in early nineteenth-century Western New York . . ."[41] Davis further states: "In a review of sermons, prophecies, exhortations, teachings, commentaries, and related oral performances in the Book of Mormon, we find that the text systematically reveals the structures and conventions of the semi-extemporaneous preaching that saturated Smith's nineteenth-century environment."[42]

Davis concludes:

> Smith's religious discourses in the Book of Mormon take up more than 100,000 words of the entire text of

approximately 269,510 words . . . [whose] religious discourses—many of which contain variations of the same fundamental Christian principles that require little or no preparation—compose just over 40 percent of the entire text of the Book of Mormon . . . [all packaged] within the narrative framework of an ancient Native American epic . . .[43]

Davis speculates:

If Smith played no role in the creation and articulation of the Book of Mormon [It is Davis's position that he did], then the real author(s)—mortal or divine, via covert manuscripts or luminous words appearing on the surface of a seer stone—managed to predict and imitate Smith's techniques so well that the results are indistinguishable from the young prophet's documented style and methods of later years.[44]

Robert L. Millet notes, "certain identifiable portions [of the *Book of Mormon*] are unmistakably nineteenth century, reflecting the culture, language, and theological worldview of Joseph Smith." Millet adds:

More recently, it seems fashionable by some [Latter-day Saints] to doubt and debate the historicity of the Book of Mormon; to speak of the contents of the Nephite record as "doctrinal fiction"; to question the reality of the Book of Mormon personalities or places; or to identify "anachronisms" in the book, specifically doctrines or principles that they feel reflect more of Joseph Smith and the nineteenth century than antiquity [an "anachronism" is thing or an idea belonging to an historical period other than that in which it is referenced].[45]

LDS Church historians, James B. Allen (born 1927), and Glen M. Leonard (born 1938) iterate, "His [Joseph Smith's] religious environment contained seeds of teachings that later become part of Mormon doctrine."[46] Richard Lyman Bushman notes: "The *Book of*

Mormon was best explained, [Fawn] Brodie argued, by Joseph Smith's 'responsiveness to the provincial opinions of his time.' "[47]

Craig L. Blomberg (born August 3, 1955), an American *New Testament* scholar, notes that "Evangelical apologists have not always drawn sufficient attention" to what he recognizes as "a substantial percentage" of the *Book of Mormon* "that simply seems out of place in the historical context to which it is attributed," but upon further examination, "fits perfectly" in the context of "the religious climate and theological concerns of the early nineteenth century."[48] What Blomberg finds more disturbing is Smith and the *Book of Mormon*'s contention that critical concepts had been suppressed and hidden (struck from both the *Old* and *New Testaments*) for centuries. He decries the credibility of this notion "even had a censor deliberately tried to destroy it all."

Blomberg further argues: "It is extremely easy, on the other hand, to imagine a nineteenth-century writer," namely Joseph Smith, "well versed in the KJV, composing such a collage of concepts." (For example, "explicit references to Christ, to his life and ministry, and to the three persons of the Godhead long before New Testament times" that are found in the *Book of Mormon* in profusion.)

Blomberg draws our attention to the fact that "The New Testament itself insists that the distinctive truths of the gospel were not as clearly known in Old Testament times as the Book of Mormon or the *JST* [*Joseph Smith Translation*] would make them (Eph 2:2-6)." He observes that because Christians have "always" pondered over what "Old Testament Saints" understood and how it is that they were redeemed, "it is understandable that Joseph Smith should have wanted them to know the entire plan of salvation." This distinctive "feature of the Book of Mormon," Blomberg contends, "makes it *more* doctrinally consistent with the New Testament" than what remains a mystery in the volume of the *Old Testament* "when taken by itself!"

The second point that Blomberg makes is, though the *KJV* was the only English translation of the *Bible* available to Joseph Smith, "the fact that the Book of Mormon frequently reproduces KJV language even where textual criticism has demonstrated the KJV to have followed an inferior and inauthentic text betrays its merely human origin." If, as Joseph Smith said, the *Book of Mormon* were "the most correct of any book on earth," Blomberg argues, "it would not parallel the corruptions that early orthodox Christianity itself introduced." Because no one knew of these deficiencies, there is strong evidence, Blomberg contends that the *Book of Mormon* was "the invention, however well motivated, of Joseph Smith."[49] (Though these substantive accusations concerning "inferior and inauthentic text[s]" may very-well be true, it has been repeatedly affirmed by Biblical scholars and textual critics over the past 200 years, that no doctrine of Scripture has been affected by these so-called textual aberrations.)

Addressing the pre-*New Testament* era Christology peculiar to the *Book of Mormon*, Terryl L. Givens notes that, "while Mormon scholars emphasize the Book of Mormon's Hebrew connections," he agrees with Stephen E. Robinson (1947-2018), a religious scholar, educator and apologist, and professor emeritus of Ancient Scripture at Brigham Young University, Provo, that the Book of Mormon's cultural belief system was highly "idiosyncratic," embracing what Robinson calls "sophisticated Christian beliefs in a pre-Christian era." Givens offers the example where Nephi's brother Jacob, speaking just prior to the *New Testament* era states: "We knew of Christ and we had a hope of his glory many hundred years before his coming, and not only we ourselves had a hope of his glory but also all the holy prophets which were before us (Jacob 4:4)." Givens concedes that the *Book of Mormon* "is, at least in part, a history of pre-Christian Christians, who 'talk of Christ, . . . rejoice in Christ, . . . prophesy of Christ' centuries before his coming (2 Nephi 25:26)."[50]

Givens further states:

> Beginning as it does in a familiar Old Testament milieu, with references to Jews and Egyptians, to Zedekiah and Jerusalem's impending destruction, **the [Book of Mormon] loses no time in upsetting expectations in regard to traditional Christology.** A mere nine verses into the record, the prophet Lehi sees in vision "One descending out of the midst of heaven," with "twelve others following him," who

"came down and went forth upon the face of the earth." **And thus we are introduced to one of the most radical and pervasive themes in the Book of Mormon—pre-Christian knowledge of Christ.** Unlike the messianic Psalms and Isaiah passages, Book of Mormon prophecies of Christ are unmistakably specific (emphasis added).[51]

Terryl and Fiona Givens write, "God . . . revealed all the ordinances of salvation to Adam . . . 'and set Adam to watch over them [and] to reveal them from heaven to man or to send Angels to reveal them' in the event of their loss."[52]

In his highly publicized and widely influential book, *Mormon Doctrine*, Bruce R. McConkie elaborates:

> Christianity is the religion of the Christians. Hence, true and acceptable Christianity is found [exclusively] among the [Latter-day Saints] who have the fulness [*sic*] of the gospel, and a perverted Christianity holds sway among the so-called Christians [both Catholics and Protestants] of apostate Christendom. In these circles it is believed and taught that Christianity had its beginning with the mortal ministry of our Lord. Actually, of course, Adam was the first Christian . . .[53]

If what McConkie says is true, why then do we read in *Acts 11:26 KJV*: "And the disciples were called Christians first in Antioch." The Gospel was not revealed to Adam and his posterity as is suggested by Joseph Smith in his so-called "inspired writings" (see *Joseph Smith Translation JTS, John 1:1*, and *Moses* 5:58-59), but are fanciful and confabulated stories that belong to the realm of pseudepigraphic literature. *John Gill's Exposition of the Entire Bible* notes:

> [The] mystery of Christ, and of the Gospel, was not made known to men in general, nor so clearly as under the Gospel dispensation. Some hints were given of it to Adam immediately after his fall [The Lord said to Adam that the seed of the woman "shall bruise" the Serpent's "head, and thou [the Serpent]

shalt bruise his heel" (*Genesis 3:15 KJV*)]; and the Gospel was before preached to Abraham ["Your father Abraham rejoiced to see my day" (*John 8:56 KJV*)], Moses [Jesus said, "Moses . . . wrote of me" (*John 5:46 KJV*)], and David [David called Jesus "my Lord" in *Psalm 110 KJV*)], and others knew something of it; and it was still more fully dispensed in the times of the prophet Isaiah [the Apostle John said, "These *things* Isaiah said when he saw His glory and spoke of Him" (*John 12:4 NKJV*)], and other following prophets; but the knowledge of it was not so extensive, nor so clear as now; it lay hid in types and shadows in obscure prophecies and short hints. . . . the time, mode, and circumstances of it were but little understood, and comparatively speaking, it was not known: however it was not so known, as it is now revealed unto his holy apostles and prophets by the Spirit. The apostles and prophets were the superior offices in the Gospel dispensation . . . (Exposition of *Ephesians 3:5*).

For what purpose were the "types" and "shadows" of those things that were to come (namely the fulfillment of Messianic promises) if, from the beginning starting with Adam, the Gospel was made manifest in all its clarity? In *Hebrews 10:1 NJKV*, we read, "For the law" (the "body" of the *Old Testament*) was but "a shadow of the good things to come, *and* not the very image . . ." The Apostle Paul wrote that the institution of the law and its practices were but "a shadow of things to come, but the substance [literally the *body*] is of Christ" (*Colossians 2:17 NKJV*).

In the Apostle Paul's letter to the *Colossians*, he speaks of "the mystery which has been hid from ages and from generations but now is made manifest to his saints" (*Colossians 1:26 KJV*). And again, in *Romans 16:25-27 KJV*, Paul writes:

Now to him that is of power to establish you according to my gospel, and the preaching of Jesus Christ according to the revelation of the mystery, which was kept secret since the world began, But now is made manifest, and by the scriptures of the prophets, according to the commandment of the everlasting God, made known to all the nations for the obedience of faith: To God only wise, be glory through Jesus Christ for ever. Amen.

Matthew Poole's Commentary on this passage states, "the whole doctrine of the gospel . . . was a hidden mystery to generations past." *Gill's Exposition of the Entire Bible* notes:

> [T]he whole gospel, and all the truths of it [were] . . . kept secret since the world began, or "from eternal times": from all the ages of the former dispensations, or that have run out from the beginning of the world . . . (*Romans 16:25*).

Jesus said, "For I tell you that many prophets and kings have desired to see what you see, and have not seen *it*, and to hear what you hear, and have not heard *it*" (*Luke 10:24 NKJV*). In *Gill's Exposition of the Entire Bible*, we read his commentary on this verse: The prophets "had a sight of Christ but a very distant one; they saw him afar off in the promises and prophecies of him; and not very clearly, but through dark types . . ."

The Apostle Paul spoke of the Gospel having once been delivered (see *Romans 1:16*). The Gospel had not been "delivered" in ages past but was manifest in due time in the Apostolic Age of the *New Testament*.

Blake Ostler (born in 1957), an American philosopher, theologian, and lawyer who received his B.A. in philosophy and B.S. in psychobiology from Brigham Young University, Provo, in answering the difficult issue of the "19th century sounding" genre that characterizes the *Book of Mormon*, proposed the "Expansion Theory" first introduced in 1987 in an article in *Dialogue: A Journal of Mormon Thought* titled "The Book of Mormon as a Modern Expansion of an Ancient Source." Ostler explains that the *Book of Mormon* is an amalgamation of an "ancient text" with Joseph Smith's "expansion" embedding 19th-century modern concepts into an otherwise ancient storyline. Ostler contends that Joseph Smith, as a prophetic voice with God given authority, "brought forth Scripture" integrating his contemporary mindset with the old. Stephen E. Robinson argues, however, that Ostler's Expansion

Theory is "inimical to the teachings of the Church" and is "merely [a] camouflaged capitulation to the arguments of the Church's opponents."[54]

Blomberg also contends:

> We see striking parallels between Joseph Smith's thought and developments in nineteenth-century liberal theology that eventuated in this century in what is known as process theology—God evolving as God oscillates between finite and infinite poles of existence. Ironically, this line of theologizing is more akin to the Greek or Hellenistic thought that Mormons like to accuse the early church of emulating than to anything that can be demonstrated from the Old or New Testament.[55]

Richard Lloyd Anderson (born 1926), emeritus professor of Church history and doctrine at Brigham Young University, admits:

> [T]he language in the sections of the Book of Mormon that correspond to parts of the Bible is quite regularly *selected* by Joseph Smith, rather than obtained through independent translation. For instance there are over 400 verses in which the Nephite prophets quote from Isaiah, and half of these appear precisely as the King James version renders them.[56]

After a brief perusal, even to the casual observer, the *Book of Mormon* appears to imitate the vernacular of the archaic Victorian English manifesting linguistic similarities with the *King James Bible*. In more than a few instances, entire passages have been duplicated word-for-word in the *Book of Mormon* that are found in the 1769 edition of the *King James Bible*. In the *Second Book of Nephi*, for example, no less than 18 chapters of the *Book of Isaiah* are quoted verbatim. Incredibly, nearly 30 percent of the *Book of Isaiah* (one source counts 478 verses) is quoted in the *Book of Mormon*. It has been noted that the *Book of Mormon* contains words and phrases that are unique to the *King James* translation (I have given several examples toward the end of this chapter) and passages that some scholars suggest are mistranslations peculiar to the *KJV*, suggesting that it was used as a direct source applied to the *Book of Mormon* (following the *KJV* into error) casting doubt on the "miraculous origin" theory of the supposed ancient text.

If what Orson Pratt (1811-1881), a vanguard member of the first Quorum of Twelve Apostles of the Church of Jesus Christ of Latter-day Saints, says is true, that ". . . almost every verse [of the *Bible*] has been corrupted and mutilated," then why is the *Book of Mormon* replete with quotations from both the *Old* and *New Testaments* (from the *King James* translation)—comprising nearly one of every nine chapters—most quoted word-for-word without addendum or correction; and, I might add, often plagiarized without attribution to the text's author of origin? The *Book of Mormon* contains approximately 27,000 words that are direct quotations from the 1611 *King James* translation of the *Bible*. Some twenty-two chapters from the book of *Isaiah* alone are found in the *Book of Mormon*, and in many cases quoted verbatim. Grant H. Palmer notes that "scholars have determined that [Joseph Smith] consulted an open Bible, specifically a printing of the King James translation . . . including its errors."[57] For example, *Isaiah 3:24* quoted in *2 Nephi* 13:24 reads "instead of a girdle a rent," when it should read "instead of a belt, a rope."

Joseph Smith used a copy of the *King James Bible* (9 inches wide by 11 inches long by 2 inches thick) published in 1828 by H. & E. Phinney, Cooperstown, New York, which he and Oliver Cowdery purchased from Palmyra printer and bookseller E. B. Grandin on October 8, 1829 for $3.75 (equivalent to $120.17 in 2022), to produce the "restored" *Joseph Smith Inspired Translation*.

Stan Larson (born 1946), who graduated from BYU with a BA in history, and an MA in Ancient Scripture, notes in his essay, "The Historicity of the Matthean Sermon on the Mount in 3 Nephi" published in 1992-1993:

> In terms of attempting to pinpoint the origin of the Book of Mormon, even more significant that Book of Mormon revisions are places where it follows the KJV into error, echoing mistranslations or including translations of late and derivative Greek texts. Certainly the Book of Mormon should not have the

same errors which displaced the original and crept into the text over the centuries. Since to plagiarize means to appropriate and use, without acknowledgment, the words of another, one must here use the term—as harsh as it may sound—to characterize Smith's dependence on the KJV. The Book of Mormon account of Jesus's sermon in 3 Nephi 12-14 originated in the nineteenth century, derived from unacknowledged plagiarism of the KJV. Smith copied the KJV blindly, not showing awareness of translation problems and errors in the KJV. Yet the Book of Mormon is not a slavish copy of the KJV—there are numerous words deleted, revised, or added to the text. Rather than translate from an ancient document, Smith seems to have quoted from Matthew 5-7 of the KJV and to have made certain revisions as a response to the English text of the KJV.

The Book of Mormon cannot be exempted from such textual criticism by emphasizing that translation inevitably introduces elements from the translator's environment.

David J. Richards, who has degrees in Hebrew & Religious Studies and in Islamic Studies, and as a postgraduate researcher has examined the *Book of Mormon* and its relationship with the *Bible*, writes in a chapter titled "The Fifth Gospel: The Ministry of Christ in 3 Nephi":

Third Nephi, particularly 3 Nephi 11-30 which narrates the visit of the resurrected Christ, has been described as 'the center of the Book of Mormon' and its 'climax' while the current introduction of the LDS version describes Christ's ministry to the Nephites as 'the crowning event' of the book. Yet the accounts close parallels with the biblical Gospels have attracted comment. Terryl Givens describes 3 Nephi as 'an account both familiar and audacious' and 'so blatantly familiar that it almost begs to be labeled [and often has been] facile plagiarism.' Grant Hardy, [a graduate of Brigham Young University and professor of history and religious studies and director of the humanities program at the University of North Carolina at Asheville], while acknowledging key differences, likewise suggests in view of the recapitulation of the Sermon on the Mount, extended biblical quotations and the narrative parallels that 'it appears that there is not much in Third Nephi that we have not already seen in the New Testament.'[58]

An additional conundrum concerning the historicity of the Book of Mormon lies in the arena of linguistics. B. H. Roberts addressed the linguistic problem in *Studies of the Book of Mormon* that he found difficult to circumnavigate:

The fact[s] . . . developed up to this point seem to be—

1. That there are a large number of separate language stocks in America that show very little relationship to each other.

2. That it would take a long time—much longer than that recognized as "historic times"—to develop these dialects and stocks where the development is conceived of as arising from a common source of origin—some primitive language.

3. That there is no connection between the American languages and the language of any people of the Old World. New World languages appear to be indigenous to the New World.

4. That the time limits named in the Book of Mormon—which represents the people of America as speaking and writing one language down to as late a period as 400 A.D.—is not sufficient to allow for these divergences into the American language stocks and their dialects.[59]

B. H. Roberts admitted:

As I proceeded with my recent investigation . . . and more especially in the . . . new field of language problems, I found the difficulties more serious than I had [previously] thought; and the more I investigated the more difficult I found the formulation of an answer . . .[60]

Roberts would reach the end of his life without finding a satisfactory answer to this enigma.

According to the *Book of Mormon*, the Nephites and the Lamanites were Jews who fled from the nation of Israel around 600 BC. It may be assumed that they continued to speak a Semitic language until at least 400 AD, the time frame when the Book of Mormon comes to a climactic conclusion. It is evident that there are no Native Americans today that speak Semitic languages, nor is there any evidence that the Native American languages have ever been influenced by Semitic language stocks at any point in their history. "Historical linguists who specialize in the languages of Native America are in agreement that the languages of Native America cannot be proven to be related to each other within the last eight to ten thousand years, let alone within the last thousand."[61]

In their book, *The Crucible of Doubt: Reflections on the Quest for Faith*, Terryl and Fiona Givens ask:

[H]ow, in the space of a mere thousand years or so, could the Hebrew of Lehi's tribe have fragmented and morphed into every one of the hundreds of Indian languages of the Western Hemisphere, from Inuit to Iroquois to Shoshone to Patagonian? Languages just don't mutate and multiply that quickly.[62]

In September of 1830, Oliver Cowdery, Parley P. Pratt, and Frederick G. Williams were sent, by revelation, to the extreme western frontiers of Missouri and of the United States to preach to the Shawnees and the Delawares whom they specifically identified as "Lamanites" who were "a remnant of the house of Israel" (see title page of the *Book of Mormon* first published in 1830). During the 1840s, Joseph Smith and the First Presidency, believing that the American Indian tribes were the "remnant of the house of Israel," also sent missionaries to the Dakota, Sioux, Potawatomi and Mohican Stockbridge, all of whom were identified as Lamanites.[63]

Joseph Smith preaching to the Lamanites. A drawing by French School.

Under the heading "North American Indian Languages," written for *Britannica* by Lyle Campbell, Professor of Linguistics, University of Hawai'i, Manoa. Author of *American Indian Languages: The Historical Linguistics of Native America,* we read:

The North American Indian languages are both numerous and diverse. At the time of first European contact, there were more than 300. . . . The North American Indian languages are so diverse that there is no feature or complex of features shared by all. . . . North American Indian languages have been grouped into 57 language families . . . These language families are independent of one another, and as of the second decade of the 21st century none can be shown to be related to any other. . . . American Indian languages . . . [were] separated from one another so long ago and changed so much in the intervening time that available evidence is insufficient ever to demonstrate any relationship. . . . In any case, no theory of common origin for the North American Indian languages has any serious following.

An article in *Mormon Stories* titled "Archaeology and the Book of Mormon," reveals:

> Philologic studies [the branch of knowledge that deals with the structure, historical development, and relationships of a language or languages] have divided the Indian languages into five distinct linguistic stocks which show very little relationship to each other. It strongly indicates that the division of the Indians into separate stocks occurred long before their language developed beyond the most primitive articulation.

Grant H. Palmer's assessment is as follows:

> [T]here is no evidence that ancient Americans practiced Hebrew or Christian rituals or held corresponding beliefs. No clearly identified Hebrew or Egyptian writing has been discovered in the New World dating before Columbus. Furthermore, linguists have determined from historical patterns the rate at which languages evolve. Given that rate, the Book of Mormon provides far too short a time (1,400 years) for the complete disappearance of the Nephite-Lamanite language. No indigenous American language has a demonstrable Hebraic or Egyptian origin.[64]

Rodney L. Meldrum, an independent researcher, author, and national lecturer on the truthfulness of the *Book of Mormon*, who has studied the origins of proposed geographical settings of the *Book of Mormon* including the Mesoamerican/Mayan connection, concedes: "[T]he written language of the Maya [among Mormon scholars, there are many who believe that the Maya civilization is conterminous with the Nephite civilization] is neither Hebrew nor Egyptian. Mayan is as unrelated to Hebrew or Egyptian as Chinese is to Latin."[65]

Richard Lyman Bushman addresses the critics' appraisal of the *Book of Mormon*'s authenticity, stating:

The modern critics write with the same confidence as the nineteenth-century skeptics. They are certain that any reasonable person who takes an objective, scientific approach to the *Book of Mormon* will recognize "the obvious fictional quality" of the book. They point to evidence in the book of the anti-Masonic agitation stirring New York in the years when it was being translated. In the doctrinal portions, they see anti-Universalist language and imitations of camp-meeting preaching. The critics complain that the Isaiah passages quoted by Nephi draw upon portions of the book now thought to be pseudepigrapha [falsely-attributed works, texts whose claimed author is not the true author, or a work whose real author attributed it to a figure of the past], composed long after the Nephites left Jerusalem. Turning to archaeology, they point out that archaeological digs have produced no evidence of Nephite civilization, yielding no horse bones, for example, an animal named in the *Book of Mormon*. ["And also all manner of cattle, of oxen, and cows, and of sheep, and of swine, and of goats, and also many other kinds of animals which were useful for the food of man. And they also had horses, and asses, and there were elephants and cureloms and cumoms; all of which were useful unto man, and more especially the elephants and cureloms and cumoms" (*Ether* 9:16-19).] Most recently, an anthropological researcher has claimed that Native American DNA samples correspond to Asian patterns [this is now well established], precluding Semitic origins. In view of all the evidence, the critics believe defense of the book's authenticity is hopeless.[66]

W. D. Davies asked, "does not the Book of Mormon rather belong to the genre of the apocalyptic and pseudepigraphical literature?" Again, Davies propounds, "does not Mormonism, in retaining so much of the literal interpretation of the apocalyptic tradition, depart from the main elements of early Christianity [?] . .

. It seems so."[67] Krister Stendahl (1921-2008), a Swedish theologian and *New Testament* expert, acknowledged: "[T]he Book of Mormon belongs to and shows many of the typical signs of the Targums and the pseudepigraphic recasting of biblical material."[68] Stendahl further states:

> [O]ne of the striking tendencies in pseudepigraphic literature [is the] hunger for further revelation, the insatiable hunger for knowing more than has been revealed so far. . . . [which] has its risks and its theological costs. . . . The apocryphal and pseudepigraphical writings, when looked at from the outside, are driven by this *horror vacui* ["the fear or dislike of leaving empty spaces"]. . . . [T]he hunger to know more engenders interpretations and new revelations. . . . It is of great importance to reflect phenomenologically on such new outpourings of revelation.[69]

Terryl and Fiona Givens concur, stating, "People have a horror of loose ends. We crave closure and certainty, wholeness and equilibrium."[70] Heikki Räisänen (1941-2015), Academy Professor Emeritus in the Academy of Finland and former Head of the Centre of Excellence in the Department of Biblical Studies of the University of Helsinki, suggested that Joseph Smith was a "creative interpreter of the Bible." Räisänen wrote: "Joseph's teachings provide solutions for most, if not all, of the genuine problems and contradictions of the Bible with which scholars have wrestled for generations."[71]

Wesley P. Walters (1926-1990), a renowned cult expert, draws our attention to the fact:

> [T]here is continual use of the 'thee', 'thou' and 'ye', as well as the archaic verb endings 'est' (second person singular). Since the Elizabethan style was not Joseph's natural idiom, he continually slipped out of this King James pattern and repeatedly confused the norms as well. Thus he lapsed from 'ye' (subject) to 'you' (object) as the subject of sentences (e.g. Mos. 2:19; 3:34; 4:24), jumped from plural ('ye') to

singular ('thou') in the same sentence (Mos. 4:22) and moved from verbs without endings (e.g. 'yields . . . putteth,' 3:19).[72]

How is it that Joseph Smith, born at the turn of the 19th-century, translated a 4th-century manuscript into 17th-century King James English from the Early Modern Elizabethan period? In Joseph Smith's defense, Joseph Fielding McConkie, Jr. offered:

> The King James Version is the Bible of Restoration. It is the Bible that Joseph Smith used as a style guide for translating the Book of Mormon and the revelations he received as they are recorded in the Doctrine and Covenants.[73]

James B. Allen and Glen M. Leonard note, "the Book of Mormon carries unmistakable marks of the language of Joseph Smith's time."[74] B. H. Roberts concedes:

> There can be no doubt, either, that the translation [of the "Golden Plates"] thus obtained was expressed in such language as the Prophet could command, in phraseology as he was master of and common to the time and locality where he lived . . . the *Book of Mormon*, though a translation of an ancient record, is, nevertheless, given in English idiom of the period and locality in which the Prophet lived; and in the faulty English, moreover, both as to composition, phraseology, and grammar, of a person of Joseph Smith's limited education; and also accounts for the general sameness of phraseology and literary style which runs through the whole volume.[75]

Samuel Langhorne Clemens (1835-1910), better known by his pen name Mark Twain, an American writer, humorist, entrepreneur, publisher, and lecturer, once said, "I like a good story well told" (Watermelon speech, 1907). Mark Twain, who was on his way to Carson City in the Territory of Nevada, accompanied by his brother Orion and one other gentleman, visited Salt Lake City on Wednesday, August 7, 1861 and were introduced to, what Twain described as "the only absolute monarch in America,"[76] President Brigham Young. Much to his disappointment, Twain, who came away from Salt Lake City, Utah, with a *Book of Mormon* tucked under his arm, thought the book was extremely drab and tedious, and referred to it as "chloroform in print." In Mark Twain's assessment of the *Book of Mormon*, he writes:

> All men have heard of the Mormon Bible, but few except the "elect" have seen it, or, at least, taken the trouble to read it. I brought away a copy from Salt Lake. The book is a curiosity to me, it is such a pretentious affair, and yet so "slow," so sleepy; such an insipid mess of inspiration. It is chloroform in print. If Joseph Smith composed this book, the act was a miracle—keeping awake while he did it was, at any rate. If he, according to tradition, merely translated it from certain ancient and mysteriously-engraved plates of copper, which he declares he found under a stone, in an out-of-the-way locality, the work of translating was equally a miracle, for the same reason.
>
> The book seems to be merely a prosy detail of imaginary history, with the Old Testament for a model; followed by a tedious plagiarism of the New Testament. The author labored to give his words and phrases the quaint, old-fashioned sound and structure of our King James's translation of the Scriptures; and the result is a mongrel—half modern glibness, and half ancient simplicity and gravity. The latter is awkward and constrained; the former natural, but grotesque by the contrast. Whenever he found his speech growing too modern—which was about every sentence or two—he ladled in a few such Scriptural phrases as "exceeding sore," "and it came to pass," etc., and made things satisfactory again. "And it came to pass" was his pet. If he had left that out, his Bible would have been only a pamphlet.
>
> The Mormon Bible is rather stupid and tiresome to read, but there is nothing vicious in its teachings. Its code of morals is unobjectionable—it is

"smouched" [Milton] from the New Testament and no credit given.[77]

In *1 Nephi* 6:1, 2 & 5, we read, "And now I, Nephi, do not give the genealogy of my fathers . . . For it sufficeth me to say that we are descendants of Joseph . . . for I desire the room that I may write of the things of God." If Nephi desired room, why then did he proceed to repeat the oft used superfluous phrase, "and it came to pass?" In one chapter alone, *1 Nephi* 16, the ubiquitous phrase, "and it came to pass," is repeated no less than 31 times!

Hugh Nibley notes: "Nothing delighted the critics more than the monotonous repetition of 'it came to pass' at the beginning of thousands of sentences in the Book of Mormon. . . . Simply outrageous—as English literature . . ."[78] The phrase "and it came to pass" occurs 1,476 times in the 1830 edition of the *Book of Mormon* comprising a full 13 pages, or 2.5% of its content. Also, a minimum of 14.7%, or 78 pages, comes from the *King James Version* of the *Bible*. This includes twenty of the twenty-seven books of the *New Testament* that are notably represented by one or more quotes.

Rev. Martin Thomas (M. T.) Lamb (1838-1912), Assistant Pastor of the First Baptist Church in Salt Lake City, Utah, observed:

[T]he prevailing style of the Book of Mormon is so verbose, so full of inelegant and uncalled-for repetitions, that any ordinary writer can greatly excel it—often reducing its wordy sentences to one-half, and one-third, and even one-fourth their present compass without any sacrifice of thought or force of beauty . . .[79]

M. T. Lamb went on to critique what he appraised as:

[A]wkwardly expressed sentences . . . [an] unnatural arrangement . . . [a] bewildering mass . . . [a] blundering, awkward narrative . . . such puerile, shallow stuff . . . barbarous in its grammatical construction . . . very limited [in its] vocabulary . . . an unfortunate choice of [words] . . . [a] climax of absurdities.[80]

Bernard DeVoto (1897-1955), an American historian, essayist, columnist, teacher, editor, and reviewer, called the *Book of Mormon* "a yeasty fermentation, formless, aimless and inconceivably absurd . . . a disintegration."[81] Harold Bloom, an American literary critic and Sterling Professor of Humanities at Yale University, said that the *Book of Mormon* "has bravura, but beyond question it is wholly tendentious and frequently tedious," and declared, "I cannot recommend that the book be read either fully or closely, because it scarcely sustains such reading."[82] Terryl L. Givens notes that the *Book of Mormon* was decried as "both clichéd and heretical, pedestrian and preposterous."[83] Charles Haddon Spurgeon (1834-1892), an English Baptist preacher who was the pastor of the congregation at the Metropolitan Tabernacle in London for 38 years, made a harsh assessment, stating, "One of the most modern pretenders to inspiration is the Book of Mormon. I could not blame you should you laugh outright while I read aloud a page from that conglomeration."[84]

Richard Lyman Bushman adds:

> The [*Book of Mormon*] has been difficult for historians and literary critics from outside Mormondom to comprehend. A text that inspires and engages Mormons baffles outside readers. . . . Histories of American literature usually ignore the *Book of Mormon*. It seems subliterary, either simple or unintelligible.[85]

Grant H. Palmer stated, "What is obvious about [certain sections] . . . of the Book of Mormon is that it was borrowed from the KJV and placed in an ancient American context."[86] Of a perplexing curiosity to me are the use of quotes from later dated sources (particularly from the *New Testament*) that appear in an historical context in the *Book of Mormon* that far antedates (600 years) the period in which they were actually written! Below is a brief sampling.

This first comparison is that of *1 Nephi* 10:8 borrowed from two *New Testament* sources, *John 1:26-27* and *Luke 3:16 KJV*.

1 Nephi 10:8—(600 years before Christ) ". . . for there standeth one among you whom ye know not;

and he is <u>mightier than I, whose shoe's latchet I am not worthy to unloose. . . .</u>"

John 1:26-27 KJV—(contemporary to Christ) ". . . but <u>there standeth one among you, whom ye know not</u>. He it is, who coming after me is preferred before me, <u>whose shoe's latchet I am not worthy to unloose</u>."

Luke 3:16 KJV—(contemporary to Christ) "John answered, saying unto *them* all, I indeed baptize you with water; but one <u>mightier than I</u> cometh . . ."

This second comparison is that of *1 Nephi* 10:18 borrowed from the epistle to the *Hebrews* verse *13:8.*

***1 Nephi* 10:18**—(600 years before Christ) "For he is <u>the same yesterday, and to-day, and forever</u> . . ."

Hebrews 13:8 KJV—(contemporary to Christ) "Jesus Christ <u>the same yesterday, and to day, and for ever</u>."

This third example is that of *2 Nephi* 4:17 borrowed from Paul's letter to the *Romans* verse *7:24.*

***2 Nephi* 4:17**—(600 years before Christ) ". . . my heart exclaimeth: <u>O wretched man that I am!</u> Yea, my heart sorroweth because of mine iniquities . . ."

Romans 7:24 KJV—(contemporary to Christ) "<u>O wretched man that I am!</u> who shall deliver me from the body of this death?"

It should also be noted:

Christ's Sermon on the Mount in the Book of Mormon and the Bible are identical. Yet later on, in the Joseph Smith translation of the Bible, Joseph corrected many of the parts of the Sermon on the Mount. So the question is, if the sermon on the mount was not translated correctly in the Bible, why then, is it the same incorrect translation in the Book of Mormon? Why is it not corrected like Joseph later did with his Bible translation?[87]

Krister Stendahl, an expert on the book of *Matthew*, acknowledges:

> I understand that this raises questions which are well known among Mormon scholars.
>
> Those verses about the daily bread and the coming of the kingdom are contained in the Inspired Version by Joseph Smith. So the question is why they are not in 3 Nephi. . . .
>
> Why the prayer for bread is missing in the 3 Nephi version [of the Sermon on the Mount] is not easy to explain.[88]

It has been proposed that Joseph Smith's inclusion of *Mark 16:15-18* in the *Book of Mormon* is a strong argument for its prevarication. Compare *Mark 16:15-18* with *Mormon 9:22-24*:

> And he said unto them, Go ye into all the world, and preach the gospel to every creature. He that believeth and is baptized shall be saved; but he that believeth not shall be damned. And these signs shall follow them that believe; In my name shall they cast out devils; they shall speak with new tongues; They shall take up serpents; and if they drink any deadly thing, it shall not hurt them; they shall lay hands on the sick, and they shall recover (*Mark 16:15-18 KJV*).
>
> For behold, thus said Jesus Christ, the Son of God . . . : Go ye into all the world, and preach the gospel to every creature; And he that believeth and is baptized shall be saved, but he that believeth not shall be damned; And these signs shall follow them that believe—in my name shall they cast out devils; they shall speak with new tongues; they shall take up serpents; and if they drink any deadly thing it shall not hurt them; they shall lay hands on the sick and they shall recover; (*Mormon 9:22-24*).

It should be noted that these same verses also appear twice in the *Doctrine and Covenants* (though paraphrased):

And these signs shall follow them that believe—
In my name they shall do many wonderful works;
In my name they shall cast out devils; In my
name they shall heal the sick; In my name they
shall open the eyes of the blind, and unstop the
ears of the deaf; And the tongue of the dumb
shall speak; And if any man shall administer
poison unto them it shall not hurt them; And the
poison of a serpent shall not have power to harm
them (*Doctrine and Covenants* 84:65-72).

And these signs shall follow him—he shall heal
the sick, he shall cast out devils, and shall be
delivered from those who would administer unto
him deadly poison; And he shall be led in paths
where the poisonous serpent cannot lay hold
upon his heel, and he shall mount up in the
imagination of his thoughts as upon eagles'
wings (*Doctrine and Covenants* 124:98-99).

Joseph Smith, while utilizing the passages in *Mark 16:15-18* (found in his *King James Bible*), had no inkling that they were, in all likelihood, spurious in nature, falling outside the canon of Scripture. This suggests, once again, that these passages were cropped (plagiarized), as were so many others from the Biblical narrative, and incorporated into Joseph Smith's so-called inspired writings—the *Book of Mormon* and *Doctrine and Covenants*.

In the final chapter of the Gospel of *Mark* in the *New Testament*, the ending appearing in most modern bibles (*Mark 16:9-20*, albeit placed in brackets or with a disclaimer) is what is known as the Longer Ending, or Apocryphal Addition. *Mark 16*: verses *9* through *20* do not appear in the oldest manuscripts (circa AD 300) creating doubt as to their authenticity, suggesting that they were not part of the original Gospel. Thomas A. Wayment, assistant professor of ancient scripture at Brigham Young University, Provo, reveals:

Mark 16:9–20 are missing completely in two
important codices, Codex Sinaiticus (fourth century
AD, containing the entire New Testament) and

Codex Vaticanus (fourth century AD, containing almost the entire New Testament, with the exception of the Pastorals and Revelation). Furthermore, many early versions (Latin, Armenian, Georgian, and Ethiopic) do not contain the final twelve verses and instead end with Mark 16:8. Metzger and Ehrman claim that "Clement of Alexandria, Origen, and Ammonius show no knowledge of the existence of these verses." While they are justified in this claim, there is no compelling reason to be alarmed at their silence on the matter and to interpret their silence as evidence of absence. Jerome acknowledged that the verses were missing in some copies of the Gospel when he stated, "In the majority of Gospel manuscripts these verses are not present" (*in raris fertur Evangeliis, omnibus Graeciae libris paene hoc capitulum fine non habentibus*). Eusebius was also aware of the difficulties associated with the ending of the Gospel of Mark when he said, "Nearly all the copies of the Gospel of Mark end in this way [i.e., at *16:8*], and the things that follow [probably *16:9–20*] are in some but not all copies and may be spurious."

Ronald V. Huggins, University of Toronto, Toronto School of Theology, 1997 MCS, Regent College, Vancouver, BC, 1987 BFA, University of Idaho, 1977 Th.D., notes:

Scholars of all theological stripes are generally agreed, though by no means universally agreed, that Mark 16:9-20 were not part of the Gospel of Mark originally, and that the Gospel either originally ended at Mark 16:8, or that the original ending was lost.[89]

Bruce Metzger (1914-2007), an American biblical scholar, Bible translator and textual critic, concludes: "Thus, on the basis of good external evidence and strong internal considerations it appears that the earliest ascertainable form of the Gospel of Mark ended with 16:8."[90]

Richard Carrier (born December 1, 1969), graduate of Berkeley and Columbia Universities, an American author and activist, whose work focuses on empiricism, atheism, and the historicity of Jesus, writes, "consensus has long since rejected [*Mark 16:9-20*] as an interpolation . . . an interpolation from manuscript and stylistic evidence."[91] Matthew D. McDill, in his introduction to "A Textual and Structural Analysis of Mark 16:9-20," echoes:

> The current consensus of scholarship is that Mark 16:9-20 was not in the original manuscript. There are a few rare exceptions to this consensus; William Farmer is the most notable example. Most of the recent writings on this passage do not attempt to establish the ending of Mark (they assume it is v. 8), but endeavor to explain what may have happened to the real ending or why Mark may have intentionally ended his gospel at v. 8.[92]

Sterling M. McMurrin emphatically stated, "You don't get books from angels and translate them by miracles."[93] Terryl L. Givens contends, "The naked implausibility of gold plates, seer stones, and warrior-angles finds little by way of scientific corroboration . . ."[94] Again Givens concedes: "Certainly inexplicable anachronisms, wildly implausible scenarios, obvious nineteenth-century imports, and the like would challenge [the *Book of Mormon*'s] divine authorship."[95] Terryl and Fiona Givens propose, "The question may remain, how does one lock onto the propositional assertions of a restored gospel that is also laden with claims about gold plates and the Book of Abraham and a male priesthood and a polygamous past and a thousand other details we may find difficult?"[96] John E. Clark capitulates that Joseph Smith's "account of the origin of the Book of Mormon is, to understate the obvious, outrageously incredible."[97]

4

The Supersession of Mormonism

I fear that the Latter-day Saints, in many cases, are blinded by their own vanity . . . (George Albert Smith, the eighth President of the LDS Church).[1]

It has been proclaimed that there is a great difference between us [The Church of Jesus Christ of Latter-day Saints] and the Christian world (Brigham Young, the second President of the LDS Church).[2]

Robert Mullen observes that, "Mormons today, as of old, tend to live in a religious world apart."[3] The supersession of Mormonism gives the LDS Church the distinction of having elevated their organization, priesthood authority, and so-called restorative doctrines well above all other Christian denominations. Joseph F. Smith said, "to become identified . . . with the rest of the [Christian] world, to become like them . . . [would] thwart . . . the purposes of God."[4] In *Doctrine and Covenants*, the God of Mormonism sternly pronounced, "[W]o unto all those who come not unto this priesthood."[5]

For nearly 200 years the Mormon Church, with their pretensions to Divine authority, religious imperialism and smug triumphalist rhetoric, has audaciously excoriated, inveighed, and vilified Christian orthodoxy—and the Lord's beloved and betrothed bride (the Church) for whom Jesus shed his precious blood, with a litany of accusations. The LDS Church's General Authorities have suggested:

> [M]any of the clearest and most precious [biblical] truths were eliminated through Satan's power over the souls of men. . . . [And] [t]hrough the mixture of the gospel with pagan [more particularly Hellenistic and Platonic] philosophy, the true nature of God had been lost. . . . [In addition, with the advent of the *Book of Mormon*,] The time had come for the light of the gospel to break through the dark cloud of superstition and false philosophy.[6]

James E. Talmage (1862-1933), an English chemist, geologist, and religious leader who served as a member of the Quorum of the Twelve Apostles of The Church of Jesus Christ of Latter-day Saints (LDS Church) from 1911 until his death, contends:

> The restored Church [The Church of Jesus Christ of Latter-day Saints] affirms that a general apostasy developed during and after the apostolic period, and that the primitive Church lost its power, authority, and graces as a divine institution, and degenerated into an earthly organization only. . . . **If the alleged apostasy of the primitive Church was not a reality, The Church of Jesus Christ of Latter-day Saints is not the divine institution its name proclaims.**[7]

Bruce R. McConkie echoes:

> Universal apostasy fell upon men between Jesus' day and our day. . . . Churches built on false gospels are false churches. They have no saving power. They may, as Jesus said, be "built upon the works of men, or upon the works of the devil" (3 Nephi 27:11). . . . The way to find the true religion and the pure gospel is to find what Jesus and the ancient apostles taught. It is, however, universally recognized by all professors of religion in all churches that such a

system no longer exists either in any one sect or in all the sects of Christendom combined.[8]

McConkie condemns the contemptible state of all so-called "false churches" that operate outside of the authority of Mormonism, "the only true Church," consigning them to "a dark and benighted world where the 'tables' of doctrine 'are full of vomit and filthiness, so that there is no place clean.' "[9]

Hugh Nibley reports that the Mormon Church has condemned "Mainstream Christianity" as "an anemic, bloodless, meaningless sort of thing, because there's no doctrine, nothing you can get your teeth into."[10] Nibley insists, "Only the Latter-day Saints honor the great traditions of Christendom by taking them literally . . ."[11]

Robert M. Bowman Jr., an American evangelical Christian theologian specializing in the study of apologetics, suggests, "If the Great Apostasy is a myth [and it is his contention that it is] then there is no basis for the LDS claim that it represents the 'Restoration' of the true church to the earth."[12]

Craig L. Blomberg contends, "I understand the argument that the church was allegedly apostate all those years, but I find that argument unpersuasive and untrue to history."

> [D]istinctively Mormon doctrines regularly rely on the Book of Mormon's claims that "plain and precious truths" have been lost from the Bible. None of the ancient manuscripts support the contention that the type of "restorations" that the JST (Joseph Smith Translation) or the uniquely LDS Scripture make were ever in the original biblical texts. Neither do any ancient manuscripts exist to support the claim that the early church left out entire books from the Bible that would have included distinctively LDS doctrine.[13]

Joseph Smith taught, however, that humankind "had apostatized from the true and living faith and there was no society or denomination that built upon the Gospel of Jesus Christ as recorded in the New Testament."[14] Joseph Fielding Smith attests:

[I]n the dark days of universal departure . . . after false teachings and organizations had been introduced, the time came when the pure gospel of Jesus was not found among men on the earth; false ordinances and doctrine had been substituted for the divine truth in all parts of the earth; and the Holy priesthood had been replaced by false creeds and a spurious order of priesthood.[15]

Again, Joseph Fielding Smith persists:

In time all ordinances of the gospel were changed, commandments were broken, and the simple principles of the gospel were mixed with pagan philosophy by the "grievous wolves" and apostate disciples who displaced the prophets and apostles who had divine communion with the heavens. Spiritual darkness set in, and unrighteous men took command and closed the heavens against themselves. Visions and contact with the heavens ceased, and the gifts of the spirit came to an end. The blessings and presence of the Twelve Apostles ceased, and the cry went forth that they were no longer needed.[16]

In an article published in the *Deseret News*, Wilford Woodruff (1807-1898), who served as the fourth president of the Church of Jesus Christ of Latter-day Saints from 1889 until his death, bemoaned: "[U]ntil the fulness [*sic*] of the gospel was revealed the [church was] like the blind groping for the wall . . . living under false doctrines, false traditions, and false teachers."[17]

Stephen E. Robinson confirms:

First of all, it should be noted that the Latter-day Saints do reject the authority of traditional Christianity after the death of the New Testament Apostles. In the LDS view the keys ["the power and right to perform certain acts on God's behalf"] and authority promised to Peter in Matthew 16:16 were *apostolic* in nature, and authority. Thereafter . . . the historical church no longer possessed the fulness [*sic*] of the gospel. This is the LDS doctrine of the Great Apostasy . . .[18]

Bruce R. McConkie gives the following definition of the so-called "keys and authority": "Keys are the right of presidency; they are divine authorization to use the priesthood for a specified purpose; they empower those who hold them to use the power of God to do the work of Him whose power it is."[19] McConkie further states:

> The President of The Church of Jesus Christ of Latter-day Saints holds the keys of salvation for all men now living because he is the only one by whose authorization the sealing power of the priesthood can be used to seal men up to salvation and exaltation in the kingdom of God.[20]

Joseph F. Smith adds, "In their fulness [*sic*], the keys ["of salvation"] are held by only one person at a time, the prophet and president of the [Church of Jesus Christ of Latter-day Saints]."[21] Robinson concludes, "For this reason Latter-day Saints reject the binding authority of subsequent developments in historical Christianity."[22] Richard Lyman Bushman emphasizes that, ". . . in the world of Joseph's revelations, the ancient authority of priests [those existing before the so-called apostasy] would become preeminent."[23]

The truth is, that the key of "Salvation [exclusively] belongs to our God, who sits on the throne, and to the Lamb [Jesus, the Son of God]" (*Revelation 7:10 NIV*), and has not been, nor will it ever be, abrogated to the prophet and president of the LDS Church. *Clarke's Commentary* on this verse emphasizes that "God alone is the author of the salvation of man; and this salvation is procured and given to them through the *Lamb*, as their propitiatory sacrifice."

In the *Doctrine and Covenants* (a book of Mormon "Scripture" that contains supposed revelations from Joseph Smith and a few other Latter-day prophets), we read:

> And my vineyard has become corrupted every whit;
> and there is none which doeth good save it be a few;
> and they err in many instances because of

priestcrafts, all having corrupt minds.[24] [Priestcraft is equivalent to professional (paid) clergy for which many Mormons find objectionable. The LDS Church, however, has 65,137 full-time paid employees (almost half that of Google or Microsoft)!]

Joseph Smith implied that all sectarian church gatherings were but the "congregations of the wicked."[25] McConkie affirms, "We live in 'a crooked and perverse generation' (D&C 34:6); the sects of the day are 'the congregations of the wicked' (D&C 60:8), and their ministers are false teachers, meaning false prophets."[26]

Smith further decried:

Christendom at the present day . . . are just ripening for the damnation of hell. They will be damned, for they reject the most glorious principle of the Gospel of Jesus Christ and treat with disdain and trample under foot the key that unlocks the heavens and puts in our possession [the Church of Jesus Christ of Latter-day Saints] the glories of the celestial world. Yes, I say, such will be damned, with all their professed godliness.[27]

[A]ll priests who adhere to the sectarian religions of the day with all their followers, without one exception, receive their portion with the devil and his angels.[28]

Joseph Fielding McConkie posits:

For nearly two thousand years mankind's knowledge of God was confined to hearsay, tradition, and speculation. . . . no church on the face of the earth possessed either the doctrines of salvation or the authority to speak on behalf of the heavens.

. . . To acknowledge that Joseph Smith was a prophet is to acknowledge the verity of the revelations that he received. It is to concede that the traditional Christian world is without the authority to speak for God and the truths of salvation are found only within the Church of Jesus Christ of Latter-day Saints.[29]

Joseph F. Smith declared:

The Church of Jesus Christ of Latter-day Saints is no partisan Church. It is not a sect. It is *The Church of Jesus Christ of Latter-day Saints*. It is the only one today existing in the world that can and does legitimately bear the name of Jesus Christ and His divine authority. . . .[30]

Spencer W. Kimball insists that the LDS Church is the "sole repository" of the Gospel's "priceless program":

The Lord Jesus Christ, our Redeemer and Savior, has given us our map—a code of laws and commandments whereby we might attain perfection and, eventually, godhood. This set of laws and ordinances is known as the gospel of Jesus Christ, and it is the *only* plan which will exalt mankind. The Church of Jesus Christ of Latter-day Saints is the sole repository of this priceless program in its fulness [*sic*], which is made available to those who accept it.[31]

To counter what Kimball confabulates as to how the Gospel is defined, this author offers that it is not a "set of laws and ordinances" that elucidates and illuminates "the gospel of Jesus Christ." The fact of the matter is the Gospel *is* Jesus Christ! Jesus, not the Church of Jesus Christ of Latter-day Saints, is the "sole repository" of the gospel. The Gospel is God's grace (fully exemplified and embodied in the Person of Jesus Christ) for the undeserving. What the Gospel (occurring 101 times in 95 verses in the *KJV* of the *Bible*) *is not*, is a prescription ("a priceless program") formulated by law. It is upon this principle ("a prescription, formulated by law") that Mormonism has chosen to define, and thus disparage, the true Gospel by adding so-called "ordinances" and "commandments" that go well beyond the scope and simplicity of the heart of God's message of the "Good News" embodied in the person of His Son. (Greek, *evangelizo*, meaning, "To bring or announce good news.") In doing so, Mormonism has become "entangled," as the Apostle Paul has well stated, "with the yoke of bondage" losing sight of "the liberty wherewith Christ has made us free" (*Galatians 5:1 KJV*). Any addendum (as Paul has duly warned) to the "simplicity of the gospel" thus becomes a detraction and an offense to Christ's finished work on the cross. The Apostle Paul wrote: "But I fear, lest somehow, as the serpent deceived Eve by his craftiness, so your minds may be corrupted from the simplicity that is in Christ" (*2 Corinthians 11:3 NKJV*).

One of the earliest creeds of the Christian church, written 54-55 AD, (pertaining to the Gospel's characterization), is found in Paul's first letter to the Corinthian church:

> Moreover, brethren, I declare unto you the gospel which I preached unto you, which also ye have received, and wherein ye stand; By which also ye are saved, if ye keep in memory what I preached unto you, unless ye have believed in vain. For I delivered unto you first of all ["of first importance" *NIV*] that which I also received [sometime before this letter was written], how that Christ died for our sins according to the scriptures; And that he was buried, and that he rose again the third day according to the scriptures . . . (*1 Corinthians 15:1-4 KJV*).

Christ's "death, burial and resurrection" is the summation of the Gospel. Jesus "died [He was crucified and was buried] for our sins," God sending His Only Son Jesus to die in our place to bridge the impassable gap between God and man. In addition, Jesus "was delivered for our offences, and was raised again [resurrected] for our justification" (*Romans 4:25 KJV*).

Joseph Fielding McConkie focuses on the elitist position of the one and only "true church" suggesting that only those who pay strict deference to the Mormon institution can have a true biblical perspective, stating:

> One cannot . . . properly understand the true meaning of the Bible and at the same time maintain membership in any church other than the [Mormon] church that the Lord has designated as the "only true

and living church upon the face of the whole earth"
(D&C 1:30). . . .

The Traditional Christian world has . . .
completely turned upside down the meaning of
everything in holy writ.[32]

The "Traditional Christian world" has taken issue with this last statement, and, instead, their hue-and-cry and common consensus suggests that it is the Mormon Church which has "completely turned upside down the meaning of everything in holy writ." Further, the "Traditional Christian world" believes Mormonism has disenfranchised itself from the theological framework of orthodoxy (going "beyond the footprint of Jesus' teachings," and outside the body of doctrine that defines Christianity) and is antithetical to mainstream Christianity. It is to this end that I have endeavored to tender, within the volume of this thesis, a vigorous polemic addressing the dogmatic mindset, religious genre and brick-and-mortar of Mormonism.

Alvin R. Dyer (1903-1977), who was an apostle in the Church of Jesus Christ of Latter-day Saints (LDS) and served as a member of the Church's First Presidency from 1968 to 1970, "reached a rhetorical apex"—entering the arena of *argumentum ad hominem*— while vehemently criticizing orthodox Christianity (which he calls "devious Christian societies"—see p. 106 of reference below) with extreme opprobrious and acrimonious condescension, suggesting:

[The traditional church's] decisions depended not
upon the voice of inspiration but upon musty
parchmental teachings [Dyer calls them "mutated
sacred writings"—p. 115; and Bruce R. McConkie,
"the musty creeds of a creaking Christendom"; and
Joseph Fielding Smith, "the dead letter of the Bible"]
of an erroneous past . . . from the corrupted concepts
["the perverted understanding"—p. 137] of a musty
and deceptive antiquity ["a bygone inspiration"—p.
199] . . . the borrowed vestige of that perverted creed
established in error by the post-apostolic church.[33]

Bruce R. McConkie, the ever-brutal antagonist of Christian orthodoxy, foments:

[V]irtually all the millions of apostate Christendom have abased themselves before the mythical throne of a mythical Christ. . . .

Indeed, it would be difficult to assemble a greater number of myths into one philosophical system than are now found in the philosophies of modern Christendom.[34]

And be it remembered that the gods of the creeds, which are the gods of Christendom, are just as false as the gods of the Assyrians, Babylonians, Muslims, Amorites, Hittites, or any other peoples, excepting only the members of the true church [the Mormons, of course].[35]

Along this vitriolic line of disparagement, Hyrum Mack Smith (1872-1918), who was a member of the Quorum of the Twelve Apostles from 1901 until his death, inveighs:

[T]he trouble with Christianity today [is that] it is not true. Christianity is . . . no truer or false than any other religion, than Mohammedanism, Confucianism, Buddhism or any other ism or philosophy . . . **that which is known as Christianity, is the falsest of all religions in the world**.[36]

Ivan J. Barrett (1910-1999), an American author, professor, and historian of The Church of Jesus Christ of Latter-day Saints, berates "the errors of Priestcraft" and the need "to dispel" the "mists of error and superstition, which have darkened the understanding, and blunted every great and noble faculty of the soul" . . . and "the foolish dogma or lame reasoning of their clergymen."[37]

Joseph F. Smith, Sr., who condemns "The clouds of error that overspread Christendom during those ages of misconception and contention,"[38] chides:

[The "Traditional Christian Church" is] led by error, superstition, ignorance, and by the cunning and craftiness of men . . . leav[ing] out here a little and there a little, here a line and there a precept . . . [and that it is] divided, disorganized, confused, and without knowledge, without revelation or inspiration, and without Divine authority of power.[39]

Elder Neal A. Maxwell (1926-2004), an American scholar, educator, and religious leader who served as a member of the Quorum of the Twelve Apostles of the Church of Jesus Christ of Latter-day Saints (LDS Church) from 1981 until his death, and for whom the Maxwell Institute (a research institute at Brigham Young University) is named, wrote:

> The word only [as in the LDS Church is "the only true and living church upon the face of the whole earth" (*D&C* 1:30)], asserts a uniqueness and singularity [about the Church] as *the exclusive ecclesiastical, authority-bearing agent* for our Father in Heaven in this dispensation.[40]

Maxwell goes on to disparage:

> [All other churches are but] "partially true as measured by divine standards . . . [and are] conceptually compromised by having been made up from doctrinal debris left over from another age . . . compromised of mere fragments of the true faith . . . a museum that houses a fossilized faith."[41]

Bruce R. McConkie, in his censure of the Biblical canon (challenging notions of the uniqueness and sufficiency of the *Bible*), bemoans that only but, "Brief fragments of truth, a sliver here and a twig there, have come down to us in the records of the past."[42] McConkie makes the oft-heard accusation from the Mormon polemicists (though contrived) that, "Satan guided his servants in taking many plain and precious things, and many of the covenants of the Lord, from the Bible, so that men would stumble and fall and lose their souls."[43] McConkie further derides the Biblical canon, stating:

> [N]either the Bible [the Authorized *King James Version* of the *Bible*], nor any Bible has been preserved in sufficient purity to enable men to find the course leading to eternal life and then to walk

therein. To gain this end—so devoutly to be desired—the world had to await the coming forth of the Book of Mormon.[44]

John G. Turner, Assistant Professor of Religious Studies at George Mason University, reveals:

> [Brigham] Young sometimes issued bitingly sarcastic critiques of the "sectarians" (i.e., Protestant Christians) of his day. In New York in late August [1843], he opined that "the greatest divine of the day [was] as ignorant as the dumm [sic] ass concerning the things of God."[45]

Brigham Young propounded, "With regard to true theology, a more ignorant people never lived than the present so-called Christian world."[46] The renowned Mormon Apostle, Orson Pratt, fomented:

> Both Catholics and Protestants are nothing less than the 'Whore of Babylon' whom the Lord denounces by the mouth of John the Revelator as having corrupted all the earth by their fornications and wickedness. Any person who shall be so corrupt as to receive a holy ordinance of the Gospel from the ministers of any of these apostate churches will be sent down to hell . . .[47]

Not to be outdone, Leonard J. Arrington and Davis Bitton speak contemptuously of "Western Christendom" (a not-uncommon chorus heard from the choir of Latter-day Saints):

> [W]hen Mormonism appeared, the religious scene was already crowded and confused, a maelstrom of frenetic activity. [This so-called "frenetic activity" was the outpouring of a religious revival that historians have called "The Second Great Awakening!" (circa 1820-1835).] Although the religious unity of Western Christendom had been broken at the time of the Reformation, the pattern in Europe was still, generally speaking, one of state churches. But the process of fragmentation continued

through the seventeenth and eighteenth centuries and reached its *reductio ad absurdum* [Latin for "reduction to absurdity"] in America, where the lack of religious consensus was becoming ever more apparent.[48]

From the *Book of Mormon*, we read:

And he said unto me: Behold there are save two churches only; the one is the church of the lamb of God [from the perspective of Mormonism this would be the Church of Jesus Christ of Latter-day Saints], and the other is the [apostate] church of the devil [which (necessarily) includes all of mainstream Christianity]; wherefore, whoso belongeth not to the church of the Lamb of God belongeth to that great church, which is the mother of abominations; and she is the whore of all the earth.[49]

Launching a head-on full-frontal attack and indictment on Christian orthodoxy, Joseph Smith (from whom all powers and authority stemmed under the auspices of the Melchizedek priesthood) asserted:

I have the truth of God, and show that ninety-nine out of every hundred professing religious ministers are false teachers, having no authority, while they pretend to hold the keys of God's kingdom on earth . . .[50]

Richard Lyman Bushman records: "Joseph [Smith] once said that Methodists [a denomination to which he once applied for membership] 'have creeds which a man must believe or be kicked out of their church [for which Joseph Smith was]. I want the liberty to believe as I please, it feels so good not to be tramelled [*sic*].' "[51] Joseph Smith announced, "I cannot believe in any of the creeds of the different denominations. . . . the creeds set up stakes, and say, 'Hitherto shalt thou come, and no further,' which I cannot subscribe to."[52] Again, Joseph Smith touts, "There are many things in the Bible which do not, as they now stand, accord with the revelations of the Holy Ghost to me."[53] "I am now going to take exceptions to the present translation of the Bible in relation to these matters."[54] It is apparent that Joseph Smith did not revere God's word! The Lord declared through the Prophet Isaiah, ". . . but to this *man* will I look, *even* to *him that is* poor and of a contrite spirit and trembleth at my word. . . ."[55]

Richard Lyman Bushman observes: "[T]he *Book of Mormon* challenges the authority of the Bible by breaking the monopoly of the Bible on scriptural truth. . . . declar[ing] the Bible to be deficient. . . . [and] recast[ing] the meaning of the original scriptures."[56] Leonard J. Arrington and Davis Bitton write, "Clearly [Joseph Smith] did not feel obligated to accept the Bible in its current authorized version as any kind of constraint on the unfolding doctrines of the [Mormon] church."[57] Richard Lyman Bushman adjudicates, "By presuming to alter the Western world's most revered literary work [the *Bible*], Joseph Smith appeared to rise above holy writ, risking the wrath of every Christian."[58]

Richard Lyman Bushman observes:

> [T]he Bible did not restrict Joseph's revelations. . . . [F]or Joseph, the Bible was a gate not a fence. Joseph's daring . . . his blasphemous audacity . . . [and] "Monstrous claims," . . . [for which] Joseph had departed for other realms entirely . . . created a transbiblical world unlike anything known in the Christian churches . . .[59]

Bushman further states:

> Joseph's theology was . . . independent and idiosyncratic . . . [and] became increasingly dramaturgical . . . [making] pronouncements on the authority of his own inspiration, heedless of current opinion ["entrenched theological traditions"] . . . [which] drove him beyond prudence.[60]

The fuselage of Mormonism was designed by Joseph Smith to carry its unsuspecting passengers beyond the creedal constraints of orthodoxy to where the deceitful "winds of doctrine" conveyed its commuters into the realms of sophistry and delusion. Sterling McMurrin relates that Joseph Smith "broke with many facets of the established theological traditions" and "revolted against the traditional Christian absolutism, and even more strenuously against the Calvinist doctrines of original sin, divine election, predestination, and salvation by grace only."[61]

John G. Turner underscores:

> Joseph Smith's challenge to the traditional canon . . . was without parallel. In addition to publishing the hefty *Book of Mormon*, he wrote or dictated scores of revelations, which his followers accepted as God's contemporary words and later compiled into additional books of scripture. "Joseph the Seer" was bound by no book [the *Bible* not excluded], no creed . . . When he bumped up against conventions and limits of nineteenth-century politics, marriage, and theology, Smith proposed his own audacious paths.[62]

When it came to the revelation of Jesus Christ, Joseph F. Smith pronounced: "But do we depend upon the Bible for this conviction and knowledge? No, thank the Lord we do not. . . . We have the Book of Mormon, the 'stick of Ephraim,' . . . [and] the collateral testimony of [Joseph Smith] who translated it."[63] Stephen H. Webb (1961-2016), a theologian and philosopher of religion, wrote:

> [Joseph Smith] read the Bible in ways so novel . . . expanded and revised the biblical narrative [and] . . . brusquely overturned ancient and impregnable metaphysical assumptions with . . . aplomb . . . [as a result,] Mormon metaphysics calls for the revision of nearly every Christian belief.[64]

Roy W. Doxey (1908-1992), who was a theologian and mid-level leader in the Church of Jesus Christ of Latter-day Saints, acknowledged:

> The Prophet Joseph Smith remarked at a conference of elders of the Church that "we are differently situated from any other people that ever existed upon this earth; consequently those former revelations cannot be suited to our conditions; they were given to other people . . ."[65]

Richard Lyman Bushman observes, "In later years, Joseph's revelations redefined the nature of God and man so radically that Mormonism has been seen as a departure from traditional Christianity as serious as Christianity's from Judaism."[66] Benjamin E. Park notes:

> James Gordon Bennett, famed editor of the *New York Herald* [wrote] that the Mormons of Commerce—rechristened Nauvoo—appeared likely to swallow up the "lukewarm Protestant sects" and incite "a religious revolution as radical as Luther's to take place in the Christian world."[67]

Alex Beam contends:

> In April 1844, [Joseph Smith] preached the most famous sermon of his life, what some regard as one of the most famous sermons ever preached in America. As if on a whim, Joseph turned nearly 2,000 years of Christian belief on its head at a funeral service for his loyal colleague King Follett. Joseph had laid the groundwork for a new world order [the Council of Fifty], and for the foundational ritual for his entire church, but that was in secret. Now, speaking in Nauvoo's East Grove, under a massive canopy of elm and chestnut trees, he unpacked some of the most radical Christian doctrine ever preached on the American continent. He spoke for two hours, shouting against a heavy wind. . . .
>
> In one long, loud sermon, he had dynamited the entire Christian cosmology, the underpinnings of every creedal [*sic*] prayer to have emerged in the previous 2,000 years.[68]

Joseph Smith, with reckless disregard to sacred, inviolate, historical boundaries, removed and unleashed well-entrenched orthodox codices, that he deemed fatuous and unnecessary tethers and hindrances, to expedite and brandish his own neo-biblical doctrines, and revolutionary path, commensurate to the exaltation and apotheosis of man, and the diminutization of God the Father; where God (Elohim) was systematically reduced to but a resurrected anthropomorphized being among a pantheon of other so-called gods. John G. Turner informs:

> The ideas expressed in the King Follett Discourse [where "God, Jesus, and human beings are, in short, [classified as] members of the same species, at different stages of development"], have often struck non-Mormons as not merely heretical but wildly hubristic for diminishing God's uniqueness and granting human beings a full measure of divine potential.[69]

Leonard J. Arrington reveals:

> God, for Brigham [Young] as for Joseph Smith before him, was once a "man" on another planet who had "passed the ordeals we are now passing through. He has received an experience, has suffered and enjoyed, and knows all that we know regarding the toils, suffering, life and death of this mortality, for He has passed through the whole of it and has received . . . exaltation." [*Journal of Discourses,*] (11:249). God, said Brigham, "is a being of the same species as ourselves; He lives as we do, except the difference that we are earthly, and He is heavenly . . . in either case we are of one species—of one family." [*Journal of Discourses,*] (4:217) . . .
>
> Brigham's sermons suggest that he saw God, angel, man, spirit, intelligence as merely different names designating related beings in various stages of development.[70]

In an article published in *Ligonier Ministries* the teaching fellowship of R. C. Sproul (1939-2017), who was an American theologian, author, and ordained pastor in the Presbyterian Church in America, we read that the "humanization of God and deification of man is antithetical to biblical orthodoxy."[71]

Craig L. Blomberg decries: "The common Evangelical *perception*, and we hope we are mistaken, is that Mormons talk a whole lot more about the process of human exaltation than about the eternal worship of a one-of-a-kind God."[72] As a prime example of Blomberg's concern, Joseph Fielding Smith propounds:

> *Those who gain . . . exaltation receive the fulness [sic] of the power, might, and dominion of that kingdom. They overcome all things. They are crowned as priests and kings and become like Jesus Christ. . . . [This doctrine of exaltation] has become one of the peculiar teachings of the Church of Jesus Christ of Latter-day Saints. . .*
>
> It is only through obedience to the principles of the gospel and the laws which pertain to this kingdom [as defined by the LDS Church] that [the] blessings [of the celestial kingdom] are obtained.
>
> Salvation comes to those who overcome all things. *We are preaching the gospel of salvation in the celestial kingdom.* **I think it would be better if we would get into the habit of speaking more of exaltation than of salvation.**[73]

This last statement is disturbing! The fact that the Mormons want to talk more about exaltation (becoming "gods" in their own right) while devaluing and demoting the message of salvation through our "great God and Savior Jesus Christ" (*Titus 2:13 KJV*) is unconscionable!

President Joseph F. Smith warned, ". . . we cannot build upon error and ascend into the courts of eternal truth and enjoy the glory and exaltation of the kingdom of our God. That cannot be done."[74] In this thesis, it is my contention that Mormonism has been fabricated *"error upon error and clout upon clout"* and has missed the *"Simplicity, simplicity, simplicity!"* of the Gospel message.[75]

It is unfortunate that Joseph Smith and his followers (the Mormons) have chosen a path that is manifestly divergent from orthodox Christianity and unconstrained by the authority of Scripture—*Sola Scriptura* (Latin ablative, "by Scripture alone"). Yielding to the age-old ploy proffered by the Lord's antagonist "Yea, hath God said . . .?" (*Genesis 3:1 KJV*), Fiona and Terryl Givens enjoin:

The Church of Jesus Christ of Latter-day Saints by contrast, could be said to have begun with a pointed and emphatic rejection of *sola scriptura*. The entire possibility of a biblically based Christianity is rendered incoherent in Joseph Smith's personal experience, which was his—and his movement's— entire rationale for a revealed religion.[76]

Mormondom has chosen, rather, *sola ecclesia*—a devotion to a monolithic church (much like Catholicism) guided and governed by an autocratic Prophet, Seer and Revelator, whose dictum demands unquestioned obedience. The devotees to the Church of Jesus Christ of Latter-day Saints are taught that so-called "modern revelation" takes absolute precedence, superseding biblical authority.

Carter E. Grant (1885-1972), in his book *The Kingdom of God Restored*, tells us that Mormonism stands ". . . as [a] beacon guidepost along **a new and unfamiliar religious highway**."[77] Richard Lyman Bushman noted that Joseph Smith "perpetually initiated new campaigns and taught new doctrines."[78]

Heber C. Kimball (1801-1868), Counselor to the First Presidency, said:

Revelation is ever the iconoclast of tradition [orthodox Christianity]; and such is the bigotry of man, his natural hatred of the **new and strange [doctrines]**, as opposed to his personal interests or private views, that the very lives of those whose mission is to introduce and establish new doctrines, . . . are ever in danger from those whose traditions would thus be uprooted and destroyed.[79]

Mark E. Petersen (1900-1984), who was an American news editor and religious leader and served as a member of the Quorum of the Twelve Apostles of The Church of Jesus Christ of Latter-day Saints (LDS Church) from 1944 until his death, asks:

Are the orthodox doctrines of the Church accepted by us [the Church of Jesus Christ of Latter-day Saints] wholeheartedly? Or do we take the liberty of putting private interpretations upon them and by preaching our own notions, thereby confuse others?[80]

In the Apostle Paul's letter to Timothy, he exhorts, "I urged you . . . that [you] teach no other doctrine" (*1 Timothy 1:3 NKJV*). The Apostle Paul cautions:

> For the time will come when **they will not endure sound doctrine**: but after their own lusts shall they heap to themselves teachers, having itching ears; And they shall turn away their ears from the truth, and shall be turned unto fables.[81]

Mark E. Petersen remonstrates, "Man-made philosophies which are at variance with revealed truth are 'fables' as truly now as they were in the days of Paul . . . And the warning is still the same: 'From such turn away.' "[82] Petersen offers: "[L]earned pastors of other churches . . . may be ever so well informed in their own lines, but their 'lines' do not happen to be Mormonism."[83]

Joseph Smith made the enduring pronouncement: "[S]ectarian religion [orthodox Christianity] was the apostate religion."[84] Brigham Young remarked:

> The sectarian world, as we call them, is a professed church of God without the Priesthood. Sectarians have not the Priesthood . . . they cannot dwell with the Father and the Son, unless they go through these ordeals that are ordained for the Church of the First born [the Church of Jesus Christ of Latter-day Saints]. The ordinances of the house of God are expressly for the Church of the First born [the LDS Church].[85]

Elder Nephi L. Morris (1870-1943), who "was educated at the Brigham Young Academy and the University of Utah, served in various capacities in the Church of Jesus Christ of Latter-day Saints, and was a popular speaker on religious and political subjects,"[86] deplores "the incompleteness of the gospel as taught by the Churches of Christendom, both Catholic and Protestant, in that the salvation which they offer is altogether inadequate to meet human needs."[87] Jana Riess, senior columnist for *Religion News Service*

(*RNS*), reports that LDS Apostle, Russel Ballard (born 1928) stated in a young adult devotional in Buenos Aires:

> Most people don't know where they came from. They don't know why they're here, and they don't know where they're going. And if they have a Catholic background they don't know who God is. They don't know who the Savior is; nor do they know who the Holy Ghost is. And we know who they are because Joseph [Smith] knelt in the presence of the Father and the Son, and our Father introduced the Savior to him in these words: "Joseph, this is my beloved son. Hear him." A boy, who then nurtured and trained by the Savior of the world to restore the fullness of the everlasting gospel of Jesus Christ to the earth.[88]

Jana Riess notes that "Elder Ballard then goes on to present Joseph Smith's sterling apostolic creeds—essentially out Catholicking the Catholics in the matter of ecclesiastical authority."[89]

According to a pamphlet produced by the Presbyterian Church (USA):

> Latter-day Saints and the historic churches view the canon of scriptures and interpret shared scriptures in radically different ways. They use the same words with dissimilar meanings. When the Church of Jesus Christ of Latter-day Saints speaks of the Trinity, Christ's death and resurrection, and salvation, the theology and practices related to these set it apart from the Orthodox, Roman Catholic and Protestant churches.[90]

John Taylor (1808-1887), the third President of the Church of Jesus Christ of Latter-day Saints, asked: "Who understood even the first principles of the doctrines of Christ? Who in the Christian world taught them? . . . It was Joseph Smith, under the Almighty, who developed the first principles, and to him we must look for further instructions."[91] Brigham Young in his typical bravado inculcated, "The Christian world, so-called, are heathens as to the knowledge of the salvation of God."[92]

Wilford Woodruff echoes:

> Where is the man or woman that comprehended anything about God or about eternity until Joseph Smith revealed the fullness of the gospel? I could read of those things in the Bible which we now believe in and receive, but I was surrounded by the traditions of the world and could not comprehend them.[93]

Brigham Young proclaimed in unmistakable language: "The Church which we represent is the Church and Kingdom of God, and possesses the only faith by which the children of men can be brought back in to the presence of our Father and God."[94] Brigham Young further proclaimed: "[W]e have got the gospel of life and salvation. I do not say that we have *a* gospel, but I say that we have *the* definit[ive] and only gospel that ever was or ever will be that will save the children of men."[95] Wilford Woodruff stated with firm conviction that, "nobody else has received the fulness [*sic*] of the everlasting Gospel; nobody else has taken hold to build up this kingdom."[96] "We believe this Church [the Church of Jesus Christ of Latter-day Saints] will prepare the way for the coming of Christ to reign as King and that this Church will then develop into the kingdom of God."[97]

The *Doctrine and Covenants* vouchsafes for the Lord that the Latter-day Saints (LDS) Church is "the only true and living church upon the face of the whole earth, with which I, the Lord, am well pleased . . ."[98] McConkie emphasizes, "Men either come to the true Church [the Church of Jesus Christ of Latter-day Saints] and sustain it and all its views and teachings or they are not of God. Only those who are of God and of his church [the LDS Church] shall be saved."[99] Melvin J. Ballard (1873-1939), who was a member of the Quorum of the Twelve Apostles, concluded, "For after all, [Mormonism] is destined, according to the word of the Lord, to become the savior and blessing of all flesh."[100]

Roy W. Doxey would have us believe that, only those "who accept 'the only true and living church upon the face of the earth' become sons and daughters of the 'Lord God.' "[101] Whereas, the Scripture explicitly instructs, "But as many as received him [Jesus, the Nazarene carpenter upon whose head was placed a crown of thorns], to them gave he power to become the sons of God, *even to them that believe on his name*."[102]

McConkie asserted: "[A]ll men in the latter days must turn to Joseph Smith to gain salvation. Why? . . . He alone stands . . . in the place and stead of the Heavenly One [Jesus Christ] in administering salvation to men on earth."[103] It is apparent that the Mormon Church has arrogated to its vainglorious organization the imperial office of God's only salvific agency, hallowing the rule and sacral power of a hierarchical "Priesthood" over the authority of the Savior. Thus, the Mormon Church has usurped the sacred and indelible mediatorship of Christ— "For *there* is one God, and one mediator between God and men, the man Christ Jesus."[104] "Neither is there salvation in any other: for there is none other name [the Mormon Church is not excepted] under heaven given among men, whereby we must be saved."[105]

Robert M. Bowman Jr., contends, "The Church [by definition] is not a religious organization run from the top down by a bureaucracy, but the body of Christ, headed by Jesus Christ alone."[106] When the scaffolding of Church hierarchy is dismantled, then will Christ alone reign. John MacArthur, (born June 19, 1939), who is an American pastor and author, and has been acknowledged as one of the most influential preachers of his time, emphasizes:

> Christ is the one true Head of the church, and whatever interferes with His headship has the seeds of apostasy in it. . . . He didn't establish an earthly priesthood [i.e., the Mormon "Priesthood"] to mediate the headship of the church . . . But by God the Father's own decree, Christ alone is Head of the church . . .[107]

Doxey continues, "Jesus' atonement for individual exaltation is of no force until the person completes his repentance through the ordinances of the gospel [as dictated by the Mormon Church]."[108] In other words, Jesus' atonement has no efficacy outside of the bounds, providence and strictures mandated by the LDS Church. Doxey adds: "[I]n order to obtain eternal life one [with "sheeplike credulity"] must obey the leaders of the [Mormon] Church."[109] Joseph Fielding Smith advocated:

> To reject the councils and testimonies of those men [the General Authorities of the Mormon Church] to carry the message of salvation to the world—or others sent under their direction—would bring down upon the heads of all who do so the judgments of the Son of God.[110]

Joseph Smith pronounced:

> [A]nd when the Lord's anointed go forth to proclaim the word, bearing testimony [of the truth of Mormonism] to this generation, if they receive it they shall be blessed; but if not, the judgments of God will follow close upon them, until that city or that house which rejects them, shall be left desolate.[111]

Joseph Fielding McConkie affirms, "Latter-day Saint theology is based on the premise that there was an apostasy—indeed, a universal apostasy—from the gospel . . ."[112] Hugh Nibley gives the following account:

> [T]he church of Christ did not survive in the world long after the Apostles. . . .
>
> The world once Christianized not only remained barbarian, but became also more and more barbaric as it passed from one century of Christian tutelage to the next.[113]

Joseph F. Smith egregiously declared:

> After Satan and wicked men [the "Gates of Hell"] had **prevailed against the Church**, crucified the Savior and killed the apostles, the keys of the kingdom were taken from the earth. . . . From the time that the keys of this Priesthood were taken from the earth until they were received by Joseph Smith, no man ever possessed that Priesthood, nor the keys thereof, with authority to build up the Zion of God,

and prepare a church or people for the second coming of Christ.[114]

Because of the Latter-day Saint's categorical assertion that the "Gates of Hell" had prevailed against the Church (contrary to Jesus' stern pronouncement—see *Matthew 16:18*), while accusing mainstream Christianity of widespread apostasy, the Church of Jesus Christ of Latter-day Saints (LDS, the Mormons) has shamelessly gone about deconstructing long held Christian concepts, while promoting their own salvific agenda (soteriology), extreme parochialism, and exclusive entitlement as God's sole administrator on "assertions of authority, truth, and liturgy." Without equivocation, the Latter-day Saints consider themselves the chosen arbiters of truth. Patrick Q. Mason (born 1976), who holds the Leonard J. Arrington Chair of Mormon History and Culture at USU, opines that there is "an authoritarian streak that has manifest itself throughout the larger Mormon tradition."[115]

Joseph Fielding Smith conceded, "I have never been able in my teachings to make the gospel plan appear easy . . . *There will not be such an overwhelming number of the Latter-day Saints who will get there* [the celestial kingdom]. . . . it will be a select few who receive these crowning blessings."[116] When Joseph Smith was asked: "Will everybody be damned, but Mormons?" he emphatically responded: "Yes, and a great portion of them [Mormons], unless they repent, and work righteousness."[117]

Joseph Fielding Smith echoes: "[W]e reject and damn all who do not accept Mormonism and the ministration of our elders."[118] Joseph Fielding Smith adds, "The fact remains that there is a spirit which accompanies the Book of Mormon [and] every man who lifts his hand or voice against it will eventually perish."[119] Parley P. Pratt, an original member of the Quorum of the Twelve Apostles of the Church of Jesus Christ of Latter-day Saints, declared, "All who will not hearken to the Book of Mormon shall be cut off from among the people . . ."[120]

Roy W. Doxey emphasized, "The world shall be judged by the teachings of the Book of Mormon . . . those who reject it will stand condemned before the Lord."[121] Wilford Woodruff echoes: "[T]he Book of Mormon [and] the book of Doctrine and Covenants . . . will rise in judgment against those who reject them."[122] Brigham Young announced, "Every spirit that confesses that Joseph Smith is a Prophet, that he lived and died a prophet and that the *Book of Mormon* is true, is of God, and every spirit that does not is of anti-Christ."[123]

Bruce R. McConkie affirmed: "[A]ll who reject [the *Book of Mormon's*] message will be damned. . . . Men will stand or fall—because of what they think of the Book of Mormon."[124]

- "[A]ll men on earth will be saved or damned because they believe or disbelieve its words . . . men will gain celestial glory or suffer with the damned in hell, all depending upon their reaction to this volume of holy writ [the *Book of Mormon*]."[125]

- "To be in opposition to the Church of Jesus Christ of Latter-day Saints . . . is to link arms with Satan and to fight against God."[126]

- "Men will gain celestial rest or welter with the damned in hell depending on how they view the Nephite record [the *Book of Mormon*]."[127]

- "Surely the day will come when all those who find fault with the revelations given to Joseph Smith and who deny the divine status of the Book of Mormon shall have cause to fear and tremble. Surely their souls shall be in turmoil and their minds filled with anxieties as they stand before the judgment bar [of God]."[128]

- " 'He that will contend against the word of the Lord, let him be accursed; and he that shall deny these things'—the things then spoken, the things written in the Book of Mormon—'let him be accursed . . .' "[129]

- "[T]he Book of Mormon . . . is the standard around which all men must either rally or be damned."[130]

Joseph Smith asks:

What will become of the world, or the various professors of religion who do not believe in revelation and the oracles of God as continued to his Church [the Church of Jesus Christ of Latter-day Saints?] . . . I tell you, in the name of Jesus Christ, they will be damned; and when you get into the eternal world, you will find it will be so; they cannot escape the damnation of hell.[131]

McConkie suggested: "[T]he way men feel about [Joseph Smith] and his prophetic successors divides true believers from those who serve another master [i.e., the Devil]."[132] Incredibly (in the following statement) Joseph Fielding McConkie, while pointing the finger of accusation at mainstream Christianity, has well defined the pathology and the stark provisional landscape of Mormonism:

> Those who have chosen to redefine the nature of God and then to redefine the meaning of the words or to rewrite scripture to accord with what they [believe] . . . have reached well beyond a [restoration]. . . of the church. They have changed gods and in so doing have changed the whole system of salvation. . . . We would liken all this to a business takeover in which the old name is preserved for goodwill, but everything else gets changed. All that is missing here is a sign that says "Under New Management."[133]

McConkie further incriminates Mormonism stating:

> Virtually every tenet of our [the Church of Jesus Christ of Latter-day Saints] faith represents a departure from the theological position of historical or traditional Christianity. What we declare to be literal, they declare to be figurative; what we declare to be figurative, they declare to be literal. Thus we share a common vocabulary while holding to an entirely different set of meanings.[134]

Just as Joseph Smith admonished and posed the question to Oliver Cowdery, so one must ask, "by what authority [Joseph Smith] took upon him . . . to alter or erase, to add to or diminish from, a revelation or commandment from Almighty God?"[135] James E. Talmage also proposed the following questions: "What right have we to turn the scriptures from their proper sense and meaning? What right have we to declare that God meant not what he said?"[136]

Wayne Jackson, who has written for and edited the *Christian Courier* since its inception in 1965, and has written several books on a variety of biblical topics including *The Bible and Science, Creation, Evolution, and the Age of the Earth*, *The Bible on Trial*, and a number of commentaries, stated: "[S]emantics are quite important. Gospel truth is a message of words, and the Christian teacher needs to be accurate in the language he employs."[137] Philip Barlow (born in 1950), a Harvard-trained scholar who specializes in American religious history, religious geography and Mormonism, writes that Joseph "Smith frequently borrowed terms from . . . traditional Christianity, then infused them with fresh, expansive meanings" renovating "the meaning of words like *translation, God, atonement, glory, light, priesthood* and more."[138]

In an article titled "The Difference Between Christian Grace and Mormon Grace" (September 17, 2012), J. Warner Wallace, a noted Christian apologist, warns:

> Words matter. Ideas have consequences. In the years that I have been engaging Mormons about matters of faith, I've learned to define terms very carefully. Christians and Mormons use many of the same terms: "grace", "heaven", "Jesus", "God", "salvation" and many more. But when the definitions of these terms are examined, it's apparent that we are talking about extremely different ideas. These differences matter. They separate Mormons and Christians and demonstrate that we are not worshipping the same God.

5

"Upon This Rock I Will Build My Church"

[I] combat the worldly wisdom and multiplied ignorance of eighteen centuries, with a new revelation, which would open the eyes of more than eight hundred millions of people (Joseph Smith).[1]

James B. Allen (born in 1927), an American historian of Mormonism and was an official Assistant Church Historian of the Church of Jesus Christ of Latter-day Saints from 1972-1979, and Glen M. Leonard (born in 1938), an American historian specializing in Mormon history, state, "Among the most distinctive characteristics of Mormonism was its claim to revelation."[2] Allen and Leonard observe that the Latter-day Saints "unique claim is that the [Mormon] Church was established by divine revelation as the only church on the face of the earth that carried the authority of God himself."[3] Joseph F. Smith pronounced, "The Church holds to the definite authority of divine revelation which must be the standard."[4] Roy W. Doxey asserts, "In all the world there was not an individual who had the right by appointment of God to receive divine communications except Joseph Smith."[5]

George Albert Smith (1870-1951), an American religious leader who served as the eighth president of The Church of Jesus Christ of Latter-day Saints, asserts:

[O]ur Father has established in this world, his Church. He has conferred upon [the Church of Jesus Christ of Latter-day Saints] in this day his authority, and there is no other authority in the world that he will recognize but that which he himself has instituted. . . . You cannot go out into the world in any other Church or in all other Churches and find . . . men holding divine authority. Do not forget that.[6]

Our Heavenly Father has made it plain to the children of men that only under the hands of those who possess divine authority [exclusively held within the jurisdiction and administered by the Saint's High Priesthood] may we obtain the power to become members of the celestial kingdom.[7]

Jeffrey R. Holland (born December 3, 1940), an American educator and religious leader who served as the ninth President of Brigham Young University and is a member of the Quorum of the Twelve Apostles of The Church of Jesus Christ of Latter-day Saints, notes that "Mormonism's modern Apostles call the 'divine authority by direct revelation' the faith's 'most distinguishing feature.' "[8]

Joseph Smith was adamant in his assertion "for nothing will save a man but a legal administrator [a representative authority of the LDS Church]: for none others will be acknowledged either by God or angels."[9] "A man can do nothing for himself unless God direct him in the right way; and the Priesthood [authority delegated through the auspices of the LDS Church] is for that purpose."[10]

Wilford Woodruff iterates:

[W]ithout this Priesthood no man, from the day the world rolled into existence, has any right to administer in any of the ordinances of his holy house . . .

No man has authority from God to administer to the children of men the ordinances of life and salvation [except] by the power of the Holy Priesthood. The power of that Priesthood is with the Latter-day Saints . . .

God has appointed [the LDS Church] to bear this Priesthood. Out of the . . . millions of people on the earth the Lord has chosen this handful of men to bear this; to ordain, to organize, to warn the world, to preach the Gospel to them.[11]

Joseph Fielding Smith indicated:

Men may search and they may study, but they will never come to a knowledge of God until they receive the gospel and obtain light through the power of the priesthood and the ordinances of the gospel [only administrated through the aegis of the Mormon Church].[12]

Joseph Fielding Smith's father, Joseph F. Smith, taught that the "Priesthood, and the ordinances of the gospel . . . are necessary to qualify men to enter into the [Celestial] kingdom of heaven."[13]

Joseph Smith insisted:

All men who become heirs of God and joint-heirs with Jesus Christ will have to receive the fulness [sic] of the ordinances of his kingdom [administered through the singular authority of the LDS Church]; and those who will not receive all the ordinances will come short of the fulness [sic] of that glory, if they do not lose the whole.[14]

Allen and Leonard emphasize, "The quest for authority was especially important to the early success of the Mormon movement." They relate, not only did Joseph Smith declare that he was "going to restore the ancient church, but [he] had also been given direct, divine authority to do so."[15] B. H. Roberts summarizes, "to Joseph Smith was given access to the mind of Deity, through the revelations of God to him; and likewise to him was given a divine authority to declare the mind of God [ex cathedra] to the world."[16]

Leonard J. Arrington and Davis Bitton reveal:

[E]specially basic to the concept of Restoration was the priesthood. The priesthood, or authority to act in God's name, had been taken from the earth sometime in the early centuries of Christian history but was now restored to earth. The Mormon church, therefore, was not only like the original Christian church but had the same sacerdotal authority, without which any attempt to restore would result only in dead forms.[17]

John Taylor comments: "This combined priesthood, it would appear, will hold the destiny of the human family in their hands and adjudicate in all matters pertaining to their affairs."[18] To this end, Robert M. Bowman Jr., argues:

> The Church's existence does not rest on the authority of an institutional priesthood held by men on earth; such a priestly order was a feature of the old covenant that had been superseded by the new covenant instituted by Jesus Christ. Rather, the church's existence rests on the authority of Christ's supreme "offices" in heaven, where he rules over the church as its king and lord and intercedes on behalf of the church as its High Priest (Romans 8:34; Ephesians 1:20-23; Colossians 1:18; Hebrews 1:3; 4:14; 6:19-20; 7:23-8:6).[19]

According to the second chapter of *Acts*, the Church (Christ's Beloved Ecclesia) was born by the very "Breath of God." Just as Adam became a living sentient being when God breathed into his nostrils, so the Church came alive and stood up ("But Peter standing up with the eleven, lifted up his voice" *Acts 2:14 KJV*) when "suddenly there came a sound from heaven as of a rushing mighty wind" (*Acts 2:2 KJV*). Pentecost (the Holy Spirit's descent upon the Apostles) defined the life and breath and "existence" of the Church from the fiftieth day after Christ's resurrection to this present day. The Spirit of God that fell upon the 120 in the upper room equipped and empowered the Church to promulgate the Gospel with "Divinely Sanctioned Authority." After Peter stood up and preached his first sermon, "about three thousand souls" were miraculously added to the Church (see *Acts 2:41*) through the sovereign will of God. Peter was not operating under the mantle of an ecclesiastical earthly authority represented by an "institutional priesthood," but, rather, was imbued with a dispensational plenipotentiary *New Testament* authority mandated from Heaven's Throne through the auspices of a Priest and King, who ever lives to make intercession for His Church. Jesus imparted authority (*exousian*) to His disciples which is the "right to exercise power." Jesus empowered and clothed His Church with His approbation ten days after His ascension where He sealed once and for all our salvation through the incomprehensible investment of His own blood on the Mercy Seat in Heaven—"By his own blood he entered once into the holy place having obtained eternal redemption *for us*" (*Hebrews 9:12 KJV*).

The Apostle Paul instructs:

> But unto every one of us is given grace according to the measure of the gift of Christ. Wherefore he saith, When he ascended up on high, he led captivity captive and gave gifts unto men . . . And he gave some [to be], apostles; and some, prophets; and some, evangelists; and some, pastors and teachers; For the perfecting of the saints, for the work of the ministry, for the edifying of the body of Christ [the Church] (*Ephesians 4:7-12 KJV*).

The Mormon Church categorically professes to be the Lord's "Only Sovereign" (the magisterial legates of heaven, and "standard [bearers] for the nations"),[20] an oligarchy guided by *modern revelation*, and their presiding President, God's mouthpiece, chief administrator of the kingdom of God on earth, and theocratic sovereign. In an article published in *Church News*, a weekly tabloid-sized supplement to the *Deseret News* and the *MormonTimes*, a Salt Lake City, Utah newspaper owned by The Church of Jesus Christ of Latter-day Saints, we read the following:

> No man holds divine authority equal to or above the president of the Church. In his position he is pre-eminent!
>
> Let us understand fully the clear identity of the president of the Church. He is the mouthpiece of God on earth for us today.[21]

Will Bagley wrote:

> The LDS church "*is not a democracy*," a modern apostle has written. "The Church is a kingdom. . . .

and the President of the Church, the mouthpiece of God on earth, is the earthly king. All things come to the Church from the king of the kingdom in heaven, through the king of the kingdom [the Church of Jesus Christ of Latter-day Saints] on earth."[22]

Eric Shuster and Charles Sale, implore:

> The President of the Church is the presiding high priest: only he can receive revelations for the Church as a whole, provide binding interpretations of scripture, or change existing doctrines of the Church. Only he holds the "keys to the kingdom" with the power to loose or bind in all temporal and spiritual matters of the Church.[23]

John G. Turner offers that "[Brigham] Young insisted that church members, and especially fellow leaders, accept him as the oracle through which divine revelation and truth now flowed to the church."[24] Bruce R. McConkie asserts: "[F]aithful saints do as they are told and go at the bidding of their prophet, for his voice is the voice of the Lord."[25] McConkie contends, "There is only one true religion [that, of course, is the LDS religion], the religion in which God rules by revelation."[26]

Stephen E. Robinson reveals, "For Latter-day Saints, the church's guarantee of doctrinal correctness lies primarily in the living prophet, and only secondarily in the preservation of the written text."[27] Joseph Fielding McConkie asserted:

> [G]ood doctrine will always sustain the idea that the living prophet, not scripture or any other document, is the constitution of the Church. The Church is not governed by canon law, we have no creed to which we must pay allegiance, nor do we have a written constitution. The governing authority of the Church is the voice of the living prophet.[28]

McConkie further states:

> [I]f a principle or doctrine does not come by way of revelation, that principle or doctrine is not a part of our religion. It may be a good principle, and it may

be a great blessing to us, but if revelation is not its source, it is not a matter of faith with us.[29]

Again, McConkie emphasizes:

The Bible . . . is not the source of our doctrine or our hope of salvation. . . . When we go forth to teach the doctrines of salvation, our commission (and it is a commandment to us) is to teach the revelations and commandments that have come to us through the Prophet Joseph Smith. . . . The Bible is what the Bible is, but the word of salvation to us comes from the prophet sent to minister as the head of our dispensation.[30]

Richard Lyman Bushman notes:

When a new edition of the revelations [of Joseph Smith] was being prepared, the editor of the Mormon newspaper [*The Evening and the Morning Star*], William W. Phelps, wrote his wife [Sally]: "The Saints must learn their duty from the Revelations [for only Joseph had the "keys of the mysteries, and the revelations"]. We must live by every word that proceeds from the mouth of God [i.e., from the mouth of His prophet], and not by what is written by man [e.g., the *Bible*] or is spoken by man."[31]

Joseph Smith offers his interpretation of a passage of Scripture as follows: "Jesus in His teachings says, 'Upon this rock I will build my Church, and the gates of hell shall not prevail against it.' What rock? Revelation."[32] In "A Course Study for the Melchizedek Priesthood Quorum of The Church of Jesus Christ of Latter-day Saints 1972-73" we read: "Revelation from God is compared to a rock upon which Christ builds his Church . . . The rock upon which the Church of Jesus Christ [the Mormon Church] is built is revelation and is not Peter."[33]

Joseph Fielding Smith asserted: "[U]pon revelation the Lord would build his church. It has always been so understood . . ."[34] In *A Sure Foundation: Answers to Difficult Gospel Questions*, James A. Carver's (one of the book's contributors) interpretation of the passage "Upon this rock I will build my Church," is that "Indeed, revelation was the issue at hand." Carver surmises: "A textual analysis of this passage clearly demonstrates that . . . the church was . . . [to be] built . . . upon . . . the 'rock' of revelation."[35]

Carver further states:

> In the Joseph Smith Translation [of the *King James Bible*], a clarifying word [this is by no means a scholarly summation, but is a purely arbitrary conclusion "pulled out of his hat" so to speak] is given: "Cephas, which is, by interpretation, *a seer*, or a stone."[36]

Bruce R. McConkie elucidates: "Seers are specially selected prophets who are authorized to use the Urim and Thummim [stones] and who are empowered to know past, present, and future things. 'A gift which is greater can no man have.' (Mosiah 8:13-18.)"[37] It is fascinating to me that Joseph Smith would conclude his so-called "inspired" rendering of the phrase "upon this rock" by incorporating and integrating "Seers" with "Stones"—for which Joseph Smith has some notoriety. Joseph Smith further states, "The white stone mentioned in Revelations 2:17 will become a Urim and Thummim to each individual who receives one, through which things of a higher order will be made known."[38] Joseph Smith's obsession with "seer stones" (i.e., the Urim and Thummim) was so pervasive that he calculated that the earth itself will someday become a great Urim and Thummim in its sanctified and immortal state.[39]

Orson Whitney (1855-1931), who was a member of the Quorum of the Twelve Apostles of The Church of Jesus Christ of Latter-day Saints from 1906 until his death, spoke of the superiority of revelation (the words of the "living prophets") over the inadequacy of the Biblical narrative to guide the Church:

> No book [the *Bible* not excluded] is good enough to preside over the Church of God and direct its activities. Books are not a sufficient guide for progressive people on their way to the celestial kingdom. They are good as far as they go, but they do not go far enough. We have something better—a living, Heaven-inspired Priesthood, with the

Restored Gospel, the gifts of the Holy Ghost, and the principle of immediate and continuous revelation. Other churches are built upon books, traditions, decrees of councils and synods, maybe-so's [*sic*] and peradventures. But the Church of the Living God stands where He has placed **the Rock of Divine Revelation** . . .[40]

Orson F. Whitney reiterated:

The Latter-day Saints do not do things because they happen to be printed in a book . . . No book presides over this Church and no books lie at its foundation. You cannot pile up books enough to take the place of God's priesthood inspired by the power of the Holy Ghost.[41]

Stephen E. Robinson confirms: "[T]he meaning of the symbol for Mormons . . . The 'rock' is . . . the principle of revelation (see Joseph Smith, *Teachings of the Prophet Joseph Smith*, sel. Joseph fielding Smith [Salt Lake City: Deseret Book Co., 1938], p. 274)."[42] Robinson contends, "Latter-day Saints believe that the General Authorities receive inspiration and revelation from God constantly in the administration of the affairs of the Church."[43]

At a meeting in Kirtland, Ohio, situated on the east fork of the Chagrin River, sixty miles northeast of Cleveland, Joseph Smith lauded the words of Brigham Young when he said: "[W]hen compared with the living oracles [the *Bible* is] nothing to me; [the *Bible* does] not convey the word of God direct to us now, as do the words of a Prophet or a man bearing the Holy Priesthood in our day and generation."[44] Eric Shuster and Charles Sale both confirm the LDS interpretation of the Biblical passage "upon this rock" in their book *The Biblical Roots of Mormonism*:

A common misconception about the Apostasy centers on the term *rock*. The name Peter in Greek is *petros* (a detached stone or small rock), and the word rock is *petros* (meaning a mass of rock). Taken from the original Greek text of the New Testament, Matthew 16:18 should be read, "Thou art Peter [*petros*, or a small rock], and upon this rock [*petra*, or foundation of rock] I will build my church." **The rock upon which the Lord intended his church to be built was and is today the rock of revelation—** not the person or personality of an apostle or some other ecclesiastical authority. It was upon continuous revelation from God the Father and the Lord Jesus Christ that the Church of Jesus Christ would be built.[45]

Joseph F. Smith announced:

The Holy Priesthood [only held within the governance of the Mormon Church] is that authority [the only legitimate authority] which God has delegated to man, by which he may speak [through the spirit of revelation] the will of God as if the angels were here to speak it themselves; by which men are empowered to bind on earth and it shall be bound in heaven, and to loose on earth and it shall be loosed in heaven; by which the words of man, spoken in the exercise of that power, become the word of the Lord, and the law of God unto the people, scripture, and divine commands. . . . It is the authority by which the Lord Almighty governs his people, and by which, in time to come, he [along with the divine organization of the Mormon Church] will govern the world.

. . . A great deal may be said in relation to the authority and rights of the [Holy] priesthood. It is the grand principle of government and of organization, by which the energies and forces of the people of God in all ages have been and will be directed. [Tell that to the *Città dell Vaticano*!] It is that principle by which God Almighty governs throughout all His universe. It is the principle by which the Church of Jesus Christ of Latter-day Saints is governed.[46]

In their co-authored book, *The Biblical Roots of Mormonism*, under the heading "Priesthood Power and Authority," Eric Shuster and Charles Sale note: "By the power of the priesthood, God created the heavens and the earth and maintains the universe in its perfect order. Through the power of the priesthood, the Lord achieves his purpose, which is to bring to pass the immortality of man."[47] By this admission, Shuster and Sale are saying that the "priesthood" is greater than its possessor, namely God! Without the "priesthood," God is essentially an impotent and powerless entity! "Mormonism teaches that the priesthood is the power and authority of God. The Lord created the heavens and the earth—indeed, the very universe is kept in perfect order—by His priesthood power."[48]

According to the teachings of Mormonism, God became God through the derivation and effectual commissioning of the priesthood, and it is by this formula that all men have the potential of becoming gods! It is the priesthood office and its puissance that transforms mere men into gods. Mormonism teaches that God is subordinate to the priesthood, and that it is the "power of the priesthood" that facilitates the process of exaltation. Bruce R. McConkie insists that, "priesthood is the eternal power and authority of Deity by which all things exist; by which they are created, governed, and controlled. . . . It is the power of God."[49]

McConkie proposed that "the knowledge of God is found only by revelation through the power of the priesthood."[50] Whereas Jesus definitively stated, "All things are delivered unto me of my Father: and no man knoweth the Son, but the Father; neither knoweth any man the Father, save the Son, and he to whomsoever the Son will reveal him" (*Matthew 11:27 KJV*). The so-called ostensible and contrived "revelation through the power of the priesthood" (born out of a false religion) cannot usurp the singular office of the Son of God as the One and Only Mediator who alone possesses the authority to reveal the Father—"[N]either knoweth any man the Father [has the knowledge of God] save the Son, and he to whomsoever the Son will reveal him."

Satan is the usurper and perverter of God's design and promises to give glory and authority over the kingdoms of this world "to whomsoever [he] will give it" (see *Luke 4:6*). The Mormon priesthood has no more authority to reveal the Father than Satan, the father of lies and deception, has the capacity to speak the truth. The God and Father as revealed by the Mormon priesthood is nothing more than an exalted and glorified man, who, in turn, promises exaltation to those who follow and conform to his dictum and pretentious guidelines. This has been the lie of Satan since the beginning of creation when he announced, "and ye shall be gods" (*Genesis 3:5 KJV*) when he successfully tempted Eve (through a counter-narrative diametrically and diabolically opposed to God's implicit pronouncement) to eat of the Tree of the Knowledge of Good and Evil and trammeled the concourse of the history of mankind to this present generation. "Nevertheless the solid foundation of God stands, having this seal: 'The Lord knows those who are His' " (*2 Timothy 2:19 NKJV*). *Ellicott's Commentary for English Readers* states: "[A]ssuredly God's firm foundation still stands unshaken. 'The firm foundation laid by God' is the Church of Christ, which is here termed a foundation laid by God . . ."

One might say that the Mormon "Priesthood" has become the "Neo Baal" of this modern era. The Prophet Elijah challenged: "How long halt ye between two opinions? If the LORD [Jehovah] be God [Elohim] follow him [Mormons do not believe in the concept that Jehovah (who they believe is Jesus) is Elohim (who they believe is the Father)]: but if Baal [the "Priesthood"], *then* follow [it]" (*1 Kings 18:21 KJV*).

Mormonism has chosen, rather, to follow their ill-conceived notion of the "High Priesthood," an office, the power and authority of which is, idolized above reason. The power of the priesthood is such that it can move the finger of God! Joseph F. Smith adds, "[W]hen a man who holds the Priesthood does that which is righteous, God is bound to acknowledge it as though he had done it Himself."[51] Drew Williams suggests, "The holy priesthood has the power and authority to act in God's behalf in all things."[52] Williams further states, "The power of the priesthood [like some magic potion conjured by witchcraft and bestowed upon the recipient] heals, protects, and inoculates all of the righteous—women and men—against the powers of darkness."[53] In *The Joseph Smith Translation* (*JST*) we read:

> [E]very one being ordained [to the "Priesthood"] after this order and calling should have power, by faith, to break mountains, to divide the seas, to dry up waters, to turn them out of their course; to put at defiance the armies of nations, to divide the earth, to

break every band, to stand in the presence of God; to
. . . subdue principalities and powers . . . (*Genesis*
14:30-32).

Like the infamous magician, Simon Magus, who idolized the
"Power" of the Apostles and was enamored by the miracles and
signs performed by the same, and desired that "whomsoever I lay
hands, he may receive the Holy Ghost" (*Acts 8:19 KJV*), so those
who desire the "Priesthood" under the pretense of wielding and
conveying "spiritual powers" to elevate themselves to a position of
prestige, have been deceived and vaunted themselves "above that
which is written" (the canon of Scripture) concerning mans'
subordinate relationship to God (*1 Corinthians 4:6 KJV*). Joseph
Smith revealed that the "priesthood continueth in the church of God
in all generations, and is without beginning of days or end of years"
(*D&C* 84:19), giving the "priesthood" Godlike status independent
of God Himself! Spencer W. Kimball explicated:

> The priesthood is the power and authority of God
> delegated to man on earth to act in all things
> pertaining to the salvation of men. It is the means
> whereby the Lord acts through men to save souls.
> Without this priesthood power, men are lost. Only
> through this power does man "hold the keys of all the
> spiritual blessings of the church," enabling him to
> receive "the mysteries of the kingdom of heaven, to
> have the heavens opened" unto him (see *D&C*
> 107:18-19).

There is a magical worldview in the Mormon perception of the
so-called spiritual powers associated with the office of the "Holy
Priesthood." It is as if the "office" itself possesses an entitlement to
some kind of potency, if you will, connecting its bearer to an
enabling force—much like the seer stone enabled Joseph Smith to
see beyond physical barriers (for which I contend he could not). I
think it would be fair to say the "office" of the "Holy Priesthood"
has superseded the Promised Counselor (the Holy Spirit) and the
Lord's gifting to the Church at large—a free gift, given through the
pleasure of God, to those who but ask.

In the Gospel of *Luke*, Jesus said, "If ye then, being evil, know how to give good gifts unto *your* children: how much more shall your heavenly Father give the Holy [Ghost] to them that ask him?" (*Luke 11:13 KJV*). By focusing on the "Holy Priesthood," Mormonism has perverted the "gift" and clothed it, instead, with a "merit" system where "worthiness" reigns supreme over grace— God's unmerited favor and love. The truth of the matter is, Mormonism's "Holy Priesthood" holds nothing of import, and is but a divisive and vain deception; a mockery and a charade of the biblical archetype.

George Albert Smith said, "Upon the rock of revelation this Church was founded and by revelation it has been guided."[54] Lorenzo Snow insisted that, "The foundation upon which the Church of Jesus Christ of Latter-day Saints is built is the rock of revelation—upon the rock that Jesus said He would build His church . . ."[55] The Traditional Christian Church, to the contrary, believes Christ (the "Rock of Ages") is the true foundation and "Chief Cornerstone" of the Church, not "revelation."

Latter-day Saints are taught that the "Rock" upon which Christ will build His Church is the rock of "Modern Revelation," whereas, the true "Rock," as understood by the adherents of traditional mainstream Christianity, is the revelation that Jesus is Messiah, the Son of the Living God! The Apostle John corroborated that, "Whosoever believeth that Jesus is the Christ [the Messiah] is born of God" (*1 John 5:1 KJV*), not "Whosoever believeth in 'revelation.' " The Apostle John again emphasized:

> And many other signs truly did Jesus in the presence of his disciples, which are not written in this book: But these are written **that ye might believe that Jesus is the Christ, the Son of God**; and that believing ye might have life [eternal life] through his name (*John 20:30-31 KJV*; emphasis added).

In Matthew's Gospel we read:

> Therefore whosoever heareth these sayings of mine, and doeth them, I will liken him unto a wise man, **which built his house upon a rock**: And the rain descended, and the floods came, and the winds blew,

and beat upon that house; and it fell not: for it was **founded upon a rock**. And every one that heareth these sayings of mine, and doeth them not, shall be likened unto a foolish man, which built his house upon the sand: And the rain descended, and the floods came, and the winds blew, and beat upon that house; and it fell: and great was the fall of it (*Matthew 7:24-27 KJV*; emphasis added).

The Apostle Paul rightly observed, "And did all drink the same spiritual drink: for they drank that spiritual Rock that followed them: and **that Rock was Christ**" (*1 Corinthians 10:4 KJV*; emphasis added). The "spiritual Rock" is not "Revelation," it is the foundation and person of Jesus Christ. The Church of Jesus Christ of Latter-day Saints is not built on an intimate and personal relationship with Jesus Christ, in spite of what its name suggests, but upon so-called "living" apostles and prophets, and the misguided and false conception of modern-day revelation, which has trapped so many thousands in its ill-conceived web of deception.

Joseph Smith testified:

All men are liars who say they are of the true Church without the revelation of Jesus Christ and the Priesthood of Melchizedek, which is after the order of the Son of God [this makes all men liars who affiliate with a house of worship outside of the domicile of the LDS Church and the *Citadel of Mormonism*].[56]

The sectarian priests [pastors of all other denominations] are blind, and they lead the blind, and they will all fall into the ditch together. They build with hay, wood, and stubble, on the old revelations, without the true priesthood or spirit of revelation.[57]

Joseph Smith insisted that it was only through the "knowledge of the priesthood" that a man can be saved and "triumph over death."[58] The LDS Church asserts: "[T]hose who [are] ordained unto this [true] priesthood . . . whatsoever they shall speak . . . shall be scripture, shall be the will of the Lord, shall be the mind of the Lord, and the power of God, unto salvation."[59] Truman G. Madsen observed that according to Mormon theology, "The canon is never closed. Revelation and scripture are therefore continual. And the Mormon refuses to harden on the all-sufficiency or only-sufficiency of any part of scripture . . ."[60] Again, Joseph Smith asserted: ["W]here there is a Prophet, a priest, or a righteous man unto whom God gives His oracles, there is the Kingdom of God; and where the oracles of God are not, there the Kingdom of God is not."[61]

Bruce R. McConkie emphasized:

> [W]herever men have the Melchizedek Priesthood, there is the Church and the kingdom of God. Conversely, when and where there is no Melchizedek Priesthood, there is no true Church and no earthly kingdom which is the Lord's, and consequently, no way to prepare men to go to the eternal church in heaven.[62]

The Mormon Church advocates, "Any kingdom less than the celestial kingdom is a conditional hell to those who abide there."[63] It is apparent that it is the prerogative and obligation of Mormons (who aspire to attain their greatest "celestial potential" in the Celestial Kingdom—the third and highest level of the LDS doctrine of the tripartite gradations of glory) to consign all of humanity to the lower Terrestrial (second) and Telestial (lowest) kingdoms who do not bow to their creeds and submit to their *ipse dixit* (unproved dogma)—the narrow, contracted notions of the Mormon Church. Joseph Fielding Smith, Jr. explains that according to Mormon theology: "[T]he term 'Heaven' as intended for the Saints' eternal home, must include more kingdoms than one."[64] Smith further states, "[T]he nation and kingdom that will not serve thee [The *Citadel of Mormonism*/Zion] will perish . . ."[65]

James G. Turner writes:

> In the early 1830s, Smith had already moved sharply away from Protestant doctrines, talking about eternal matter and intelligences (as opposed to creation *ex nihilo*, out of nothing), distancing himself from the Protestant (and Catholic) understanding of the

Trinity, and describing three tiers of heavenly glory.[66]

In his preface to *Joseph Smith: Rough Stone Rolling*, Richard Lyman Bushman notes:

> A rhetorical problem vexes anyone who writes about the thought of Joseph Smith. Are his ideas to be attributed to him or to God? Some readers will consider it obvious that the revelations came from Joseph Smith's mind and nowhere else. His revelations of the afterlife, for example, can be summed up by saying "Joseph Smith imagined a heaven divided into three degrees of glory." Only a Mormon reader would say bluntly, "God revealed a heaven with three degrees of glory," without any disclaimer. Out of respect for the varied opinions of readers, it would seem judicious to compromise with "Joseph Smith *purportedly* received a revelation about a heaven with three degrees of glory."[67]

NOTE: James R. White (born December 17, 1962), director of Alpha and Omega Ministries, an evangelical Reformed Christian apologetics organization based in Phoenix, Arizona, writing for the Christian Research Institute (CRI), states:

> [Joseph] Smith assumed, incorrectly, that there had to be a direct correspondence between the sun/moon/stars analogy of [*1 Corinthians 15*] verse 41 and the "celestial/terrestrial" terms of verse 40. This was prompted also by Smith's interpretation of a later verse in Paul's second letter to the Corinthians, even though it appeared in an entirely different context. When Paul sought to defend his apostleship against his critics in Corinth, he wrote, "I know a man in Christ who fourteen years ago—whether in the body I do not know, or out of the body I do not know, God knows—. . . was caught up to the third heaven" (2 Cor. 12:2 NASB).
>
> Here [where Paul was "caught up to the third heaven"], the third heaven is the abode of God: the

"first" heaven would be the atmosphere above us, where birds fly; the "second" heaven would be where the stars are located, that which we call "space" today. Paul is saying he was taken up to the very presence of God. The context here is completely different than the discussion of resurrection bodies in 1 Corinthians 15. This has no connection to the discussion of celestial and terrestrial glories in his previous letter to the Corinthians, but the connection Smith made between the two is what provided him with his "three levels of glory."

Would Smith have been thrown as far off track had the King James used the more common words "heavenly" and "earthly" instead of "celestial" and "terrestrial"? We cannot know, but surely, it would have been less of a temptation for Smith to come up with a never-before-seen word like "telestial" had the King James consistently translated the underlying Greek terms. . . .

Smith's basic error in reading this text [*1 Corinthians 15:40-41* where Paul speaks of the "celestial bodies, and bodies terrestrial," and *2 Corinthians 12:2* where Paul said that he was "caught up to the third heaven"] combined with some unfamiliar English terminology and some translational inconsistency on the part of the KJV, has led to the entire concept of levels of glory and exaltation. A sobering reminder to handle the Word of God with care and accuracy![68]

The "first heaven" (our atmosphere) whose boundary is called the Kármán line begins at an altitude of about 62 miles. The "second heaven" encompasses the vast expanse of the known universe estimated at 46.5 billion light years in any direction, or 96 billion light years in diameter. The "Third Heaven" is descriptive of a division of heaven in religious cosmology. The concept of a third Heaven, also called *shamayi h'shamayim* (שמי השמים or "Heaven of Heavens"), is mentioned in such passages as *Genesis 28:12*, *Deuteronomy 10:14* and *1 Kings 8:27* as a distinctly spiritual realm traversed and occupied by the angels and God.

6

"The Keys of the Kingdom"

The Book of Mormon is a controversial book. It has . . . been condemned as a fraud, as the worst kind of deception perpetrated in the name of religion (American educator, Lowell L. Bennion).[1]

It has been said that the Book of Mormon has fraud written upon every page of it (Heber J. Grant, the seventh President of the LDS Church).[2]

In any criticism of Mormonism, much turns on whether the observer believes Joseph was who he said he was and did what he said he did. To the observer who accepts Joseph's claim of prophetic calling, the miraculous events that Joseph described are as believable as any that are recorded in the Bible. To the observer who rejects this claim, Joseph was—indeed had to have been—a fraud (Eric Shuster and Charles Sale, who co-authored the book, *The Biblical Roots of Mormonism*).[3]

The Mormon Church teaches that their Prophet is the highest and only presiding ecclesiastical authority on the earth today. In 1976, as President Spencer W. Kimball stood before the Thorvaldsen statues of the *Christus* and the Twelve Apostles (where Judas Iscariot is replaced by St. Paul) in the Vor Frue Kirke (the Church of Our Lady) in Copenhagen, Denmark:

> [H]e turned to President [Johan] Bentine [the stake president] and with unaccustomed sternness pointed his finger at him and said with firm, impressive words, "I want you to tell every Lutheran [prelate] in Denmark that they do not hold the keys! I [Spencer W. Kimball] hold the keys! ["The consummate authority on this earth . . . to act in the name of God."] We [the Church of Jesus Christ of Latter-day Saints] hold the real keys and we use them every day."[4]

President Kimball pointed to the statue of Peter and the keys explaining the symbolism and said, "We are the living apostles. We hold the real keys, as Peter did, and we use them every day. They are in use continually."[5] Bruce R. McConkie adamantly stated: "The President of the Church [of Jesus Christ of Latter-day Saints] is the only person on earth at any given time who does or can exercise these or any other priesthood keys in their eternal fulness [*sic*]."[6] The "Saints" presumption of license and elite guardianship over the so-called "Restored Gospel" is not simply a supremacy based on reason, but of a monopolistic priesthood conveyed by divine investiture of dispensational "keys," thus arrogating to themselves the title of God's Magisterium and only vice-regents on earth.

In the Gospel of *Matthew*, we read where Jesus asks His disciples:

> But whom say ye that I am? And Simon Peter answered and said, Thou art the Christ, the Son of the living God. And Jesus answered and said unto him, Blessed art thou, Simon Barjona: for flesh and blood hath not revealed *it* unto thee, but my Father which is in heaven. And I say also unto thee, That thou art Peter, and upon this rock I will build my church; and the gates of hell shall not prevail against it. And I will

give unto thee the keys of the kingdom of heaven: and whatsoever thou shalt bind on earth shall be bound in heaven: and whatsoever thou shalt loose on earth shall be loosed in heaven (*Matthew 16:15-19 KJV*).

Thorvaldsen's Peter holding the keys to the Kingdom.

In 1819, Bertel Thorvaldsen (1770-1844), a preeminent Danish/Icelandic sculptor, teamed with architect Christian Fredrik Hansen (1756-1845), was commissioned by the Church of Our Lady in Copenhagen, Denmark to cast, model, and create the *Christus* (also known as *Christus Consolator*) and the Twelve Apostles. The statues were ultimately sculpted in marble quarried in the Apuan Alps near the city of Carrara in Tuscany, in central Italy, and were completed and installed in the Vor Frue Kirke in 1838. The Apostles—six to a side—line the cathedral's interior walls, with the resurrected *Christus*—arms raised and outstretched—prominently featured at the front.

A century later, after visiting the cathedral of the Church of Our Lady in Copenhagen, Elder Stephen L. Richards (1879-1959) was so impressed with the marble statue of the *Christus* that he commissioned an 11-foot-high replica be built for the LDS Church now on display in a glass rotunda at the North Visitor's Center in Salt Lake City, Utah. The replica of the *Christus*—completed in 1959—was quarried from the same Apuan Alps above the city of Carrara where Bertel Thorvaldsen's statue was quarried.

Thorvaldsen's *Christus*

The final presentation of the *Christus* was not open for public viewing, however, until 1967. Subsequent statues have been sculpted and displayed by the LDS Church at various temple visitor's centers from Los Angeles to Washington D.C., and from France to New Zealand. As of January 2019, a replica of the *Christus* (standing at 13-feet) and the Twelve Apostles—scaled to three-quarters of the originals in Copenhagen, and sculpted from the same Carrara marble—can now be viewed by the public in the piazza style LDS rotunda Visitor's Center within view of the Rome Italy Temple.

Before the Commissioning of the *Christus* now on display in Salt Lake City, and also prominently featured in Rome, Elder Stephen L. Richards had commented, "You know, the world thinks we're not Christian because they see no evidence of Christ on this square. They hear the words, but see no evidence."[7]

NOTE: The *Christus* sculpture in Salt Lake City has recently been removed (in 2021) from the now deconstructed North Visitors' Center on Temple Square and has been placed in temporary storage until the proposed four-year-renovation project of the Salt Lake Temple and the surrounding areas are completed.

Allen F. Harrod wrote that the prevailing self–appraisal of Mormonism is that they see themselves as "uniquely endowed by the hand of God and [hold] exclusive rights as His divine instrument . . ."[8] Joseph Smith categorically stated that "The learned, the eloquent, the philosopher, the sage, the divine—all are ignorant."[9] "The world is full of technicalities and misrepresentation, which I calculate to overthrow . . ."[10]

Joseph Smith proudly announced:

- I hold the keys of the last kingdom [dispensation] . . . I was ordained to this very office in that Grand Council [of heaven] . . . and I intend to lay a foundation that will revolutionize the whole world.[11]

- Now, I have received, as the Prophet, Seer, and Revelator, standing at the head of this dispensation, every key, every ordinance, every principle and every priesthood that belongs to the last dispensation and the fulness [*sic*] of times.[12]

- I have got all the truth which the Christian world possessed, and an independent revelation in the bargain, and God will bear me off triumphant.[13]

- Then I think of the sectarian priests boasting of what they know. Why I have forgotten a thousand times more than they ever knew.[14]

- I have the whole plan of the kingdom before me, and no other person has.[15]

- It is my meditation all the day, and more than my meat and drink, to know how I shall make the Saints of God comprehend the visions that roll like an overflowing surge before my mind.[16]

- I defy all the world to destroy [this] work of God.[17]

- I defy all the world to refute me.[18]

- I shall triumph over my enemies: I have begun to triumph over them at home and I shall do it abroad. All those who rise up against me will surely feel the weight of their iniquity upon their own heads.[19]

- [L]earned men who are preaching salvation . . . are unlearned in the things of God . . . But I am learned, and know more than all the world put together.[20]

- I know better [than] all learned men and doctors of divinity.[21]

- [T]he Almighty . . . will give me dominion over all and every one of them.[22]

- I defy all the learning and wisdom and all the combined powers of earth and hell together . . .[23]

- I testify that no man has power to reveal it but myself—things in heaven, in earth and hell. . . .[24]

- What many people call sin [Joseph Smith remarked on one occasion], is not sin. I do many things to break down superstition, and I will break it down . . .[25]

- If I were not in your midst to aid and counsel you, the devil would overcome you.[26]

- I could go back and trace every subject of interest concerning the relationship of man to God, if I had time. I can enter into the mysteries; I can enter largely into the eternal worlds . . .[27]

- [Y]ou know no more concerning the destinies of the Church and kingdom than a babe upon its mother's lap. You don't comprehend it.[28]

- I am a lawyer; I am a big lawyer and comprehend heaven, earth and hell, to bring forth knowledge that shall cover up all lawyers, doctors and other big bodies.[29]

- I am at the defiance of the world, for I will take shelter under the broad cover of the wings of the work in which I am engaged. It matters not to me if all hell boils over; I regard it only as I would the crackling of the thorns under a pot.[30]

- The Lord has constituted me so curiously that I glory in persecution. . . . All hell boil over! Ye burning mountains, roll down your lava! For I will come out on top at last.[31]

- I have the truth, and am at the defiance of the world to contradict me, if they can.[32]

- When did I ever teach anything wrong from this stand? When was I ever confounded? . . . there is no error in the revelations which I have taught. . . .[33]

- Why do not my enemies strike a blow at the doctrine? They cannot do it: it is truth, and I defy all men to upset it.[34]

- I bear record this morning that all the combined powers of Earth and hell shall not and cannot ever overthrow or overcome this boy.[35]

- I combat the errors of ages . . . I cut the Gordian knot of power, and I solve mathematical problems of universities, with truth—diamond truth; and God is my 'right-hand man.'[36]

- In your hands or that of any other person, so much power would, no doubt, be dangerous. I am the only man in the world whom it would be safe to trust with it. Remember, I am a prophet.[37]

- I calculate to be one of the Instruments of setting up the Kingdom of Daniel, by the word of the Lord, and I intend to lay a foundation that will revolutionize the whole world . . .[38]

- [I]f you will follow the revelations and instructions which God gives you through me, I will take you into heaven as my back load.[39]

- I myself hold the keys of this last dispensation, and I forever will hold them in time and in eternity. So set your hearts at rest, for all is well.[40]

- The whole earth shall bear me witness that I, like the towering rock in the midst of the ocean, which has withstood the mighty surges of the warring waves for centuries, *am impregnable* . . .[41]

Jesus taught that, "[O]ut of the abundance of the heart the mouth speaketh" (*Matthew 12:34 KJV*). The preceding quotes (so full of self-righteous blather and hubris) clearly depict one who has a towering ego, is insular and self-absorbed, pretentious and arrogant, if not narcissistic! The Apostle Paul, perhaps the greatest apostle of all time, on the other hand, said, "But God forbid that I should glory, save in the cross of our Lord Jesus Christ, by whom the world is crucified unto me, and I unto the world" (*Galatians 6:14 KJV*). Authentic prophets of God do not spend a lot of time talking about themselves. The Lord chooses men, rather, who walk in humility to be intermediaries and a prophetic voice to the nations, first to Israel, and then to the Gentiles.

Sally Denton addresses the "seeds of . . . grandiosity that would eventually overtake [Joseph Smith's] personality."[42] Richard

Lyman Bushman iterates, "He [Joseph Smith] believed in himself and the cause to the point of arrogance, as more than one critic pointed out."[43] Again, Bushman relates: "Joseph was hated for twisting the common faith in biblical prophets into the visage of the arrogant fanatic . . ."[44] Joseph Smith's ego was beyond pale!

Jesus warned, "He that speaketh of himself seeketh his own glory: but he that seeketh his glory that sent him, the same is true . . ." (*John 7:18 KJV*). The presumptive conclusion in Jesus' statement is that when one speaks of himself and seeks his own glory that he does not speak the truth. *Proverbs 27:2 KJV* warns, "Let another man praise thee, and not thine own mouth; a stranger, and not thine own lips."

Joseph Fielding Smith, Jr. concurs:

> When a man comes in the name of the Lord . . . performing mighty works, he will not come with the blare of trumpets, nor will he advertise his performance. . . . When a man comes preaching his own doctrine . . . he does all of this to be seen of men and by advertising his deeds to the world, it is a sure sign that he has not been called by divine appointment.[45]

Joseph F. Smith, Sr. raises the "yellow flag of warning" classifying the most dangerous false teachers as: "The proud and self-vaunting ones, who read by the lamp of their own conceit; who interpret by rules of their own contriving; who become a law unto themselves, and so pose as the sole judges of their own doings."[46] John Taylor implored:

> [N]o man has a right to plume himself upon any position he occupies in this Church, for he is simply a servant of God and a servant of the people, and if any man attempts to use any kind of arbitrary authority and act with any degree of unrighteousness, God will hold that man to an account for it, and we all of us have to be judged according to the deeds done in the body. We are here as saviors of men and not as tyrants and oppressors.[47]

John A Widtsoe (1872-1952), a member of the Quorum of the Twelve Apostles of The Church of Jesus Christ of Latter-day Saints from 1921 until his death, entreated: "[C]losely related to the feeling of superiority, are false interpretations of scripture. These rise to such magnitude, though at variance with accepted, revealed doctrine, that they endanger the spiritual life of the individual."[48] In spite of Joseph Smith's provocative declarations of vainglorious self-importance and superiority, Joseph Fielding Smith counters, "It is contrary to reason to think that the Lord would establish his Church upon any man, no matter how faithful and wonderful he might be."[49]

Heedless of what Joseph Fielding Smith asserted, Bruce R. McConkie adulated:

> From the opening of our dispensation [the founding of the LDS Church in 1830] down to the Second Coming of the Son of Man; and for that allotted period of earth's history, the word of the Lord, the word of salvation, the word of light and truth are going to the world through Joseph Smith and in no other way and through no one else.[50]

Joseph Fielding McConkie (son of Bruce R. McConkie) sounds off his own praises of Joseph Smith, asserting:

> He [Joseph Smith] would be called upon to write more scripture than the dozen most prolific writers of the Bible combined . . .[51]

> No man in earth's history has been responsible for restoring more truth than has the Prophet Joseph Smith . . .[52]

> [H]e taught more truth about the Son of God than any other gospel teacher or writer of whom we have record. . . . he was the most competent witness of Deity upon the earth.[53]

> At his hand more truths and knowledge about Christ are available to the honest seeker of truth than by the labors of any other man who ever lived. . . . Joseph Smith's labor gives more clarity, power, and

purpose to the Old Testament than do those of all the scholars in earth's history combined.[54]

Brigham Young idolized and elevated Joseph Smith next to Jesus Christ himself:

> I honor and revere the name of Joseph Smith. I delight to hear it; I love it. I love his doctrine . . . I do not think a man lives on earth that knew him better than I did; and I am bold to say that, Jesus Christ excepted, no better man ever lived or does live upon this earth.[55]

> If we ask who will stand at the head of the resurrection in this last dispensation, the answer is— Joseph Smith, Junior, the Prophet of God. He is the man who will be resurrected and receive the keys of the resurrection, and he will seal this authority upon others, and they will hunt up their friends and resurrect them when they shall have been officiated for and bring them up.[56]

Jesus said, "**I am the resurrection**, and the life: he that believeth in me, though he were dead, yet shall he live . . ." (*John 11:25 KJV*; emphasis added). Jesus **is the resurrection**. The resurrection is not a kinetic, or potential-like energy or designated "key" that lies in His possession because of some entitlement that can be conveyed to just anyone, but is an innate attribute of Jesus the "Creator" of all transient life and the "ground of all being" and embodiment of "Life Eternal." Only Jesus the eternal "I Am" can both define and endow imperishable life!

Parley P. Pratt plaudits:

> Ages yet unborn will rise up and call [Joseph Smith] blessed. A thousand generations of countless myriads will laud [Joseph Smith's] name and recount his deeds, while unnumbered nations bask in the light and enjoy the benefits of the institution founded by his instrumentality.[57]

Wilford Woodruff enjoins with the encomium: "I will say myself that I do not believe there ever was a man . . . that was more closely united and associated with God the Father, and God the Son, and God the Holy Ghost, than the Prophet Joseph Smith."[58] Joseph F. Smith, with enraptured praise, said, "no man or combination of men possessed greater intelligence than [Joseph Smith], nor could the combined wisdom and cunning of the age produce an equivalent for what he did."[59]

William W. Phelps (1792-1872), who was an early leader of the Latter-day Saint movement, printed the first edition of the Book of Commandments and wrote numerous hymns that became standard works of the church, memorialized Joseph Smith's martyrdom on June 27th, 1844 with exuberant praise:

Praise to the Man (originally titled "Joseph Smith")

Praise to the Man who communed with Jehovah!

Jesus anointed that Prophet and Seer.

Blessed to open the last dispensation,

Kings shall extol him, and nations revere. . . .

Hail to the Prophet, ascended to Heaven! . . .

Mingling with Gods . . .

Great is his glory and endless his priesthood.[60]

B. H. Roberts suggests that these overt and excessively flattering indulgences from Joseph Smith's "immediate and enthusiastic disciples" who had "come under the magic spell of his personality," were spawned by a "superstitious reverence that magnifies every virtue and blinds them to every fault," and "who see only the perfection of the object they adore."[61] In spite of Roberts' reservations concerning Joseph Smith's overzealous admirers, he was not beneath expressing his own approbations. Roberts, enraptured by the Prophet Joseph Smith, trumpeted:

[I believe] in him without reservation . . . I was influenced by the boldness of his claims, for the tremendous intellectual daring . . . for the very sway and swagger of him, and for his unschooled eloquence. . . . To me and for me, [Joseph Smith] is the Prophet of the Most High, enskied and sainted![62]

B. H. Roberts

Merriam-Webster informs: "The very first, and most famous, use of 'ensky' occurs [in 1603] in Shakespeare's *Measure for Measure*, when Lucio tells Isabella, a novice in a convent, 'I hold you as a thing **enskied and sainted**.' " *Merriam-Webster* lists the following synonyms for "ensky": aggrandize, canonize, deify, dignify, elevate, ennoble, enshrine, enthrone, exalt, glorify, magnify. *Merriam-Webster* states that, "Someone who has been enskied has been raised, figuratively, as high as the sky."

This author will reserve his praise and adulation for Jesus, the King of Glory! In the Apostle John's *Apocalypse*, we read:

> And I beheld, and I heard the voice of many angels round about the throne and the beasts and the elders: and the number of them was ten thousand times ten thousand, and thousands of thousands;
>
> Saying with a loud voice, Worthy is the Lamb that was slain to receive power, and riches, and wisdom, and strength, and honour, and glory, and blessing (*Revelation 5:11-12 KJV*).

7

God's Blanket Denouncement

From the beginning of mankind those things which are the most genuinely pure—even Godlike—ofttimes become the first to be imitated—reproduced in counterfeit effect— deceiving many, even the elect if it were possible (Carter E. Grant, who wrote numerous articles on Western and Mormon history).[1]

Most card-carrying Latter-day Saints would probably admit that the events [concerning the "First Vision"] that followed Joseph after he entered that grove of trees would be nothing short of preposterous to accept (Drew Williams, author of *The Idiot's Complete Guide to Understanding Mormonism*).[2]

In *The Pearl of Great Price* (one of Mormonism's "Standard Works"), we read of God's so-called blanket denouncement of the world-body of "believers at large"—the multifaceted Christian Church (Catholics, Protestants—Methodist, Presbyterians, Baptists, etc.)—as recorded in Joseph Smith's "First Vision":

> [A]ll their creeds were an abomination in His sight; that those professors were all corrupt; that "They draw near to Me with their lips, but their hearts are far from Me, they teach for doctrines the

commandments of men, having a form of godliness, but they deny the power thereof."[3]

In this caustic declaration, "all" other faiths are clearly marginalized—their pastors and clergy demoralized—while their cherished creeds are resoundingly dismissed with aplomb. Hoyt W. Brewster Jr. (born 1939), manager, curriculum planning and development, Church Curriculum Department, admits that, "this statement [as recorded in Joseph Smith's "First Vision"] has given a great deal of offense."[4] Terryl and Fiona Givens concede, "Many readers of Joseph Smith's First Vision account feel the sting of a wide-net rebuke, with its reference to the Christian creeds as 'an abomination' in God's sight."[5]

William Edwin Berrett (1902-1993), who was a Vice President of Brigham Young University and a Latter-day Saint author, notes: "The assertion on the part of the Saints that they possessed the gospel in its fulness [sic] while all other denominations were wrong, continued as it had done from the time of the first vision, to arouse opposition."[6] James B. Allen and Glen M. Leonard concede, "Occasionally Latter-day Saint preachers created resentment themselves with unrestrained enthusiasm or dogmatic insistence on the superiority of their religion."[7] Entitlement, elitism and arrogance would well-define an organization that trumpets and self-reflects as "the only true and living church upon the face of the whole earth" (D&C 1:30)—the "Chosen People."

D. Michael Quinn notes, "By obedience to its increasingly centralized hierarchy, the aggressive Mormon community altered—and usually disrupted—the social landscape wherever it established its headquarters."[8] Quinn further acknowledges:

> Fear of being overwhelmed politically, socially, culturally, economically by Mormon immigration was what fueled anti-Mormonism wherever the Latter-day Saints settled during Joseph Smith's lifetime. Religious belief, as non-Mormons understood it, had little to do with anti-Mormonism. On the other hand, by the mid-1830s Mormons embraced a religion that shaped their politics, economics, and society. Conflict was inevitable.[9]

Gordon B. Hinckley conceded that "Such teachings, flying in the face of traditional Christianity, were bound to stir the indignation of the intolerant ["intolerant," of course, would include all who oppose the "teachings" of Mormonism]."[10] Sally Denton notes:

> Setting themselves apart as the chosen ones—calling all non-Mormons "Gentiles"—created a suspicion and animosity not easily assuaged. The "us" versus "them" mentality, begun as a survival tool and forged into a pathology, would serve as both cohesion and division, and, in any case, plague the new religion for years to come.[11]

Denton further states:

> The Mormons' millennialist fervor, coupled with assertions that their scriptures were equal to the Bible and their faith the only true one, added to the conflict, as did what two historians described as "the anti-democratic tendencies of their dogmatic, crusading spirit."[12]

Again, Denton writes:

> [The Mormons] were peculiarly oblivious to "the provocative nature of their more radical doctrines"— including their apocalyptic goal of ushering in the new messiah—which led to what two historians called "the myth of persecuted innocence."[13]

Denton concludes, "The Mormons' clannishness and radical theology would be both their strength and their curse." Denton suggests the Church created its own "atmosphere of persecution and insularity, piety and spiritual supremacy, zealotry and vengeance."[14] Joseph Fielding Smith asks, "Is it not horrible to contemplate that gospel truth has been perverted and defiled until it has become such an abomination?"[15] On the heels of Smith's suggested contemplation, B. H. Roberts offers a semblance for the reason why Mormonism was (historically) so often dismissed and critically assessed:

> It must be admitted . . . that there is something very irritating in the message which the Church of Jesus

Christ of Latter-day Saints has to proclaim to the world: the churches are all wrong; their creeds are an abomination to the Lord; they teach for doctrine the commandments of men; they draw near to the Lord with their lips, but their hearts are far from him; they have a form of godliness but deny the power thereof—and hence a New Dispensation of the gospel has become necessary. All this of course was not likely to appeal sympathetically to the ministry or people of supposedly orthodox Christian churches, especially when such a message was delivered, as sometimes it must be admitted it was delivered, without due regard to the feelings of those to whom it was addressed.[16]

Leonard J. Arrington and Davis Bitton intimate: "A group that succeeds in turning friends and the far more numerous 'neutrals' into enemies, as the Mormons did in one place after another, must have exhibited some repellent characteristics, at the very least."[17] Charles R. Harrell expounds:

Since its inception, many Mormons have taken an exclusivist stance towards other belief systems, acknowledging that, while other religions have a portion of the truth (mingled with error), only Mormonism contains the full and undiluted truth. This has sometimes led to feelings, and certainly an external perception, of doctrinal superiority and elitism among Latter-day Saints.[18]

Joseph Smith and his followers left a trail of expulsions from Palmyra, New York to Harmony, Pennsylvania; from Harmony to Fayette, New York; from Fayette to Colesville, New York; from Colesville to Kirtland, Ohio; from Kirtland to Independence, Missouri; from Independence to Clay County, Missouri; from Clay County to Far West, Missouri; from Far West to Nauvoo, Illinois and from Nauvoo to the Great Basin (their final hegira to the Salt Lake Valley) in the sparsely-inhabited Utah Territory.

The *Salt lake Tribune* commented that, "Wherever the [Latter-day Saints] settled they stirred up strife with their neighbors, until they became so generally hated, that they were compelled to seek a home in the inaccessible wilderness in order to get away from the human race." Elder George A. Smith (1817-1875), who was an early leader in the Latter Day Saint movement, and served in the Quorum of the Twelve Apostles and as a member of the First Presidency of the Church of Jesus Christ of Latter-day Saints, describes the Salt Lake Valley as "so desolate and God-forsaken that no mortal upon earth ever would covet it . . ."[19] Brigham Young pontificated, "This country suits us merely because no other well informed people can covet its possession. If they do, it is because they grudge us an existence upon any part of God's footstool."[20] Though the Mormon Church now occupied Utah Territory, a "sparsely-inhabited," "desolate and God-forsaken" enclave, the LDS Church soon found itself embroiled in a conflict with the armed forces of the United States Government that became known as the "Utah War," or the "Mormon Rebellion."

Richard Lyman Bushman notes:

> [The early expansion of Mormonism] had met defeat after defeat. None of the Mormon settlements had lasted in Ohio or Missouri. Joseph's seven-year stay in Kirtland was the longest in any gathering place. At Far West, the Saints survived barely two years. The gathering led to one disaster after another, as local citizens turned against the expanding Mormon population. Joseph lost old friends and trusted supporters: Oliver Cowdery, David Whitmer, Frederick G. Williams, William W. Phelps, Orson Hyde, Martin Harris, and Thomas B. Marsh all left him in 1838, worn down by failures and perceived missteps.[21]

Joseph Fielding Smith contends: *"Nothing by way of ordinance* and *very little by way of doctrine*, given by revelation in the days of our Savior and during the lives of the apostles, was left remaining. . . ."[22] Smith claims that at the time Joseph Smith had his "First Vision":

> There was not one fundamental truth belonging to the plan of salvation that was not, in the year 1820, so

obscured by false tradition and ceremonies, borrowed from paganism, as to make it unrecognizable; or else it was entirely denied. By heavenly direction and command of our Lord Jesus Christ, Joseph Smith restored all these principles in their primitive beauty and power . . .[23]

Again, Joseph Fielding Smith asserts:

Therefore, we have [the *Book of Mormon* and the *Bible*], besides which we have the *Doctrine and Covenants*, these three witnesses [three of the "Standard Works" of Mormonism] enable us to occupy a different position from any other religious denomination upon the face of the earth.[24]

We must have faith in the mission of Joseph Smith. Because the world had lapsed into spiritual darkness, changed the ordinances and broken the everlasting covenant, the Church of Jesus Christ had to be brought again from the heavens.

. . . We are far ahead of any other people in the world. We have greater faith because we have a better understanding of the truth, and because we are to a greater extent striving to keep the commandments of the Lord. . . .

[T]he world . . . cannot or do not comprehend the mission of Jesus Christ. They do not understand what salvation means. They do not know upon what it is based.[25]

. . . [T]he whole world ought to come to us [the Latter-day Saints] with songs of everlasting joy, singing their hosannas to embrace the truth . . .[26]

This author will reserve his "hosannas" for the Lord and His Christ! For Jesus alone is worthy of our praise and adulation. Even God's mighty holy angels refused adoration commanding us to "Worship God" (*Revelation 22:8-9 NKJV*). The exclusivity of worshipping Christ alone is a magisterial doctrine that guards his followers from

184

looking for salvation in an institutionalized church promulgating a superseding formula of ordinances and commandments.

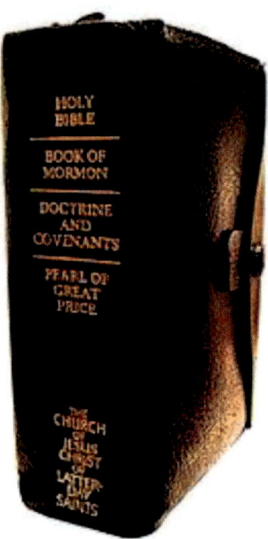

The Four Standard Works of Mormonism (the "Quad" Scriptures).

Joseph Fielding Smith boasts that the *Ensign* of "*the Church of Jesus Christ of Latter-day Saints*, which was established" in this last dispensation, "was the greatest event the world has seen since that day that the Redeemer was lifted upon the cross and worked out the infinite and eternal atonement."[27] Gerrit de Jong, Jr. (1892-1978), the first dean of the college of Fine Arts at Brigham Young University, clarifies, "What we really try to convey when we say we know that the Gospel is true, is that Mormonism, so-called, is the true Gospel of Jesus Christ."[28] Joseph Smith declared, "Truth is 'Mormonism.' God is the author of it."[29] Heber J. Grant confirms:

> Mormonism is in very deed the plan of life and salvation, the gospel of the Lord Jesus Christ. . . . There is nothing in all the world for which I am so grateful as an absolute knowledge that we, the Latter-day Saints, have the true gospel of Jesus Christ.[30]

Roy W. Doxey trumpets: "The Church of Jesus Christ of Latter-day Saints, or the kingdom of God, is the perfect organization, for it is the divine way in which mankind may work out its salvation, the most important work which should have man's attention in this life."[31] Bruce R. McConkie bloviates:

> [The Mormon Church] is the only true and living church upon the face of the whole earth and is the one place where salvation may be found. It is, in the true and literal sense of the word, the kingdom of God on earth, and as such it is preparing men to go to the kingdom of God in heaven, which is the celestial kingdom.[32]

Again, McConkie affirms, "The Church of Jesus Christ of Latter-day Saints is the Lord's kingdom on earth and the only place where salvation may be found. Again these are absolute, eternal, ultimate truths."[33] George Albert Smith insists: " 'Mormonism,' so-called, is the Gospel of Jesus Christ, consequently it is the power of God unto salvation to all those who believe and obey its teachings."[34] B. H. Roberts concurs: "[The LDS Church] is the sacred depository of his truth. It is his instrumentality for promulgating all those spiritual truths in which he would have mankind instructed."[35]

Roy W. Doxey adds, "Joseph Smith's . . . theological teachings paved the way for a far nobler understanding of God than that conceived by an apostate world."[36] Mark E. Petersen explains:

> Man-made doctrines lead to denominationalism. Denominationalism leads away from basic doctrine [and "a wide departure from original Christianity"]. But only basic doctrine can save. If we worship according to the doctrines of men our worship is in vain, that is, without effect.
>
> That means then that church unity can come only through acceptance of the divine teachings as provided by Christ and the prophets, who are authorized by the Almighty to minister in His affairs.

But this premise is rejected by uninspired denominations [this includes all denominations], which in effect, then, reject not only church unity, but the very salvation which they claim to seek.

Revelation, true authority, direction by living prophets [here it is implied that they are only found in the Mormon Church] can point the way to salvation.

Which of all the [other] denominations in the world can provide them?[37]

Wilford Woodruff insinuates:

The very fact that generation after generation have risen up and established systems and organizations, all professing to be according to the plan of salvation, and yet opposed one to another, until they have raised up scores of churches all differing on points of doctrine, proves that there has been something out of the way.[38]

For 52 years, the "Mormon Miracle Pageant" held each year (until 2019) in Manti, Utah, the Church of Jesus Christ of Latter-day Saints began their production by introducing three sectarian congregations and their clergy, all preaching conflicting messages. The exhibition's lead-in was orchestrated by design as a prelude to prepare the audience for the much- celebrated appearing of Joseph Smith and the so-called restoration of the ancient Gospel in all its purity. Declaring that the Mormon Church is the only true expression of the Christian faith, denouncing the "Denominational Theory"—where diversity is fully expressed in the multifaceted body of Christ and in the symbiotic ecclesiastical structure of the Church at large—the LDS Church insists that they have cornered the market on sacramental authority and divine revelation.

Ezra Taft Benson, the 15th United States Secretary of Agriculture during both presidential terms of Dwight D. Eisenhower, pronounced, "This is not just another Church. This is not just one of a family of Christian churches. This is the Church and kingdom of God, the only true Church upon the face of the earth

. . ."[39] President Spencer W. Kimball likewise announced, "This is not another church. This is *the* Church. This is not another gospel or philosophy. This is the church and gospel of Jesus Christ."[40] Martin Marty (born in 1928), an American Lutheran religious scholar, in responding to a query posed by a member of the LDS Church's Public Affairs department proposed, "The most important issue facing Mormons in the next ten years is maintaining the posture that you are the only true church, to the exclusion of all others and then trying to get along with those you exclude."[41]

In an article titled "Why Are There Different Denominations," posted October 24, 2016 in the Galli Report, JoHanna Reardon, a student of Church history, writes that the "denominational theory of the church [is] based on certain guiding principles:"

1. Considering the human inability to see the truth clearly at all times, differences of opinion about the outward form of the church are inevitable.

2. Even though these differences do not involve fundamentals of faith, they are matters of importance.

3. Since no church has a full grasp of divine truth [the LDS Church would argue this point], the true church of Christ can never be fully represented by any single ecclesiastical structure.

4. Finally, the mere fact of separation does not of itself constitute schism. It is possible to be divided at many points and still be united in Christ.

A principle example chronicled in the *Old Testament* that reflects unity in the face of diversity is the nation of Israel. Each of the "Twelve Tribes" of Israel was unique in its disposition. In *Genesis 49:1-11*, the prophecy given by Jacob when he had gathered his sons together was specific to their progeny—"each tribe according to his blessing he blessed them"—who descended and denominated from the patriarchs to become their eponymous tribes. No two tribes were alike, each following his own predilection or blueprint, so to speak, whose prescription—"That I may tell you that which shall befall you in the latter days"—given by Jacob described their lineage's journey throughout the concourse of the nation's history. Four hundred years later, Moses gathered the tribal leaders of Jacob's clan of Israel once more (see *Deuteronomy 33:1-29*) and blessed the descendants of the children of Israel in like manner emphasizing each tribe's defining characteristics as the succeeding generations followed suit. Even though Israel would become one nation in the land of Canaan, each tribe continued to maintain its own autonomy and individuality.

Just as no one tribe can define Israel, its history, or its final evaluation as a nation, so no one denomination can delineate the Kingdom of God in its fullness. It took "Twelve Tribes"—whose names would be forever inscribed upon the gates of the New Jerusalem (see *Revelation 21:12*)—to best represent the nation of Israel, and seven first-century churches "which are in Asia" (see *Revelation 1:11-3:22*) to unfold the full spectrum of the ecclesia in John's *Apocalypse*—hear "what the Spirit says to the churches [plural]." Jesus said that He "walks in the midst of the seven golden lampstands [which are the seven churches]" (*Revelation 2:1 NKJV*). Mormonism's one-size-fits-all or one-stop-shopping approach to the Kingdom of God—declaring that they are the only "true church" (singular)—is inviable and ill advised, if not conceited and unconscionable.

God not only reveals Himself in His unity (Jesus said, "I and *my* Father are one." *John 10:30 KJV*) but also in His diversity through the triune expression of the Godhead (Father, Son, and Holy Spirit). The Apostle Paul wrote, "for we being many are one bread and one body" (*1 Corinthians 10:17 KJV*). And again, "There are differences of ministries, but the same Lord" (*1 Corinthians 12:5 KJV*). *Matthew Henry's Concise Commentary* on this verse states that in the church (the "Body of Christ"), "There are various gifts, and various offices to perform, but all proceed from one God, one Lord, one Spirit." Just as God's gifts are distributed and denominated in the "Body of Christ," as He has ordered them in His providence for the multiformity and edification of the whole, so too, the "Church-at-large"—defined by its diversification of denominational expressions, yet bound by central tenets—is mutually benefited through the "family," and wide-ranging network, of Christian churches. The Church is not represented by a stiff statuesque-like monochrome image, but is personified by a vibrant multifaceted mosaic of many colors whose portraiture can only be seen from a distance.

Diversity does not necessarily result in divisiveness. In God's wisdom, He has allowed a broad latitude in the multifaceted community of believers in the ecclesia to achieve His purposes. Unity in the corporate "Body of Christ" (the Church) is not necessarily achieved through uniformity. In the Apostle Paul's letter to the church in Galatia we read: "There is neither Jew nor Greek, there is neither bond nor free, there is neither male nor female: for ye are all one in Christ Jesus" (*Galatians 3:28 KJV*).

In the *Book of Revelation,* we read:

> After this I beheld, and, lo, a great multitude, which no man could number, of all nations, and kindreds, and people, and tongues, stood before the throne, and before the Lamb, clothed with white robes, and palms in their hands;
>
> And cried with a loud voice, saying, Salvation to our God which sitteth upon the throne, and unto the Lamb (*Revelation 7:9-10 KJV*).

Carl Moser, who holds a Ph.D. in *New Testament* studies from St. Andrews University, Scotland, writes:

> It is a foundational belief of Mormonism that the church Christ founded in the first century apostatized but was restored through the work of Joseph Smith in 1830. It is claimed that Joseph Smith reintroduced to the world a pristine Christianity replete with truths and insights that had been lost in the "Great Apostasy." According to the apostasy thesis, the process of Hellenization and the influence of pagan Greek philosophy corrupted Christianity. Precious truths were forgotten, the transmission of the Bible was interfered with, inspired books were lost, and the canon was inappropriately deemed closed. The lenses of Hellenistic thinking caused and continue to

cause traditional Christianity to misread and misunderstand the Bible. The Christian tradition of theological absolutism and ontological Trinitarianism is unbiblical, and creedal orthodoxy has much to do with Athens but little to do with Jerusalem. As evidence of Joseph Smith's restoration of Christianity and the soon return of Christ, God allowed Smith to miraculously restore ancient texts and doctrines that had been lost for nearly two millennia.[42]

Moser, however, observes that because ". . . Mormon teachings depart [so] radically from biblical and historical Christian faith . . . I do not believe that at this time Mormonism can be categorized as Christian in any very useful or theologically significant sense . . ."[43]

Joseph Smith conceded: "[I]t may seem to some to be a very bold doctrine that we talk of" (*Doctrine and Covenants* 128:9). Benjamin E. Park writes matter-of-factly that, "Joseph Smith [was] known for his doctrinal innovations."[44] Bruce A. Van Orden, associate professor of Church history and doctrine at Brigham Young University (BYU) in Provo, Utah, presents Joseph Smith as "a revealer and **innovator of new and unusual doctrine** and religious practices."[45] Historians James B. Allen and Glen M. Leonard report: "Even for the Saints, some of the newly revealed doctrines were difficult to accept," where Joseph Smith himself "concluded with a discouraged recognition of how hard it was to accept such things." Allen and Leonard admit that, "Mormon doctrine departed significantly from some current, well-established religious tenets of the day."[46] Leonard J. Arrington and Davis Bitton attest: "At each stage some Mormons were left behind, disagreeing with the latest revelatory changes." Arrington and Bitton further state: "[S]ome of these 'advanced' doctrines did not reach scattered members of the church at once, and there is evidence of reluctance on the part of some to go beyond the simple Mormonism [the "Old Standard"] they had accepted in the early 1830s . . ."[47]

Gerrit de Jong, Jr. concedes:

Many of the tenets held by the modern [LDS] Church were considered so startling in the earlier days as to call for frequent explanation and defense by all who professed belief in Joseph Smith's mission. Even mere sympathetic consideration of any of the modern prophet's teachings made it necessary for a person to give a convincing explication in order to escape ridicule and persecution.[48]

Leonard J. Arrington and Davis Bitton intimate:

To begin with, there was the repugnance felt for a religion that challenged many accepted values. Except for the small minority who greeted Mormonism as the answer to unmet spiritual needs, most felt that its beliefs were superstitious, disgusting and repellent. What was apparently most galling was a mixture in Mormonism of what seemed to outsiders as a primitivistic reversion to "unenlightened," even "un-American," beliefs.[49]

Joseph Smith recorded in his journal: "If the [LDS] Church knew all the commandments, one-half they would condemn through prejudice and ignorance."[50] Again, Joseph Smith proffers: "Had I inspiration, revelation, and lungs to communicate what my soul has contemplated in times past, there is not a soul in this congregation but would go to their homes and shut their mouths in everlasting silence on religion till they had learned something."[51] Joseph further bloviated: "I could explain a hundred fold more than I ever have of the glories of the kingdoms manifested to me in the vision, were I permitted, and were the people prepared to receive them."[52]

The Mormon Church asserts that the "apostasy" of Christianity's mainstream ecclesia necessitated the "restoration of the Gospel" and reestablishment of God's truths that were lost, corrupted and sullied by the folly of men. (Thus the extra-Biblical revelations—*The Book of Mormon, Doctrine and Covenants* and *The Pearl of Great Price.*) This noble, albeit beguiling ruse subsumed under the misleading banner of "RESTORATION," continues to be successfully exploited by Mormonism as a "red herring" to proselytize hundreds of thousands of unsuspecting initiates into their organization. Joseph Smith expeditiously conscripted the machination of "RESTORATION" as a peg and leitmotif on which to hang his heretical mantle!—a corrupt morass and miasma of false teachings (theological perversions) that is a mockery of the sacred. Mormonism is (as I will address throughout this thesis) an unauthorized franchise that is off the beaten path— the narrow road that leads to life as defined by orthodoxy and embraced by mainstream Christianity.

Joseph Smith did not bring "restoration" to the Gospel by any stretch of the imagination. He, rather, audaciously and single-handedly concocted a maverick religion that is so eccentric and has so distanced itself from orthodoxy that it has no affinity, or resemblance to the long-held sacred and cherished beliefs of mainline Christian institutions. It is under this insidious cloak of "RESTORATION," that the Mormon Church has introduced their menagerie of sordid and peculiar doctrines to fill a void—whether real or imagined—left in the wake of an alleged inept and "apostatized" Church.

The high-sounding and cleverly orchestrated ploy of "restoring the fullness of the Gospel," however, must face the resonating charge that Joseph Smith's so-called "revelations" and "cunning craftiness" cannot bear up under the rigorous unveiling and relentless examination of the historical records, and of the rightly divided word of truth and the refiner's fire of the One who tests all things. We can rest assured, and remain confident that the "Living Word of God" will search out and try "Them which say they are apostles and are not and [will expose them as] liars" (*Revelation 2:2 KJV*); those prevaricators whose machinations were set in motion to deceive. Instead of getting back to the so-called first-century church, the LDS Church would do well to get back to the first-century Savior! For it is "Christ in us the hope of glory" that defines His true Church (see *Colossians 1:27*).

Paul's letter to the Ephesians offers a stern warning: "That we *henceforth* be no more children, tossed to and fro, and carried about with every wind of doctrine, by the sleight of men, *and* cunning craftiness, whereby they lie in wait to deceive" (*Ephesians 4:14 KJV*).

8

Was there a Great Apostasy?

From Adam to the present, the whole history of the world has been one recurring instance of personal and group apostasy after another. . . . Apostasy consists in abandonment and forsaking of . . . true principles, and all those who do not believe and conform to them are in an apostate condition, whether they are the ones who departed from the truth or whether they inherited their false concept from their apostate fathers. . . .

With the loss of the gospel, the nations of the earth went into a moral eclipse called the Dark Ages. Apostasy was universal. . . . And this darkness still prevails except among those who have come to a knowledge of the restored gospel (Bruce R. McConkie, a member of the Quorum of the Twelve Apostles of the LDS Church).[1]

The arguments put forth by those who would prove the survival of the Church are enough in themselves to cast serious doubts upon it. The first thing that strikes one is the failure of the ingenuity of scholarship to discover any serious scriptural support for the thesis. There are remarkably few passages in the Bible that yield encouragement even to the most determined exegesis, and it is not until centuries of discussion have passed that we meet with the now familiar interpretations of the "mustard seed" and "gates-of-hell" imagery, which some now hold to be eschatological teachings having no reference whatever to the success of the Church on Earth (Hugh Nibley, an apologist for the LDS Church).[2]

Craig J. Hazen, Associate Professor of Comparative Religion and Christian Apologetics at Biola University and Director of the Graduate Program in Christian Apologetics, notes:

Mormon apologists have a very long way to go to produce a convincing case for the truth of the Restoration [and the "Great Apostasy"] through Joseph Smith, Jr. I do not envy their task, because so many of the raw materials for a robust defense are missing. Mormon scholars have inherited a less-than-coherent metaphysic, a continued mistrust of the Bible, some difficult theological conundrums, and a devastating drought of "threshold" evidence that does not allow the broader scholarly community to take seriously the claims in and about LDS sacred texts.[3]

Christian apologist, Robert M. Bowman Jr. contends:

The LDS Church's rationale for its own existence is the complete disappearance of the true and living church on the earth—called the Great Apostasy—sometime after the passing of the New Testament apostles. Mormons commonly appeal to both the New Testament and church history to support this claim. However, the LDS explanation of the so-called Great Apostasy is contrary to teaching of the New Testament and makes no sense when one considers the facts about the history of the church era. . . .

The New Testament predicts [but] a partial apostasy of people in the church, not a complete apostasy of the church itself. . . .

The New Testament does speak of *apostasy*, a term that means a falling away. However, nowhere does it speak of a complete or total "Great Apostasy" as the LDS Church teaches. In the New Testament, apostasy is something that *people* do, never something that was to happen to the whole *church*. Throughout the New Testament, then, warnings of apostasy are directed to individuals, never to the whole church. The New Testament knows nothing of a worldwide "Great Apostasy."

Not only does Jesus not envision a seventeen-century hiatus in this process [of the gospel dispensation and its dispersion among the nations via the "Great Commission"], but his promise explicitly states that he will be with his disciples "always" until the task of evangelizing the nations is complete and the end of the age comes.[4]

Luke Wayne, a writer-researcher for CARM (Christian Apologetics and Research Ministry), who holds a Masters of Arts in Theological Studies from Midwestern Baptist College and a Masters in Divinity from Midwestern Baptist Theological Seminary, wrote an article entitled "Was there a 'great apostasy,' of the church after the time of the New Testament?" (11/19/2018), in which he states:

[A]t the very heart of Mormon teaching is the idea of the "great apostasy" . . . Thus, the entire Mormon system hinges on this idea that there was a total apostasy of the early church after the death of the apostles. If this event did not occur [and it is Wayne's contention that it did not], nothing else that Mormonism teaches even makes sense. The problem for Mormonism, however, is that this "great apostasy" is utterly unbiblical and contrary to the very promises and teachings of Jesus Himself. It certainly did not happen. It's not that the Bible doesn't teach it. The Bible explicitly teaches *against* such a notion. [Italics in original.]

In the Gospel of Matthew, we read of Jesus' "Great Commission" delivered to His disciples:

> Go ye therefore, and teach all nations, baptizing them in the name of the Father, and of the Son, and of the Holy Ghost: Teaching them to observe all things whatsoever I have commanded you: **and, lo, I am with you alway,** *even* **unto the end of the world**. Amen.[5]

Mormon theology would have us believe that the promise of God to His Church, wherein Christ said "and lo, I am [the Name of the Eternal God is] with you alway, *even* unto the end of the world, Amen" (*Matthew 28:20 KJV*), went amuck and ran into a wall of resistance, thus spawning the Great Apostasy—collapsing His ecclesia beyond repair—and sidelining the Great Commission for 1700 years! Though Christ's Church, no doubt, faced great opposition, it should be understood that the Lord's unconditional promises as stated above were never dependent upon favorable circumstances. God is unquestionably sovereign, and as the Chief Architect and Builder of His indomitable kingdom, the gates of hell would never (I repeat NEVER!) be allowed to prevail. Christ's Church triumphant will have (and has always had) the assurance of ascendancy over all its enemies. The Church shall "possess the gates of those who hate them" (*Genesis 24:60 NKJV*). "What shall we then say to these things? If God *be* for us who can *be* against us?" (*Romans 8:31 KJV*).

The Lord spoke through the prophet Isaiah pronouncing:

> "No weapon formed against you shall prosper [prevail], And every tongue *which* rises against you in judgment You shall condemn. This *is* the heritage of the servants of the LORD, And their righteousness *is* from Me," Says the LORD (*Isaiah 54:17 NKJV*).

Jesus will never leave, nor has He ever abandoned, His church. Jesus' promise to His Church (His beloved bride) is, "I will never leave thee, nor forsake thee" (see *Hebrews 13:5*) "even unto the end of the world." The Apostle Paul wrote that we are "Persecuted, but not forsaken; cast down, but not destroyed" (*2 Corinthians 4:9 KJV*). Was the apostolic labor in vain and the apostles sowing in tears (and their ultimate martyrdom) for naught? Were there no songs of joy to be reaped? The Psalmist sings with jubilation, "He that goeth forth and weepeth, bearing precious seed, *shall doubtless come again* with rejoicing bringing his sheaves with him" (*Psalm 126:5-6 KJV*; italics added). Was the divine law of sowing and reaping—scripted by heaven's design—violated? "May it never be! Rather, let God be found true, though every man be found a liar" (*Romans 3:4 NASB*).

Tertullian (155-240 AD) propounded, "The blood of the martyrs is the seed of the church."[6] Jesus said, "Verily, verily, I say unto you, Except a grain of wheat fall into the ground and die, it abideth alone: but *if it die, it bringeth forth fruit*" (*John 12:24 KJV*; italics added). It is evident that the word of God (often referred to as *the seed*; see *Luke 8:11*) will not return void "but it shall accomplish that which I please, and it shall prosper *in the thing* whereto I sent it" (*Isaiah 55:11 KJV*). The Lord promised, "They shall not labour in vain, nor bring forth for trouble; for they *are* the seed of the blessed of the LORD, and their offspring with them" (*Isaiah 65:23 KJV*). Mormonism's theory of a general apostasy that took place shortly after the Apostles died would be a violation of the axiom— God's eternal law—of sowing and reaping! Brigham Young iterated, "It is natural for me to believe that, if I plough the ground and sow wheat, in the proper season I shall reap a crop of wheat; this is the natural result."[7]

Just as LDS Prophet John Taylor suggested that the "idea of the Church being disorganized and broken up because of the Prophet [Joseph Smith] and patriarch [Hyrum Smith] being slain is preposterous,"[8] so too, it would seem, the apostasy of the Church after the martyrdom of the Apostles in the first century would likewise be even more "preposterous!" So too, the Church had the "seeds of immortality in its midst."[9] The death of the Apostles was by no means a portal through which the "Gates of Hell" was allowed to come against the Church signaling its defeat, nor could it be measured as the crucible of Christianity's demise as is portrayed by Mormonism's "Doctrine of Apostasy and Restoration." The Church was not conceived by man, nor was it born of man, but was "born of God" (*1 John 5:4*) and is the "offspring of God" (*Acts 17:29*). To this end the Church is assured and attested to by the One to whom was given "all authority in heaven and earth" (*Matthew 28:18*), and under whose authority we stand. Jesus said, "I will build my church; and the gates of hell will not prevail against it" (*Matthew 16:18 KJV*). John MacArthur writes:

> [W]e follow a Commander who has been given all authority—absolute lordship—in heaven and on earth (Matthew 28:18). As Paul said, Christ is "far above all principality and power and might and dominion, and every name that is named, not only in this age but also in that which is to come. And [God] put all *things* under His feet, and gave Him to be head over all *things* to the church" (Ephesians 1:21-22).[10]

"*As* the mountains *are* round about Jerusalem, so the LORD *is* round about his people from henceforth even for ever." (*Psalm 125:2 KJV*). "For the LORD will go before you, And the God of Israel *will be* your rear guard" (*Isaiah 52:12 NKJV*). God has put a hedge around us on every side (*Job 1:10*). The hosts of heaven garrison themselves about us as warring servants of the redeemed. One can see that the place where the Church has taken refuge is one of privilege where we are invited into His very presence to abide with Him and He with us. We have been sealed to God with the "Holy Spirit of promise" (*Ephesians 1:13 KJV*). The "Holy Spirit of promise" wherein Christ dwells in us and is our "hope of glory" (*Colossians 1:27 KJV*), our "earnest expectation" (*Romans 8:19 KJV*), and "the earnest of our inheritance until the purchased possession" (*Ephesians 1:14 KJV*). We are God's "signet ring" (see *Haggai 2:23*), chosen and designated to represent His authority, championing the Kingdom of God. We are to God the sweet fragrance of Christ (*2 Corinthians 2:15*), His living epistle "known and read of all men" (*2 Corinthians 3:2 KJV*).

"For the gifts and the calling of God *are* irrevocable" (*Romans 11:29 NKJV*). What God has done, cannot be undone. To this end, the Scripture is clear, "Yes, before the day was I am he; and there is none that can deliver out of my hand: I will work, and who shall let it" (*Isaiah 43:13 KJV*). The *New International Version* renders this verse, "Yes, and from ancient days I am he. No one can deliver out of my hand. When I act, who can reverse it?" Again, in *Isaiah 14:27* we read, "For the LORD of hosts hath purposed, and who shall disannul *it*? And his hand *is* stretched out, and who shall turn it back?" (*KJV*). God's work is unstoppable! Christ, who lives in us (His Church), is unconquerable! Christ's Great Commission (to propagate and take the Gospel to the world) is guaranteed success! Jesus said, "As *my* Father hath sent me, even so send I you" (*John 20:21 KJV*). As Jesus, with "His face set like flint" (see *Isaiah 50:7* and *Luke 9:51*) completed His mission, even so, the Church, without faltering, will also complete the Great Commission to preach the Gospel to all the world.

According to Mormonism's theory of apostasy, the promise of Christ to be with His Church to the end of the age was disannulled, leaving His bride forsaken—left to the designs of wicked men— spawning a corrupt priestcraft that left Christianity languishing for 1700 years (failing God's purposes), only to be rescued and resuscitated by Joseph Smith's so-called "Restoration." The problem with Joseph Smith's theory is that Jesus is not only the author of our faith, He is also the finisher and the author of all the machinations that lie between the conception and the conclusion of His broad visage and beatific vision. The Church continues to move forward "from faith to faith" (*Romans 1:17 KJV*); "from strength to strength" (*Psalm 84:7 KJV*); God giving His measure of "grace for grace" (*John 1:16 KJV*). Ours is an "everlasting gospel" (See *Revelation 14:6*) that will endure throughout the ages. The Apostle Paul wrote, "Unto him *be* glory in the church by Christ Jesus throughout all ages, world without end. Amen" (*Ephesians 3:21 KJV*). *Barnes' Notes on the Whole Bible* on this verse states that, "The church [the habitation of God] was to be the instrument by which the glory of God would be shown . . ." throughout all ages.

His plans cannot be thwarted—plans that were settled in the mind of God before time began—God's power and will deciding beforehand what should happen (*Acts 4:28*), working out everything to the satisfaction of His will and desire (*Ephesians 1:11*). God declares from the beginning the finality of all things. "The counsel of the LORD standeth for ever, the thoughts of his heart to all generations" (*Psalm 33:11 KJV*). God will definitively accomplish all that He purposes (*Isaiah 46:10*), its execution never faltering. "What I have said, that will I bring about; what I have planned, that will I do" (*Isaiah 46:11 NIV*). The book of *Job* expounds, "I know that you can do all things, no purpose of yours can be thwarted" (*Job 42:2 NIV*). "But the plans of the LORD stand firm forever, the purposes of his heart through all generations" (*Psalms 33:11 NIV*).

The Apostle Paul wrote, "But thanks be to God, who in Christ **always leads us in triumphal procession** . . ." (*2 Corinthians 2:14 ESV*, emphasis added). Jesus said, "And when he putteth forth his own sheep [i.e., commissions them], **he [Jesus] goeth before them**, and the sheep follow him: for they know his voice" (*John 10:4 KJV*). "Their king will pass before them, With the LORD at their head" (*Micah 2:13 NKJV*). As the head of the Church, the Lord utters His voice before His army (*Joel 2:11 ESV*), while the kingdom of God advances by force. The Lord is awesome in His procession, breaking forth both "conquering and to conquer" (*Revelation 6:2 KJV*). The Bride of Christ (the Church), like a fierce and mighty army in battle array, moves forward in formation marching in line, not veering from the desired course, the Lord's columns steadily advancing straight ahead, obedient to His command (*Joel 2:2-11*). There is no jostling or breaking rank as God's army "appears like the dawn, fair as the moon, bright as the sun, majestic as the stars in procession" (*Song of Solomon 6:10 NIV*), "*And* terrible as *an army* with banners" (*Song of Solomon 6:10 KJV*). God's advance battalion of warriors, endued with God's power, charge through all opposing forces with the boldness of a lion. "Before them fire devours, behind them a flame blazes" (*Joel 2:3 NIV*). "Like a mighty army drawn up for battle. . . . They charge like warriors [and] scale walls like soldiers. . . . Before them the earth shakes, [and] the heavens tremble" (*Joel 2:3, 5, 7, & 10 NIV*). "I will help thee, saith the LORD, and thy redeemer, the Holy One of Israel. Behold, I will make thee a new sharp threshing instrument having teeth: thou shalt thresh the mountains, and beat them small, and shalt make the hills as chaff" (*Isaiah 41:14-15 KJV*).

Charles Spurgeon taught:

The Church of Christ is continually represented under the figure of an army; yet its Captain is the Prince of Peace; its object is the establishment of peace, and its soldiers are men of a peaceful disposition. The spirit of war is at the extremely opposite point to the spirit of the gospel.

Yet nevertheless, the church on earth has, and until the second advent must be, the church militant, the church armed, the church warring, the church conquering. And how is this?

It is in the very order of things so it must be. Truth could not be truth in this world if it were not a warring thing, and we should at once suspect that it were not true if error were friends with it. The spotless purity of truth must always be at war with the blackness of heresy and lies.[11]

As the Apostle Paul approached the end of his life's ministry while imprisoned in Rome, and as his departure (his martyrdom) drew near, he said, "I have fought a good fight, I have finished *my* course, I have kept the faith . . ." (*2 Timothy 4:7 KJV*). Paul affirmed that our battle is against the citadel of the kingdom of darkness (the "Gates of Hell"): "For we wrestle not against flesh and blood, but against principalities, against powers, against the rulers of the darkness of this world, against spiritual wickedness in high *places*" (*Ephesians 6:12 KJV*). The Apostle Paul admonished, "You therefore must endure hardship as a good soldier of Jesus Christ" (*2 Timothy 2:3 NKJV*).

As Christians, we are called to a field of battle with formidable foes who are enemies of Christ and His Kingdom, but it is to our satisfaction, however, that we have Divine assurance and the pledge of certain victory with Jesus as our "Leader and Commander" (see *Isaiah 55:4*), "Captain of the host of the LORD" (*Joshua 5:14 KJV*), and "Captain of [our] salvation" (*Hebrews 2:10 KJV*). Though we are in the thick of battle, our fight is from the position of inevitable victory! "This says the LORD to you: 'Do not be afraid nor dismayed because of this great multitude, for the battle is not yours, but God's' " (*2 Chronicles 20:15 NKJV*). "But thanks *be* to God, which giveth us the victory through our Lord Jesus Christ" (*1 Corinthians 15:57 KJV*). "For whatsoever is born of God overcometh the world: and this is the victory that overcometh the world, *even* our faith" (*1 John 5:4 KJV*). Jesus said, "In the world ye shall have tribulation: but be of good cheer; I have overcome the world" (*John 16:33 KJV*). "Ye are of God, little children, and have overcome them: because greater is he that is in you, than he that is in the world" (*1 John 4:4 KJV*). "Nay, in all these things we are more than conquerors through him that loved us" (*Romans 8:37 KJV*).

Jesus did not leave his apostles to be martyred for naught. He, rather, endowed His apostles and empowered His Church with δύναμιν (Greek *dunamin*; power), to be His disciples when they received the promised "Baptism of Fire" from the Father and the earnest of their expectation!—the Holy Spirit, Counselor, and Comforter. Jesus said, "For thine is the kingdom, and the power [Greek dynamis; δύναμις]."

In an article scripted by Justin Taylor posted in *The Gospel Coalition* on August 18, 2017, we read:

> *Mormons claim that "total" apostasy overcame the church following apostolic times, and that the Mormon Church (founded in 1830) is the "restored church."*
>
> If the Mormon Church were truly a "restored church," however, one would expect to find first-century historical evidence for Mormon doctrines like the plurality of gods and God the Father having once been a man. Such evidence is completely lacking.
>
> Besides the Bible disallows a *total* apostasy of the church (e.g., Matt. 16:18; 28:20; Eph. 3:21; 4:11-16), warning instead of *partial* apostasy (1 Tim. 4:1) [Justin Taylor is senior vice president and publisher for books at Crossway and blogs at *Between Two Worlds* and *Evangelical History*] (italics in original).

1 Timothy 4:1 KJV states:

Now the Spirit speaketh expressly, that in the latter times *some shall depart from the faith*, giving heed to seducing spirits, and doctrines of devils; Speaking lies in hypocrisy; having their conscience seared with a hot iron (emphasis added).

NOTE: The passage in *1 Timothy 4:1* states: "*[S]ome* shall depart from the faith", not "*all*."

Jesus made absolutely no prediction concerning a so-called "Great Apostasy," but, rather, made the compelling and uncompromising pronouncement that, "I will build my church; and the gates of hell shall not prevail against it" (*Matthew 16:18 KJV*). As the Church's chief "Architect and builder" (*Hebrews 11:10 KJV*), God has given zero allowance or tolerance for its being disassembled. Jesus continues to be consumed with a great and unrelenting zeal and devotion for God's house—"For the zeal of thy house hath eaten me up" (see *Psalm 69:9*, and *John 2:17 KJV*). We read in *Barnes' Notes on the Bible*: "[T]he meaning of the passage ["the gates of hell shall not prevail against it"] is, that all the plots, stratagem, and machinations of the enemies of the church would not be able to overcome it . . ." In *Matthew Poole's Commentary*, we learn: "[T]he power of the devil and his instruments shall never prevail against it utterly to extinguish it . . . This is a plain promise for the continuance of the gospel church to the end of the world."

When our Redeemer pronounced the enduring words "Upon this rock I will build my church, and the gates of hell shall not prevail against it," His words were no less omnipotent in their conveyance than was His command when He called the cosmos into existence or when he made His "covenant of the day, and . . . covenant of the night . . . that there should not be day and night in their season" (*Jeremiah 33:20 KJV*). In *Psalm 127:1 KJV*, we read, "[E]xcept the LORD build the house they labor in vain that built it." And in *Hebrews 12:28 KJV*, the author speaks of "a kingdom which cannot be moved [shaken]", and in *Hebrews 11:10 KJV*, the author envisions "A city whose builder and maker *is* God."

The Apostle Paul said that "Jesus Christ himself [was] the chief corner *stone*" of "the household of God," the Church (see *Ephesians 2:19-20 KJV*). The Church is built on an immovable rock—the surest of foundations. "For other foundation can no man lay than that is laid, which is Jesus Christ" (*1 Corinthians 3:11 KJV*). Jesus said that if a house (i.e., the Church) is built upon the rock (the sure foundation of Christ's teachings) that the house will stand when the rains descend, and the floods come, and the winds of adversity "beat upon that house . . . for it was founded upon a rock" (*Matthew 7:24-25 KJV*).

In the book of *Daniel*, the Lord made the proclamation, "[H]is dominion *is* an everlasting dominion which shall not pass away, and his kingdom *that* which shall not be destroyed" (*Daniel 7:14 KJV*). His kingdom is like a "stone that was cut out without hands . . . [and] became a great mountain, and filled the whole earth" (*Daniel 2:35 KJV*). That the Kingdom of God is like a stone that is cut out of a mountain "without hands," does not escape my attention. Clearly, the oversight, enterprise and magnification of God's Kingdom is His labor, and not of men. The "Stone" rolled on until it "became a great mountain, and filled the whole earth" (*Daniel 2:35 KJV*), thus establishing God's enduring and everlasting Kingdom "which shall never be destroyed" (*Daniel 2:44 KJV*). In the *Book of Mormon*, we read, "For the eternal purposes of the Lord shall roll on until his promises shall be fulfilled" (*Mormon 8:22*).

In *MacLaren's Expositions* on *Isaiah 49:16*—"Behold I have graven you on the palms of my hands; your walls are continually before me" (*KJV*)—MacLaren writes: "He will not slack, nor stay His hand on which Zion [His Church] is graven until it has 'perfected that which concerneth us [*Psalm 138:8 KJV*],' and fulfilled to each of us that 'which He has spoken to us of [*Hebrews 1:2 KJV*].' "

Jesus emphatically stated: "And I give unto them eternal life, and they shall never perish, neither shall any *man* pluck them out of my hand. My Father, which gave *them* me, is greater than all, and no *man* is able to pluck *them* out of my Father's hand" (*John 10:28-29 KJV*). It is impossible that the Church would ever be plucked out of God's hand, and severed from His Divine protection, thereby succumbing to a so-called "Great Apostasy."

"I am zealous for Zion and with great zeal; With great fervor I am zealous for her" (*Zechariah 8:2 NKJV*). " 'For I,' says the LORD, 'will be a wall of fire all around her, and I will be the glory in her midst' " (*Zechariah 2:5 NKJV*). Again, the Psalmist exhorts: "As the mountains *are* round about Jerusalem [and as its walls are ever before Him], so the LORD *is* round about his people from henceforth even for ever" (*Psalm 125:2 KJV*). To wit, following a "sublime and triumphant conclusion," the Apostle Paul asks with impassioned conviction: "What shall we then say to these things? If God *be* for us, who *can be* against us?" (*Romans 8:31 KJV*). God who has entrusted us with a "Divine Commission" will by all means enable us to obey the call! For God takes pleasure in the posterity of His servants (see *Psalm 35:27*).

One of the defining characteristics of the church is that of its sustained growth in spite of opposition. The Scripture never describes the ecclesia as succumbing to a dreadful "Great Apostasy," nor is the church depicted as waxing and waning. Jesus said:

> [T]he kingdom of heaven is like to a grain of mustard seed, which a man took and sowed in his field: which indeed is the least of all seeds: but when it is grown, it is the greatest among herbs and becometh a tree, so that the birds of the air come and lodge in the branches thereof (*Matthew 13:31-32 KJV*).

The story of the Mustard Seed, found in all three synoptic Gospels (*Matthew 13:31-32; Mark 4:30-32; Luke 13:18-19*), is a parable symbolic of the Kingdom of God. The mustard seed (the so-called "least of all seeds"; one to two millimeters in diameter) metaphorically and allegorically represents the Church in its obscure, supple and incipient appearance as a "little flock" divested with enormous inherent potential hidden within its minutia and embryonic nuclei. Joseph Smith interprets (wrongly, I might add) that the fowls of the air that lodge in its branches are "angels come down" to help "gather their children."[12]

The correct rendering of this passage is, the "birds of the air come to lodge in the branches thereof" are representative of demonic entities and/or false teachers invading the church. In *Matthew's* Gospel, Jesus identifies the birds of the air as "the wicked one" (*Matthew 13:4, & 19*). In *Mark*, Jesus connects the fowls with

"Satan" (*Mark 4:4, & 15*), and in *Luke*, Jesus again links them to "the devil" (*Luke 8:5, & 12*). In *Genesis 15:11*, when fowls swoop down on the carcasses of Abraham's sacrifices, he is obliged to drive them away (see also *Deuteronomy 28:26*). In the book of *Revelation*, the Babylonian kingdom becomes "the habitation of devils, and the hold of every foul spirit, and a cage of every unclean and hateful bird." (*Revelation 18:2 KJV*).

These "Fowls"—fallen angels led by "the prince of the power of the air" (*Ephesians 2:2 KJV*), are "deceitful spirits" determined to both influence and infiltrate the Church sowing "doctrines of demons" (see *1 Timothy 4:1*). Just as God permitted Satan to tempt Job (see *Job 1:12 & 2:6*) and to sift Peter as wheat (*Luke 22:31*), so He has allowed antichrists to lodge within the branches of His beloved Church (see *1 Corinthians 11:18-19*).

Richard Lyman Bushman writes that Joseph Smith, announced in a meeting of "forty-four elders, four priests, and fifteen teachers [who] met in a log schoolhouse near Isaac Morley's farm":

> Christ's kingdom, like a grain of mustard seed, [according to Levi Hancock (1802-1883), an early convert to the Mormon Church and a general authority for nearly fifty years] "[W]as now before him and some should see it put forth its branches and the angels of heaven would . . . come like birds to its branches."[13]

Incredibly, in Joseph Smith's announcement there seems to be a convocation where demonic spirits were invited ["come like birds to its branches"] to mingle with those in attendance! Indeed, Bushman tells us:

> Then the meeting [soon] unraveled. Joseph ordained Harvey Whitlock to the high [Melchizedek] priesthood, the most important business of the meeting, and Whitlock reacted badly. "He turned as black as Lyman was white," Hancock reported. "His fingers were set like claws. He went around the room and showed his hands and tried to speak, his eyes were in the shape of oval O's." Astonished at the turn of events, Hyrum exclaimed, "Joseph, that is not of

God." . . . Then Hancock said, Leman Copley, who weighed over two hundred pounds, somersaulted in the air and fell back on his back over a bench. . . . The evil spirit, according to Hancock, was in and out of people all day and the greater part of the night. . . .

This was not the spiritual endowment the elders had expected, and the outburst may have contributed to "trouble and unbelief" among the disciples. John Whitmer noted about this time "some apostatized, and became enemies to the cause of God, and persecuted the saints." . . .

During the turbulent meeting, Joseph ordained five men to the high [Melchizedek] priesthood, and Lyman Wight ordained eighteen others including Joseph. The ordinations to the high priesthood marked a milestone in Mormon ecclesiology. Until that time, the word "priesthood," although it appeared in the *Book of Mormon*, had not been used in Mormon sermonizing or modern revelations. Later accounts applied the term retroactively, but the June 1831 conference marked its first appearance in contemporary records.[14]

The parable of the "Mustard Seed" is similar to the "Parable of the Wheat and Tares," where the "enemy" sowed weeds among the good seed:

The servants said unto him, Wilt thou then that we go and gather them up? But he said, Nay; lest while ye gather up the tares, ye root up also the wheat with them. Let both grow together until the harvest: and in the time of harvest I will say to the reapers, Gather ye together first the tares, and bind them in bundles to burn them: but gather the wheat into my barn (*Matthew 13:28-30 KJV*).

Again, Jesus said:

So is the kingdom of God, as if a man should cast seed into the ground. And should sleep, and rise night and day, and the seed should spring and grow up, he knoweth not how. For the earth bringeth forth the fruit of herself; first the blade, then the ear, after that the full corn in the ear. But when the fruit is brought forth, immediately he putteth in the sickle, because the harvest is come (*Mark 4:26-29 KJV*).

The triumphant achievement of the apostolic commission to go into the world and "preach the gospel to every creature," and the inevitable growth and maturation of the church against which "the gates of hell would not prevail" is expounded upon, in part, by LDS Apostle Lorenzo Snow:

[The Apostles] were bound to succeed; no power could cross their path and prevent them reaping the most sanguine success because they went forth in the strength of the Almighty to perform His will, and it was His business to sustain and support them and furnish them all the means of success. . . . [The Apostles] had the assurance that in their labors no power on earth could successfully oppose them.[15]

John MacArthur contends that, "The kingdom of God advances by the power of God alone."[16] The glorious emergence of the "Bride of Christ" (the Church) is the sovereign work of God and will never be despoiled or confounded by the futile efforts of heaven's foes. Nor will the Church ever devolve through faith's disavowment. The untold legions of betrothed born-again believers, whose Bridegroom stands forever fast at the ready as His lover's Guardian, Commander and Protector, are destined for the climactic union, and wedding supper of the Lamb in God's eternal kingdom. God has unfurled His banner over His church. Jesus is the ever-vigilant Watchman—"I have set watchmen upon thy walls, O Jerusalem, *which* shall never hold their peace day nor night: ye that make mention of the LORD, keep not silence, And give him no rest, till he establish, and till he make Jerusalem a praise in the earth" (*Isaiah 62:6-7 KJV*). The Protector of His people never slumbers:

Behold, he that keepeth Israel shall neither slumber nor sleep. The LORD is thy keeper: the LORD is thy shade upon thy right hand. The sun shall not smite thee by day, nor the moon by night. The LORD shall preserve thee from all evil: he shall preserve thy soul. The LORD shall preserve thy going out and thy coming in from this time forth, and even for evermore (*Psalm 121:4-8 KJV*).

The Church's sustained growth and maturation "unto a perfect man, unto the measure of the stature of the fulness of Christ" (*Ephesians 4:13 KJV*)—"the full corn in the ear"—is not dependent upon man (though he is invited to actively participate)—"For the earth bringeth forth fruit of herself" (*Mark 4:28 KJV*). "Except the LORD build the house [the Church], they labour in vain that built it: except the LORD keep the city, the watchman waketh *but* in vain" (*Psalm 127:1 KJV*). We are "The branch of [His] planting, The work of [His] hands, That [He] may be glorified" (*Isaiah 60:21 NKJV*). The Lord's Church moves forward, inexorably and supernaturally, by His sovereign will and not by the fingerprints of man. We have been well-advised not to "steady the Ark of God" (to keep our hands off)—the Ark being a representation of the "House of God," His Church (see *2 Samuel 6:6-7*)—for the Lord is well able to transport His Church to her desired haven. The Scriptures inform us that "the builder of the house is greater than the house itself. For every house is built by someone, but God is the builder of everything" (*Hebrews 3:3-4 ESV*). The Church is the Body of Christ—living stones that are being built up into a spiritual house—"whose Builder and Maker *is* God" (see *Hebrews 11:10*).

"Through wisdom a house is built, And by understanding it is established; By knowledge the rooms are filled With all precious and pleasant riches" (*Proverbs 24:3-4 NKJV*). *Gill's Exposition of the Entire Bible* on this verse states:

> The house of God, the church of the living God, is built by Wisdom, that is by Christ; on a good foundation, a rock, upon himself, against which the gates of hell can never prevail . . . the church of God is established by Christ, who is understanding as well as wisdom.

God orchestrates the growth of the Church from its inception and the planting of the seed to its fruition and harvest. We are but laborers in His harvest. There are those who plant, and those who water, "So then neither is he that planteth any thing, neither he that watereth; but God that giveth the increase" (*1 Corinthians 3:7 KJV*). "The body, [which is] nourished and knit together by joints and ligaments, grows with the increase which is from God" (*Colossians 2:19 NKJV*). It is the Lord who adds "to the church [additional members of His body] daily such as should be saved" (*Acts 2:47 KJV*). "Christ is [the] head of the church," His body—"For we are members of His body, of His flesh and of His bones"—"and He is the Savior of the body." With meticulous care, Christ both "nourishes and cherishes . . . the church," His bride-to-be, and would never leave her forsaken (see *Ephesians 5:23, 29, & 30 NKJV*).

Jesus said, "The kingdom of heaven is like leaven, which a woman took and hid in three pecks of flour until it was all leavened" (*Matthew 13:33 KJV*). Once the leavening agent has initiated its fermentation effect on the dough, yeast's ongoing chemical reaction progresses unabated until the whole is transformed, realizing its desired outcome. Speaking metaphorically, the Apostle Paul asks, "Know ye not that a little leaven leaveneth the whole lump?" (*1 Corinthians 5:6 KJV*). The active catalytic reagent that Christ infused within His ecclesia cannot, nor will it ever, be purged out! His influence (As the Chief Executor who holds the scepter of authority) is designed to persistently, and effectively proliferate until the redemption of "the whole." The very Presence of Christ— through the agency of the Holy Spirit—is irremovable ("I will never leave thee nor forsake thee"—*Hebrews 13:5 KJV*), and irreversible ("When I act, who can reverse it?"—*Isaiah 43:13 NIV*). Just as "a little leaven leaveneth the whole lump," so Paul likewise stated, "For if the firstfruit *is* holy, the lump *is* also *holy*; and if the root *is* holy so *are* the branches" (*Romans 11:16 NKJV*). The part that is dedicated to the Lord consecrates and is extended to the whole.

Charles Spurgeon called Christ's crucifixion "the very hinge of the history of the world. . . . the great turning point of all the world's history . . ."[17] Jesus said, "And I, if I be lifted up from the earth [even as he was lifted up on the cross], will draw all men unto me." (*John 12:32 KJV*). To lift Jesus up on the cross was the Father's way of exalting His Son, and giving Him a Name that was above all other names "That at the name of Jesus every knee should bow, of things in heaven, and things in earth, and things under the earth" *(Philippians 2:9 KJV)*. The "Great Commission" is dependent upon Jesus being "lifted up." Jesus said, "as Moses lifted up the serpent in the wilderness, even so must the Son of man be lifted up" *(John 3:14 KJV)*. Once Jesus was crucified, assuring victory over death and the ruler of this world (Satan), men from every nation began to be drawn to the Savior as if by an irresistible magnetizing force. The *Pulpit Commentary* emphasizes:

> The attraction of the cross of Christ [would] prove to be the mightiest and most sovereign motive ever brought to bear on the human will, and when wielded by the Holy Spirit as a revelation of the matchless love of God, will involve the most sweeping judicial sentence that can be pronounced upon the world and its prince.

Concerning the men who were drawn to Christ, J. R. Thomson notes:

> The apostles were Christ's lieutenants and captains in his holy war. The early history of the Church tells how capable and devoted men were raised up, to teach and preach, to organize and administer, to write and expound, to suffer, to witness, and to die. . . . brave, self denying men have . . . been drawn to the Savior by the magnetism of the Spirit's influence, and qualified to render service to the Church . . . the history of which is . . . one of incessant progress.[18]

The inexorable force of humanity's attraction to Christ (as he was "lifted up") could never be diminished (not even by a fraction) by the so-called "Great Apostasy," let alone blotted out for 1700 years! This claim on the part of the LDS Church is not only presumptuous, but preposterous, and represents an arrogance that defies God's plan of redemption that can never be retracted, rescinded, diminished, or hidden. The Apostle Paul said, "But if our gospel be hid, it is hid to them that are lost" *(2 Corinthians 4:3 KJV)*.

Surely the Gospel was neither hidden nor lost, as the LDS Church has suggested, for generations.

To say that the Church of Jesus Christ of Latter-day Saints—which they claim to be "the only true Church on the face of the whole earth" (*Doctrine and Covenants* 1:30) is the sole repository of God's plan of salvation, decrying the simplicity of the Gospel—"Jesus Christ and him crucified" (*1 Corinthians 2:2 KJV*)—is to arrogate to themselves a moniker that undermines the authority vested in Jesus Christ alone. Jesus said, "that [He] openeth, and no man shutteth; and shutteth and no man openeth" (*Revelation 3:7 KJV*). When Jesus opened the door to salvation by allowing Himself to be "lifted up" on the cross, an effectual door that gave all of mankind an entrance into heaven through the propitiation of their sins was opened that "no man shutteth." Jesus announced that He was the "Door," and it is only through Him that we have access to the Father. The fact that Jesus was "lifted up" on the cross (and the events that followed—His death, burial, and resurrection) cannot be undone, and remains the manifesto of the Gospel's central message.

The crucible of the cross out of which our Lord forged the salvation of humanity, both gave birth to, and defines the Church Triumphant. The shedding of Christ's innocent blood will not congeal without vindication, neither will His indescribable suffering—as He drank the cup of God's wrath that was consummated in the agony of His death—ever lose its unmitigated potency nor experience an attenuation in its efficacy. The personal investment that Jesus made—His precious blood nonetheless, along with the Holy Spirit of promise—gave our Lord an irrevocable purchase. Together, these dynamic influences have become the primary impetus for the indomitable will, and unstoppable growth of the "Body of Christ." The "Temple of the Lord" (the Church)—a "spiritual house" of "living stones"—*1 Peter 2:5 KJV*—will continue its unprecedented advancement by an inexorable Divine Fiat until His Bride, holy and radiant, reaches "the measure of the stature of the fulness of Christ" (*Ephesians 4:13 KJV*), and is crowned as the diadem of the Lord's betrothed; ". . . a crown of glory in the hand of the LORD" (*Isaiah 62:3 KJV*). "But the path of the righteous is like the light of dawn That shines brighter and brighter until the full day" (*Proverbs 4:18 NASB*).

Isaiah prophesied:

> Of the increase of *His* government and peace *there will be* no end, Upon the throne of David, and over His kingdom, To order it, and establish it with judgment and justice From that time forward, even forever. The zeal of the LORD of hosts will perform this (*Isaiah 9:7 NKJV*).

The Apostle Paul said, "I know [in] whom I have believed, and am persuaded that he is able to keep that which I have committed unto him [namely the church] against that day [the day of Christ's Second Coming]" (*2 Timothy 1:12 KJV*). Jesus is both the Savior and Guardian of the Church—His beloved bride—, and as the Chief Shepherd of His flock, He offers His divine protection against all assailants (both from within and without) to the exclusion of any possibility of a "Great Apostasy." The Apostle Paul said, "Being confident of this very thing, that he which hath begun a good work in you will perform *it* until the day of Jesus Christ" (*Philippians 1:6 KJV*). God is both "the author and finisher of *our* faith" (*Hebrews 12:2 KJV*). In Paul's letter to the Corinthians he writes:

> [God] will also confirm [preserve, sustain and establish] you to the end *that ye may be* blameless [free from reproach] in the day of our Lord Jesus Christ. God *is* faithful, by whom ye were called unto the fellowship of his Son Jesus Christ our Lord (*1 Corinthians 1:8-9 KJV*).

In his prayer to the Ephesians (and the Church-at-large), the Apostle Paul exults:

> Now unto him that is able to do exceeding abundantly above all that we ask or think, according to the power that worketh in us, Unto him *be* glory in the church by Christ Jesus throughout all ages, world without end. Amen (*Ephesians 3:20-21 KJV*). "[T]hroughout all generations . . ." (*NIV, ESV.*)

In this passage, Paul is declaring that the Church will continue to manifest God's glory, to His praise and honor, **to all generations** (Latin, *pasas tas geneas*), excluding any possibility of a so-called

"Great Apostasy" that endured for seventeen-hundred years! There is no way in hell (literally) that the Church—the beloved bride of Christ—could ever succumb to the "powers-that-be" that would cause her to stray from Christ's tenacious embrace! Jesus, who is the Chief Cornerstone of His Church, would never allow this to happen on His watch. "What therefore God hath joined together [Christ and His bride, the Church that he purchased with His precious blood] let not man put asunder [i.e., "the Great Apostasy"]" (*Mark 10:9 KJV*).

In *Ephesians 5:29-32 KJV*, we read:

> [The Lord] nourisheth and cherisheth . . . the church: For we are members of his body, of his flesh, and of his bones. For this cause shall a man leave his father and mother, and shall be joined unto his wife, and they two shall be one flesh. This is a great mystery: but I speak concerning Christ and the church.

In the Gospel of *Luke*, we read where Jesus asked:

> For which of you, intending to build a tower, sitteth not down first, and counteth the cost, whether he have sufficient to finish *it*? Lest haply, after he hath laid the foundation, and is not able to finish *it*, all that behold it begin to mock him, Saying, This man began to build, and was not able to finish (*Luke 14:28-30 KJV*).

Jesus laid the foundation of His Church (counting the cost) knowing full well the ultimate sacrifice He would have to make to see His bride continue to mature (without faltering) to her final consummation. To suggest that that Jesus was not able to sustain the work that He began is to mock (along with what Mormonism has perceived as) a fallible plan that fell into an apostatized tailspin for 1700 years!

Proverbs 14:28 KJV advises, "In the multitude of people *is* the king's honour: But the want of people *is* the destruction of the prince." The so-called "Great Apostasy" of the church, as it is so dramatically emphasized and portrayed by the LDS Church's foundational "Doctrine of Apostasy and Restoration," does nothing but confound God's purposes. The Mormon Church's false accusation of universal apostasy for no less than 1700 years foments a betrayal and disservice to Christ, bringing both dishonor and destruction to the Prince's Kingdom! Jesus, the One who laid down His life, and is the irrepressible and pivotal foundation of the "Kingdom of God," has become both the Kingdom's "Chief Corner Stone" (elect and precious) as well as its "Capstone." As the "Capstone," Jesus "is the head of the body, the church . . ." (*Colossians 1:18 NKJV*). Our Savior, Jesus Christ, counted the cost—"for the joy that was set before him [he] endured the cross" (*Hebrews 12:2 KJV*)—and paid the ultimate price—"for ye are bought with a price" (*1 Corinthians 6:20 KJV*); "with the precious blood of Christ" (*1 Peter 1:19 KJV*)—to bring the tower and citadel of His dominion to completion (see *Luke 14:28*) to the praise of His glory and honor! Christ's Church will continue to follow an indomitable linear eschaton until its final summation. His plan is unimpeachable and bulwarked against common failure, and any propensity for a general apostasy is left without formulae.

It is impossible that the Church would ever be shipwrecked (fall into a general apostasy) with Jesus at the helm. For we are "fully persuaded that what he had promised [that he would never leave us nor forsake us], he was able also to perform" (*Romans 4:21 KJV*). In *Romans 8:24*, we read that Jesus is at the right hand of the Father (and is ever at the "helm" of His Church) making intercession for His beloved Bride. Charles Spurgeon exulted:

> The thought that there beats a heart in heaven that is always loving us; that there moves a tongue that always pleads for us; that there is an arm in heaven that always fights for us; and that there is a foot in heaven that will be swift to run for our defense—Oh! This is precious consolation.[19]

John MacArthur writes:

> [W]e are preserved in Christ and guaranteed to triumph in the end.
>
> That is the starting point of Jude's epistle. That is also precisely where Jude *ends* his epistle, commending his readers to "Him who is able to keep

you from stumbling, and to present you faultless before the presence of His glory with exceeding joy" (v. 24). . . . "kept by the power of God through faith for salvation ready to be revealed in the last time" (1 Peter 1:5).[20]

The Scripture assures us that "if this counsel or this work [the Gospel as revealed to and proclaimed by the Apostles] be . . . of God, ye cannot overthrow it . . ." (*Acts 5:38-39 KJV*). Jesus said, "No man can enter into a strong man's house, and spoil his goods, except he will first bind the strong man; and then he will spoil his house" (*Mark 3:27 KJV*). Jesus is the "strong man" of the house of God—"Ye also, as lively stones, are built up a spiritual house [His house], an holy priesthood, to offer up spiritual sacrifices, acceptable to God by Jesus Christ" (*1 Peter 2:5 KJV*)—and will never be bound, or His house (the Church) despoiled. "The word of God is not bound" (*2 Timothy 2:9 KJV*), nor can it ever be quarantined or silenced, let alone plundered and contravened as has been suggested by Mormonism's "Doctrine of Universal Apostasy and Restoration." Jesus said, "When a strong man, fully armed, guards his own palace [as Jesus faithfully watches over His house, His beloved Church], his goods are in peace" (*Luke 11:21 NKJV*).

The Apostle Paul asks:

> Who shall separate us from the love of Christ? *shall* tribulation, or distress, or persecution, or famine, or nakedness, or peril, or sword? As it is written, For thy sake we are killed all the day long; we are accounted as sheep for the slaughter. Nay, in all these things we are more than conquerors through him that loved us. For I am persuaded, that neither death, nor life, nor angels, nor principalities, nor powers, nor things present, nor things to come, Nor height, nor depth, nor any other creature, shall be able to separate us from the love of God, which is in Christ Jesus our Lord (*Romans 8:35-39 KJV*).

Our Lord and Master proclaimed:

> You [the Church, my Beloved] are the light of the world. A city [*De civitate Dei*—the Elect of God (see

> Augustine's *The City of God*)] that is set on a hill
> *cannot be hidden.* Nor do they light a lamp and put it
> under a basket [i.e., the so-called "Great Apostasy"],
> but on a lampstand, and it gives light to all who are
> in the house (*Matthew 5:14-15 NKJV*; italics added).

Jesus would never allow His Church, whom He has designated as the "light of the world," to be put "under a basket"—out of sight—leaving those who are in darkness, destitute and without hope for 1700 years. Christ in us the "hope of glory" (*Colossians 1:27*), a glory held in earthen vessels proclaiming the only hope for this fallen world, will never be sequestered away while we, His Church, are in the world.

Elder Alexander B. Morrison (1930-2018), a Canadian scientist, academic, and public servant and was a general authority of the Church of Jesus Christ of Latter-day Saints (LDS Church) from 1987 until his death, conceded:

> The view that changes in the early church resulted in
> the descent of stygian darkness over the entire earth,
> such that humankind had no contact with God or the
> Spirit for nearly two millennia, simply doesn't stand
> up to the scrutiny of modern scholarship.[21]

The One who committed unto us, His Church, the "word of reconciliation" (see *2 Corinthians 5:19*) so that the world could then be reconciled to God, would not leave the world without a witness, floundering in sin and darkness for untold centuries! Jesus emphatically stated: "But ye shall receive power, after that the Holy Ghost is come upon you: and ye shall be witnesses unto me both in Jerusalem, and in all Judaea, and in Samaria, and unto the uttermost part of the earth" (*Acts 1:8 KJV*). It is through the sustaining power of the Holy Spirit that the Church continues to fulfill the "Great Commission" in a hostile world to make disciples of all nations to the very end of the age (see *Matthew 28:19-20*). For the duration of history until He returns, Jesus (with all confidence) passed the baton/torch and the perpetuation of His ministry and the declaration of the Gospel to His Church, guaranteeing its success by the Holy Spirit's empowerment.

> (For the weapons of our warfare [spiritual powers given by the Eternal Spirit] *are* not carnal, but mighty through God to the pulling down of strongholds;) Casting down imaginations, and every high thing that exalteth itself against the knowledge of God, and bringeth into captivity every thought to the obedience of Christ . . . (*2 Corinthians 10:4-5 KJV*).

Jesus said, "Behold, I give you ["as of something already bestowed [to His Church] in its completeness"] the authority to trample on serpents and scorpions ["symbols of spiritual powers of evil"],[22] and over all the power of the enemy, and nothing shall by any means hurt you" (*Luke 10:19 NKJV*). The Apostle Paul declared, "And the God of peace will crush Satan under your feet . . ." (*Romans 16:20 KJV*; compare with *Genesis 3:15*).

> Wherefore we receiving a kingdom [the Gospel Dispensation] which cannot be moved ["shaken" as in the dispensation of the Old Covenant when Mount Sinai trembled violently (see *Exodus 19:18*)], let us have grace, whereby we may serve God acceptably with reverence and godly fear (*Hebrews 12:28 KJV*).

Barnes' Notes on the Bible commentary on this verse (*Hebrews 12:28*) reads:

> Wherefore we [have received] a kingdom which cannot be moved . . . that is permanent and unchanging . . . never to pass away . . . nor is there any power that can destroy it . . . its great principles and laws will endure to the end of time . . . destined never to fall. . . .
>
> The "argument" which [the Apostle Paul] presents is, that this kingdom is permanent. There is no danger of its being overthrown. It is to continue on earth to the end of time; it is to be established forever. . . . there is the assurance:
>
> (1) That all our interests there are safe;
>
> (2) That all our exertions will be crowned with ultimate success,

(3) That the efforts which we make to do good
will have a permanent influence on mankind,
and will bless future ages; and

(4) That the reward is certain.

The Old Covenant with its ceremonial laws was ordained to be abrogated while the New Covenant with its enduring promises (for all the promises of God are "Yes" and "Amen" in Christ Jesus—see *2 Corinthians 1:20*) has ushered in an unshakable and unalterable kingdom. Brigham Young pronounced: "The Lord sits in the heavens and laughs at man's puny efforts to thwart His purpose and to render His word into promises of non-effect."[23] Jesus assured his disciples stating: "Fear not little flock; for it is your Father's good pleasure to give you the kingdom" (*Luke 12:32 KJV*). "He that spared not his own Son, but delivered him up for us all, how shall he not with him also freely give us all things" (*Romans 8:32 KJV*). Our title to the "Kingdom" (a "Kingdom" that cannot be rescinded) is assured through the unflappable and indomitable will of the Father.

In an article published by Mormon Research Ministry (MRM) under the heading, "The Great Apostasy," Aaron Shafovaloff comments:

> BYU history professor Eric Dursteler observes that early LDS treatises on the apostasy were "clearly" influenced by "the highly polemical, popular, confessional, historical literature of the nineteenth century and the anticlerical literature of the eighteenth-century enlightenment." He further notes that, although the characterization of the Middle Ages as a dark and decadent era and the Renaissance as an era of spiritual awakening has been repudiated by virtually all modern historians of the past century, "Latter-day Saint treatments of the apostasy . . . have retained much of their binary vision of the Middle Ages and Renaissance."

The Latecomers of the Church of Jesus Christ of Latter-day Saints (circa 1830 to present) have obfuscated and dismissed the light of historic Christianity, thereby justifying their so-called "restored gospel," plunging humanity into darkness for seventeen centuries, while supplanting themselves as the only true defenders of the faith; when, in fact, their "false apostles and deceitful workers" (see *2 Corinthians 11:13*) have suppressed the truth in lies and unorthodox doctrines while masquerading another fabricated gospel (that is not the true light) as the true. Jesus ominously cautioned: "If therefore the light that is in thee be darkness [i.e., the so-called "Restored" Gospel with all of its heterodox machinations], how great *is* that darkness!" (*Matthew 6:23 KJV*). We must exercise the utmost caution lest we put our trust "in the sweetest frame" whose foundation is built upon the shifting sands of deception and our house comes to utter ruin!

My house is built on nothing less

Than Jesus Christ, my righteousness;

I dare not trust the sweetest frame,

But wholly lean on Jesus' name.

On Christ, the solid Rock, I stand;

All other ground is sinking sand,

All other ground is sinking sand.

(Opening stanza to Edward Mote's (1797-1874)
"My Hope Is Built.")

The Apostle Paul confidently declared that the unfaltering Church would continue to grow with expediency "Till all come in the unity of the faith, and the knowledge of the Son of God, unto a perfect man unto the measure of the stature of Christ" (*Ephesians 4:13 KJV*). The mystical body of Christ, the Church, will continue on its inevitable concourse—driven by God's Divine Fiat—until it reaches "the measure of the stature of the fulness of Christ." The supreme objective of the maturation of the Bride of Christ will yet be realized as the Church, with its many members, will someday be joined to her Bridegroom in perfect unity to be wholly like Him.

This passage in *Ephesians 4:13* speaks of the unabated continuance of the Church in its expected path to fruition and fullness and final termination leading up to the Parousia—for "When Christ *who is* our life appears [the Parousia] then you [the

Church] will appear with Him in glory" (*Colossians 3:4 NKJV*). The mystical body of Christ is inexorably predestined for a climactic conclusion—for we were "predestine[ed] *to be* conformed to the image of his Son" (*Romans 8:29 KJV*). "But we all [the Church/the bride of Christ], with open [unveiled] face beholding as in a glass [mirroring] the glory of the Lord, are changed [metamorphosed] into the same image [the image of Christ—the *imago Dei*] from glory to glory, *even* as by the Spirit of the Lord" (*2 Corinthians 3:18 KJV*). When we gaze steadfastly into Christ's face, our countenance is transformed into His image by the power of the Holy Spirit. "For **HE WILL FINISH THE WORK** and cut it short in righteousness" (*Romans 9:28 KJV*; capitalization and emphasis added). At that time, He will present His bride to Himself "a glorious church not having spot or wrinkle or any such thing, but that it should be holy and without blemish" (*Ephesians 5:27 NKJV*). The Apostle Paul exulted: "For what *is* our hope, or joy, or crown of rejoicing? *Is it* not even you [His beloved Church] . . . blameless in holiness before our God and Father at the coming of our Lord Jesus Christ . . ." (*1 Thessalonians 2:19 & 3:13 NKJV*). The Apostle John wrote:

> Beloved, now we are the children of God; and it has not yet been revealed what we shall be, but we know that when He is revealed [at the *Parousia*], we shall be like Him, for we shall see Him as He is. And everyone who has this hope in Him [longing for His appearing] purifies himself, just as He is pure (*1 John 3:2-3 NKJV*).

The Apostle Paul declared:

> Creation itself also will be delivered from the bondage of corruption into the glorious liberty of the children of God. For we know that the whole of creation groans and labors with birth pangs together until now. And not only *they*, but we also who have the firstfruits of the Spirit, even we ourselves groan within ourselves, eagerly waiting for the adoption, the redemption of our body (*Romans 8:21-23 NKJV*).

The word "groan," as in the groaning of creation and the "Body of Christ," comes from the Greek root word *sustenazo*, and is related to the sounds of a woman groaning in labor when she is about to deliver a baby. Mormonism teaches that the groaning and labor pains of both creation and the "Body of Christ" (the Church) were silenced, suspended and forestalled in a neonatal Fetal Growth Restriction (FGR) for 1700 years (the uterus of conception becoming the Church's antepartum grave). We know that contractions become stronger and occur with more regularity and frequency (manifesting at shorter intervals) over time. The intensity of birth pangs escalates and the frequency of uterine contractions increase in correlation with the greater dilation of the cervix as the birthing (the Parousia and the revelation of Christ's Church) becomes immanent. The reality is, the gestation and developmental process never becomes stalled, but continues unabated until conception and the fetus (in this case the Church) has reached maturation. The delivery after a given period, is inevitable, within a narrow margin and latitude within its parturiency. " 'Shall I bring to the time of birth, and not cause delivery?' says the LORD. 'Shall I who cause delivery shut up *the womb*?' says your God" (*Isaiah 66:9 NKJV*).

In *Psalm 139:13-16 KJV*, we read:

> For thou hast possessed my reins: thou hast covered me in my mother's womb. I will praise thee; for I am fearfully and wonderfully made: marvellous are thy works; and that my soul knoweth right well. My substance was not hid from thee, when I was made in secret, and curiously wrought in the lowest parts of the earth. Thine eyes did see my substance, yet being unperfect; and in thy book all my members were written, which in continuance were fashioned, when as yet there was none of them.

We are "made in secret" (Hebrew, סָתַר *sather*, or *cether*, meaning covering, hiding place, or to be concealed). "In the secret place of His tent He will hide me" (*Psalm 27:5 NAS*). And we are "curiously wrought" (Hebrew, רקם *raqam*, meaning embroidered with different colored threads as a tapestry or variegated garment). From conception (zygote) to birth, we are the workmanship of the

Creator. Albert Barnes writes: "No one but God can perform the work of creation. . . . We are not self-created" (see *Barnes' Notes on the Bible, Psalm 100:3*). We are His by creation, adoption, and regeneration. "As thou knowest not what is the way of the spirit, nor how the bones do grow in the womb of her that is with child: even so thou knowest not the works of God who maketh all" (*Ecclesiastes 11:5 KJV*). "And I will lay sinews upon you, and [I] will bring up flesh upon you, and [I will] cover you with skin, and [I will] put breath in you, and ye shall live; and ye shall know that I *am* the LORD" (*Ezekiel 37:6 KJV*). The Psalmist declared, "Know ye that the LORD he is God: It is he that hath made us, and not we ourselves; We are his people, and the sheep of his pasture (*Psalm 100:3 KJV*).

Gill's Exposition of the Entire Bible on *Psalm 100:3* states: "In him we live, move and have our being; and as new creatures, we are his workmanship, created in him, and by him, regenerated by his spirit and grace and formed for himself, his service and glory; and made great and honourable by him." If left to our own devices as the corporate "Body of Christ," submitting to formulas prescribed in the context of ordinances and commandments to work out our salvation (a house built on sand and the precepts of men), we would inevitably fail. Our identity as Christians is not crafted by our own hands. "We [the Church] are His workmanship, created in Christ Jesus" (*Ephesians 2:10 NKJV*). The Church, "a building made without hands" (*2 Corinthians 5:1*), a house built upon a rock, is sculpted and modeled by the Lord, the "Divine Artificer," where we, as "living stones, are being built up a spiritual house" (*1 Peter 2:5 KJV*) "fitly joined together" (*Ephesians 4:16 KJV*). "Except the LORD build the house, they labour in vain that build it" (*Psalm 127:1 KJV*).

"And the temple, when it was being built, was built with stone [costly "Melekeh" limestone] finished in the quarry, so that no hammer, chisel *or* any iron tool was heard in the temple while it was being built" (*1 Kings 6:7 NKJV*). The sound of the iron tools represents the attribution of man's efforts and personal achievement for which God was requiring that man abstain. If God is the "Divine Atrificer"—Jesus emphatically stated, "I will build my church"— He has left no provision for its demise or disenfranchisement as has been suggested by Mormonism's theory of a general apostasy. "For we are His workmanship, created in Christ Jesus for good works, which God prepared beforehand ["finished in the quarry"] that we should walk in them" (*Ephesians 2:10 NKJV*). The Temple of the Lord is designed by His specifications. " 'All *this*,' said David 'the LORD made me understand in writing, by *His* hand [Divine guidance] upon me, all the works of these plans' " (*1 Chronicles 28:19 NKJV*). The literal rendering of this verse in Hebrew is: "The whole in a writing from the hand of Jehovah, to me he made clear; all the works of the model [the Temple]." David himself sketched out the whole design of the temple under Divine inspiration. *Matthew Henry's Concise Commentary* states that the temple was "framed according to the Divine counsels, and the plan laid in the Divine wisdom, ordained before the world, for God's glory and our good." "Know ye not that ye are the temple of God, and that the Spirit of God dwelleth in you?" (*1 Corinthians 3:16 KJV*).

The Latter-day Saint apologists might ask: *"But what are we to make of Amos 8:11-12?" Amos 8:11-12 KJV* reads:

> Behold, the days come, saith the Lord GOD, that I will send a famine in the land, not a famine of bread, nor a thirst for water, but of hearing the words of the LORD: And they shall wander from sea to sea, and from the north even to the east, they shall run to and fro to seek the word of the LORD, and shall not find *it.*

In an article posted in the *Institute for Religious Research* (*IRR*) on August 16, 2011 under the heading "Amos 8:11-12 and the LDS doctrines of Apostasy and Restoration" by Robert M. Bowman Jr., we read:

> Mormons have long held that Amos 8:11-12 specifically predicted the "Great Apostasy" that the LDS Church teaches stretched from about 100 AD (when the New Testament apostles passed from the scene) to 1830 (when Joseph Smith founded the LDS Church).

Bowman argues: "This understanding of Amos 8:11-12 as a prediction of the so-called Great Apostasy . . . has nothing to do with the Christian church during or after the New Testament era." Bowman further states: "There is no connection between what Amos said and anything that happened following the passing of the New Testament apostles more than 800 years after the time of Amos." Bowman quotes Duane Crowther, a well-known and respected LDS author, theologian, lecturer, teacher and choral director, who graduated from Brigham Young University with high honors as stating that the passage in *Amos 8:11-12* does not "in its original context, refer to the Great Apostasy" but rather specifically refers to the *Old Testament* period of the nation of "Israel in Amos's immediate future, not to people worldwide living centuries later." Crowther "questions the wisdom of . . . LDS expositors of the scriptures who have, in his view, forced the interpretation of this passage with gross disregard for context and the true intention of the prophet Amos." Bowman asks: "Can a religious group that so badly mishandles biblical texts like this one really be a divinely authorized and uniquely inspired restoration of the truth?"

In his book *This Is My Doctrine: The Development of Mormon Theology*, Charles Harrell, a retired associate professor in Brigham Young University's School of Technology, writes that "The earliest recorded LDS teachings give little indication of a universal apostasy, especially in the way it is currently understood." Harrell further states: "Biblical scholars explain that in its historical context, the 'famine' alluded to in this passage [*Amos 8:11-12*] refers to the imminent consequence of the wickedness and apostasy of ancient Israel as seen in the Assyrian conquest (see Amos 7:11). . . . This prophecy was uttered around 760 BC and Israel was invaded by the Assyrians about 40 years later." Harrell concludes that "the scholarly consensus is that in their original context [*Amos*'s] prophecies were expressly directed at ancient Israel's apostate condition"[24] and were neither related to nor indicative of the so-called "Great Apostasy" following the death of the *New Testament* apostles.

Again, the Latter-day Saint apologist will ask, *"Does not the passage in 2 Thessalonians 2:3 speak of an apostasy or the 'Great*

Falling Away?' " In the balance of this chapter, I will address this question.

In 1970, I visited Faith Center on the corner of 13th and Polk Street in Eugene, Oregon and listened to a message Roy Hicks Jr. (1943-1994) was preaching on the "Rapture of the Church." (Roy later became General Supervisor of the International Foursquare Churches.) The Rapture is a term in Christian eschatology which refers to the "being caught up" as discussed in *1 Thessalonians 4:17*, when the "dead in Christ" and "we who are alive and remain" will be "caught up in the clouds" to meet "the Lord in the air."

Roy was teaching on the phrase *caught up* stating that the Greek word, *harpazó*, rendered caught up, literally means to take by force, or to snatch away suddenly as if by robbery, using an open display of force. The term *Rapture* finds its equivalent transliteration in the *Latin Vulgate Bible*—that was in use for a thousand years—whose translation of the Greek *harpazó* appears as *rapiemur*.

> Harpazó means to take suddenly and vehemently, often with violence and speed or quickly and without warning. The idea is to take by force with a sudden swoop and usually indicates a force which cannot be resisted. In eschatological terms (future events, prophetically related) as in the present verse, **harpazó** refers to what is often known as the "rapture" (Latin = **rapture** = seizing or Latin = **rapio** = seize, snatch) (*Precept Austin Commentary* on *1 Thessalonians 4:17-18*).

Roy Hicks Jr. was teaching about the immanency of Christ's return, and the prophetic fulfillment of events defining the *Last Days*, and the generation of those "who are alive and remain" at the time the "Lord Himself will descend from heaven" (see *1 Thessalonians 4:16 & 17 NASB*).

In *1 Corinthians 15:51-52*, Paul wrote, "Behold, I tell you a mystery; we will not all sleep [die], but we will all be changed, in a moment, in the twinkling of an eye, at the last trumpet; for the trumpet will sound, and the dead will be raised imperishable, and we will be changed" (*NASB*). The Greek word for "in a moment" is the word, *atomos*, which implies an indivisible moment of time. It is the only place in the *Greek New Testament* where the word is used. To the Greek, *atomos* was the smallest conceivable indivisible entity. "In the twinkling of an eye" (which is a reflected particle of light), from an observer's perspective, is equated to an infinitesimally small fraction of time equivalent to about a billionth of a second when calculating the speed of light at 983,571,056 feet per second (300,000 km/sec). The Greek word for *twinkling* is *rhipe*, and is also the only mention of this expression in the *Greek New Testament*. Jesus said, "For as the lightening cometh out of the east and shineth even unto the west; so shall the coming of the Son of man be" (*Matthew 24:27 KJV*). Jesus will come "in a moment" as the Church's transformation is completed and our earthly bodies are changed in an instant into the likeness of His glorious image. Jesus said, "And, behold, I come quickly; and my reward is with me" (*Revelation 22:12 KJV*). The word "quickly" as used in this context is the Greek word *tachu* which can have the connotation of something that happens suddenly.

"If a man dies, will he live *again*? All the days of my struggle I will wait **Until my change comes**. You will call, and I will answer You; You will long for the work of Your hands" (*Job 14:14-15 NASB*; emphasis added).

I was born by the river in a little tent

Oh, and just like the river I been runnin' ever since

It's been a long, a long time comin'

But I know a change a gon' come

Oh, yes it will

It's been too hard livin' but I'm afraid to die

'Cause I don't know what's up there beyond the sky

It's been a long, a long time comin'

But I know a change gon' come

Oh, yes it will

(Charles Moore [Sam Cooke] 1963—"A Change is Gonna Come").

The disciples, Peter, James and John, saw the *Kingdom of God* coming with power when they stood in Jesus' transfigured presence. Jesus was literally *metamorphosed* (used in the context of a physical transformation) on the *Mount of Transfiguration*. There was a marked change in his appearance. His face "became different" (*Luke 9:29 NASB*) and "shone like the sun" (*Matthew 17:2 NASB*). Even his garments changed and became "white as light" (*Matthew 17:2 NASB*), "became white *and* gleaming" (*Luke 9:29 NASB*), "radiant and exceedingly white, as no launderer on earth can whiten them" (*Mark 9:3 NASB*). Jesus' garments were but earthly vestments aging by way of detrition, no different than our own bodies, yet suddenly transformed. ". . . [T]he earth [as well as our earthly bodies] shall wax old like a **garment . . .**" to be cast off (*Isaiah 51:6 KJV*; emphasis added).

From the oldest book in the *Bible*, written around 1500 BC, we read Job's provocative declaration:

> As for me, I know that my Redeemer lives, And at the last He will take His stand on the earth. Even after my skin [his fleshly garment] is destroyed, Yet from my flesh I shall see God; whom I myself shall behold, And whom my eyes will see and not another (*Job 19:25-27 NASB*).

It is obvious that the "outer man is decaying" (*2 Corinthians 4:16 NASB*)—some more gracefully than others, nevertheless decaying. The apostle Paul, writing by the Spirit's inspiration, said:

> For we know that if the earthly tent which is our house [our body] is torn down, we have a building from God [a new body], a house not made with hands, eternal in the heavens. For indeed in this *house* we groan, longing to be clothed with our dwelling from heaven, inasmuch as we, having put it on, will not be found naked (*2 Corinthians 5:1-3 NASB*).

> For our citizenship is in heaven, from which we also eagerly wait for a Savior, the Lord Jesus Christ; who will transform the body of our humble state [In the Greek text it is, "the body of our humility."] into

conformity with the body of His glory, by the exertion of the power that He has even to subject all things to Himself (*Philippians 3:20-21 NASB*).

Roy Hicks Jr. spoke specifically of *2 Thessalonians 2:1-4*:

Now we beseech you, brethren, by the coming of our Lord Jesus Christ, and *by* our gathering together unto him, That ye be not soon shaken in mind, or be troubled, neither by spirit, nor by word, nor by letter as from us, as that the day of Christ is at hand. Let no man deceive you by any means: for *that day shall not come*, except there come a falling away first, and that man of sin be revealed, the son of perdition; who opposeth and exalteth himself above all that is called God, or that is worshipped; so that he as God sitteth in the temple of God, shewing himself that he is God (*KJV*).

Roy's understanding of the passage *falling away*, was that the Greek word *apostasia* could be rendered *departure*, speaking of the rapture (the "catching away") of the church. The basic meaning of *apostasia* is to *depart from*, or *go away* from *Apo, to move away*, and *stasis*, meaning *to stand*. Roy said that the hindering factor keeping the "man of sin" (the Antichrist) from being revealed, is the presence of the Church on the earth, and the restraint of the Holy Spirit. But once the Church *departs* from the earth, all hell will break loose. Jesus said that the Church was to be the "salt of the earth" (see *Matthew 5:13*), understanding that salt was an inhibiter of corruption. When the Church departs from the earth, there will be uninhibited degradation!

The Greek article "*the*" in front of *apostasia* makes the *going away*, or *departure*, more than a general thesis, but belies, rather, a specific event Paul's audience was familiar with in the context of his first letter (see *1 Thessalonians 4:13-18*). Paul writes, "Do you not remember that while I was still with you, I was telling you these things?" (*2 Thessalonians 2:5*). The Greek article "*the*" (ἡ, *hee*) is used in the anaphoric sense in that it is referencing a concept of an idea that was previously mentioned (i.e., the rapture in *1 Thessalonians 4:13-18*).

Many have rendered the debatable passage as a falling away from the faith, which is the secondary meaning of *apostasia*. I am sure the equivocation will continue, but one thing is certain, the *event horizon* of the coming of our Savior is drawing near and is fast approaching its perigee.

> I'm going home on the morning train,
>
> I'm going home on the morning train
>
> Evening train might be too late
>
> Oh, I'm going home on the morning train. . .
>
> ("Morning Train"—a traditional African-American Spiritual).

In Paul's second letter to the church in Thessalonica, he wrote:

> Now brethren, concerning the coming of our Lord Jesus Christ and our gathering together to Him . . . Let no one deceive you by any means; for *that day will not come* unless the falling away [Greek ἀποστασία, apostasia] comes first, and the man of sin is revealed, the son of perdition . . . (*2 Thessalonians 2:1 & 3 NKJV*).

The first seven English translations of the *Bible* all rendered the noun ἀποστασία (apostasia) as either "departure" or "departing." The *Wycliffe Bible* (1384); *Tyndale Bible* (1526); *Coverdale Bible* (1535); *Cranmer Bible* (1539); *Breeches Bible* (1576); *Beza Bible* (1583); *Geneva Bible* (1608), all supported the notion that the word (later translated in the *King James Version* as "falling away") truly means "departure." Jerome, who was commissioned by Pope Damasus I in 382 to translate the *Bible* into Latin, known as the *Vulgate*, translated ἀποστασία (apostasia) with the word "*discessio*," meaning "departure." The translators of the *King James Version* were the first to introduce the new rendering of ἀποστασία (apostasia) as "falling away."

Thomas D. Ice, who received his BA from Howard Payne University in 1975, his masters in theology from Dallas Theological Seminary in 1981, and a Ph.D. from Tyndale Theological Seminary in 1995, notes that, "The word is a Greek compound of *apo* 'from' and *istemi* 'stand.' Thus, it has the core meaning of 'away from' or 'departure.' " Ice further states:

> Understanding departure as the rapture would satisfy the nuance of this text. . . . Whatever Paul is referring to in his reference to "the departure," was something that both the Thessalonian believers and he had discussed in-depth previously. When we examine Paul's first letter to the Thessalonians, he never mentions the doctrine of apostasy, however, virtually every chapter in that epistle speaks of the rapture (cf. 1:9–10; 2:19; probably 3:13; 4:13–17; 5:1–11).[25]

The LDS Church does not teach that there will be a rapture and has instructed its members *to* prepare to endure the days of tribulation when the earth will experience the wrath of Almighty God. The LDS Church's "modern revelation" (see *Doctrine and Covenants* 29:8) makes it clear that the saints will remain on the earth through the tribulation period until Christ's coming. And so they shall.

Dr. Wayne House (ThD, Concordia Seminary, St. Louis; JD, Regent University School of Law) is Distinguished Research Professor of Biblical and Theological Studies at Faith Evangelical College and Seminary in Tacoma, Washington, and Professor of Law, Trinity Law School in Santa Ana, California, observes:

> Remember, the Thessalonians had been led astray by the false teaching (2:2–3) that the Day of the Lord had already come. This was confusing because Paul offered great hope, in the first letter, of a departure to be with Christ and a rescue from god's wrath. Now a letter purporting to be from Paul seems to say that they would first have to go through the Day of the Lord. Paul then clarified his prior teaching by emphasizing that they had no need to worry. They could again be comforted because the departure he had discussed in his first letter, and in his teaching while with them, was still the truth. The departure of Christians to be with Christ, and the subsequent revelation of the lawless one, Paul argues, is proof

that the Day of the Lord had not begun as they had thought. This understanding of apostasia makes much more sense than the view that they are to be comforted (v. 2) because a defection from the faith must precede the Day of the Lord. The entire second chapter (as well as 1 Thessalonians 4:18; 5:11) serves to comfort (see vv. 2, 3, 17), supplied by a reassurance of Christ's coming as taught in his first letter.[26]

Dr. Daniel Davey, Virginia Beach Theological Seminary President and Senior Editor for the forthcoming *New Testament Exposition Commentary* series, averred, "It is with full assurance of proper exegetical study and with complete confidence in the original languages, that the word meaning of *apostasia* [as mentioned in *2 Thessalonians 2:3*] is defined as departure."[27] Davey further notes concerning the definite article "*the*" (indicating specificity) with the noun *apostasia*:

> Since the Greek language does not need an article to make the noun definite, it becomes clear that with the usage of the article, reference is being made to something in particular. In II Thessalonians 2:3 the word *apostasia* is prefaced by the definite article which means that Paul is pointing to a particular type of departure clearly known to the Thessalonian church.[28]

Kenneth S. Wuest (1893-1961), a noted Evangelical Biblical *Greek New Testament* scholar wrote:

> The author is well aware that *apostasia* was used at times both in classical and *koine* Greek in the sense of a defection, a revolt, in a religious sense, a rebellion against God, and of the act we today call apostasy. Liddell and Scott [in their *A Greek-English lexicon*; a standard lexicographical work of the Ancient Greek language] give the above as the first definitions of the word. Moulton and Milligan [the *J. H. Moulton and G. Milligan's Lexicon*] quote a papyrus fragment where the word is used of a rebel.

But these are acquired meanings of the word from the context in which they are found, not the original, basic, literal meaning, and should not be imposed upon the word [*apostasia* in *2 Thessalonians 2:3*] where the context does not qualify the word by these meanings.[29]

Wuest further states:

In 1 Thessalonians 4:13-18, Paul had given these saints teaching on the Rapture, and the Greek article here ["*the*" (Greek ἡ, *hee*) in *2 Thessalonians 2:3*] points to that which was well known to both the reader and the writer, which is another use of the Greek definite article.[30]

Raymond (Ray) Charles Stedman (1917-1992), one of the twentieth-century's foremost evangelical Christian pastors and biblical expositors, wrote in his book, *Waiting for the Second Coming*:

I must point out that there is considerable evidence that the word translated "rebellion" or "apostasy" [in *2 Thessalonians 2:3*] should more properly be translated "the departure." Read that way, the apostle is clearly saying that the Day of the Lord cannot come until the departure (of the church) has first taken place.

E. Schuyler English (1899-1981), a biblical scholar, author and a prominent figure in the evangelical Christian community, defended the view that the passage in *2 Thessalonians 2:3*, that has been interpreted as a "falling away" (Greek, apostasia), is a reference to the rapture. (See his book *Rethinking the Rapture: An Examination of What the Scriptures Teach as to the Time of the Translation of the Church in Relation to the Tribulation*.) English concluded:

[*A*]*postasia* in 2 Thessalonians 2:3 meant "departure" or "withdrawal" rather than the more common translations of "falling away" or "rebellion." English based his case on lexical possibilities and contextual considerations to solve a theological problem.[31]

Chuck Smith (1927-2013), an American pastor who founded the Calvary Chapel movement, admitted that interpreting "this word 'apostasy' [as mentioned in *2 Thessalonians 2:3*] . . . as meaning departure . . . [was] definitely a possibility."[32] In his book, *The Final Curtain*, Chuck Smith writes:

> The term "falling away" is an interesting translation of the Greek word apostasia. The root verb from which apostasia comes means "to depart from." This verb is used fifteen times in the New Testament and only once translated "fall away." In other instances it is translated "to depart from" or "to leave from."
>
> William Tyndale, one of the first people to translate the Bible into English, and many other early translators of the New Testament, rendered apostasia as "a departure." If this is the case, this verse can be read, "For the day shall not come, except there come a departure first, and that man of sin be revealed, the son of perdition." This "falling away" could very easily refer to the departure, or rapture, of the Church.[33]

Brian Brodersen, Chuck Smith's son-in-law, and senior pastor at Calvary Chapel Cost Mesa, California, notes:

> In my opinion there has been a mistake in this verse's [*2 Thessalonians 2:3*] interpretation . . . . I think it could very possibly be that [Paul is] talking about the rapture here. . . . I believe [*2 Thessalonians 2:3*] speaks of the departure of the church.[34]

In an article published by the Institute for Creation Research under the heading, "Falling Away" *2 Thessalonians 2:3*, we read:

> The "falling away" (Greek apostasia) has commonly been transliterated as "the apostasy" (the definite article in the Greek indicates Paul had already told them about it), and then assumed to apply to the final great religious apostasy at the end of the age. The

context, however, as well as the etymology of the word itself, makes this interpretation unlikely. In this precise form it is used nowhere else in the New Testament, so its meaning must be defined by its context here. It is derived from two Greek words, apo (meaning "away from") and stasis (meaning "standing"). It thus could properly be rendered "standing away" instead of "falling away." In Paul's previous letter, he had made no reference whatever to a coming departure from the faith, but he had discussed at length a coming departure from the earth by all believers, when Christ returns to meet them in the air (I Thessalonians 4:13-18). Thus this "standing away from," in context, seems to refer to all the raptured believers standing away from the earth, as they stand before their returning Lord when they meet Him in the heavens. Paul here is simply reminding them that the "sudden destruction" that would come upon unbelievers when "the day of the Lord" begins could not happen until the rapture—"the standing-away" from the earth before Christ (note Romans 14:10)—had taken place. The entire context, before and after, fits this understanding of the text better than the idea of the apostasy from the faith.

Manfred E. Kober, who received his Th.M. and Th.D. degrees from Dallas Theological Seminary in Dallas, Texas, and is a professor in the Theology department at Faith Baptist Bible College, implores: "The Biblical writers speak of the rapture as being a blessed hope (Titus 2:3); a purifying hope (1 John 3:3); a comforting hope (1 Thess. 4:18); and a sure hope (2 Peter 1:19)."[35]

The notion that there should be a "falling away" or "apostasy" of the faith at the end of the "Modern Christian Era" prior to Christ's Second Coming appears to be a non-sequitur when one considers the Church's continuance in "its inevitable concourse—driven by God's Divine Fiat" until His ecclesia reaches "the measure of the stature of the fullness of Christ" (*Ephesians 4:13 KJV*). The Church was never destined to collapse through unbelief and disassemblement, but is, rather, predestined by God's command (i.e., the "Great Commission") to rise to its pinnacle of influence as the "salt of the earth" to a dispirited world bereft of the truth. The Church Triumphant will "run with endurance the race that is set before" her and will not be left destitute ("I will never leave thee nor forsake thee") nor in any way be defeated ("[for] we are more than conquerors through him that loved us") as she reaches the threshold of her journey's end and final destination (see *Hebrews 12:1, & 13:5*, and *Romans 8:37*). Christ's New Testament Church (His Bride-to-be) will not faint nor will she be weary as she crosses the finish line at the end of the age, but will exult in triumph as she eagerly runs—in her full strength—mounting up with wings like an eagle to meet her Bridegroom in the air (see *Isaiah 40:31* and *1 Thessalonians 4:17*).

The Lord's beloved Church will not be reduced to a placid, battle-fatigued, washed-out refugee of a bygone Christian era, but will dramatically continue in her unstoppable ascendancy as the "crown of glory . . . and a royal diadem in the hand of [the LORD]" (*Isaiah 62:3 KJV*). "And the LORD shall make thee the head, and not the tail; and thou shalt be above only, and thou shalt not be beneath . . ." (*Deuteronomy 28:13 KJV*). "I will build [the church] and not pull [it] down, and I will plant [the church] and not pluck [it] up . . . and they shall be my people, and I will be their God" (*Jeremiah 24:6-7 NKJV*). The invincible Church is preordained to "possess the gate[s] of [her] enemies" (see *Genesis 22:17* and *Matthew 16:18*). The Temple (the "Body of Christ") must come to its completion that the Lord "may take pleasure in it and be glorified" (*Haggai 1:8 NKJV*).

Jesus said, "Occupy till I come" (*Luke 19:13 KJV*). The word "occupy" as used in this context means not only to "possess" but also to "improve" for the purpose of increasing the Lord's investment until He returns to make a final accounting. *Gill's Exposition of the Entire Bible* exposits:

> "Till I come" suggests the certainty of Christ's coming, the continuance of the Gospel ministry to that time; and there is no rest nor ease for Christ's ministers, but a continued series of labour and service, until then; when, for their encouragement, they shall receive their reward.

The Church has yet to see its finest hour. "Greater things are still to come." The Scripture tells us "The end of a thing is better than its beginning" (*Ecclesiastes 7:8 NKJV*). I believe God has saved the best for last, and that the Church will continue to be a beacon of light resonating God's truth shining "brighter and brighter until the full day" (*Proverbs 4:18 NASB*).

We Are The Church Invincible

We are the hands of God
Our task to do His will
To lay our hands upon this world
And by His Spirit see it healed
We are the Church invincible
The flesh and blood of Christ
We are the Gospel visible
Our lives the Saviour's light to the world

We are the word of God
And by the things we say
This world will judge the Prince of life
And be drawn in or turn away

We are the feet of God
Who walk the narrow way
And every step we take is watched
By those for whom we fast and pray

Though persecution comes
And governments oppose
Beneath the crushing weight of law
The church of Jesus grows and grows

John Pantry

©1990 Thankyou Music

9

"The Spirit of Man is the Candle of the Lord"

Once in the world's history we were to have a Yankee prophet, and we have had him in Joe Smith. For good or for evil, he has left his track on the great pathway of life; or, to use the words of Horne, "knocked out for himself a window in the wall of the nineteenth century," whence his rude, bold, good humored face will peer out upon the generations to come (John Greenleaf Whittier, an American Quaker, poet and an advocate of the abolition of slavery).[1]

Whether one believes that the faith he spawned is the world's only true religion or a preposterous fable, Joseph emerges from the fog of time as one of the most remarkable figures ever to have breathed American air (Jon Krakauer, author of *Under the Banner of Heaven*).[2]

The word of God reveals, "The spirit of man *is* the candle of the LORD searching all the inward parts of the belly" (*Proverbs 20:27 KJV*) examining the dispositions and motives of the heart. It is my prayer (which as God who considers every religious institution accountable, and holds forth the candle of the spirit of the LDS Church) that the heart of the *Citadel of Mormonism* will be exposed and laid bare for the entire word to see. I pray, also, that God, who knows "what is in man," (see *John 2:25*) will reveal the heart of Joseph Smith, the moniker and founder of Mormonism— "the remarkable individual who had fashioned the mould [*sic*] which was to shape the feelings of so many thousands of his fellow-mortals."[3] For "Wherever the name of Joseph Smith is known the *Book of Mormon* is also known."[4] Ivan J. Barrett emphasizes, "without Joseph Smith and his visions there would be no Mormon religion. They are the core, the foundation, and the substance of the structure."[5] Paul C. Gutjahr emphasizes:

> Absolutely central to any understanding of the religious power and influence of the [*Book of Mormon*] is the prophetic figure who ushered it into the world. The book and the Prophet functioned in a symbiotic relationship of mutual credentialing. The presence of a new sacred text testified to the special status and powers of Joseph, who had translated it, and in turn Joseph testified to the truth of the book through his continuing revelations from God. Neither the Prophet nor the book would, without the other, wield the oracular power each enjoyed.[6]

Joseph Smith strongly criticized orthodoxy, stating, "The scriptures are a mixture of very strange doctrines to the Christian world; who are blindly led by the blind."[7] Again, Joseph Smith derides what he calls, "the muddy stream of tradition,"[8] and Joseph Fielding McConkie categorizes as "the dense theological fog . . . and truths long hidden."[9]

Dr. Robert L. Millet and Joseph Fielding McConkie, blatantly and shamelessly patronize the Church—whom they call "our friends" (as the saying goes: "with friends like those who needs enemies!")—while leveling the following accusations against orthodox Christianity:

> The theologies of the world are a mass of confusion.
> They evidence the apostasy [of the orthodox Church]

and attest to the puniness of the mind of man when unaided by the Spirit of God. They [the Church] lack mercy and are devoid of justice, for they portray a God with power to save but a portion of his creatures, and that too on an inequitable basis. They are founded in uncertainty and some even in ambiguity. They deny revelation and yet in their doctrines freely add to the scriptural canon. Some promise salvation to the wicked and faithless by grace alone; others damn innocent and pure children. But the Latter-day Saint reader ought to be reminded that without a divine dispensation we would be no better informed than our friends from other churches. Were it not for the restoration of the gospel and the advent of living prophets, our understanding would reach no higher than theirs.[10]

Joseph Smith denigrated orthodox Christianity to the point where he went so far as to suggest: "What is it that inspires professors of Christianity generally with a hope of salvation? It is that smooth, sophisticated influence of the devil, by which he deceives the whole world."[11] Bruce R. McConkie brazenly imputes that, "the great creeds of Christendom were formulated so as to conform to [the] whispered promptings [of "evil spirits"]. And the "Sectarian views of the Godhead" are "incomprehensibly garbled" [with reference to the Trinity].[12]

McConkie further remonstrates:

It follows that the devil would rather spread false doctrine about God and the Godhead, and induce false feelings with reference to any one of them, than almost any other thing he could do. The creeds of Christendom illustrate perfectly what Lucifer wants so-called Christian people to believe about Deity in order to be damned.

. . . We [the Church of Jesus Christ of Latter-day Saints—unlike mainstream Christianity] do not worship the Son . . . Our relationship with the Son is one of brother and sister in the premortal life [where Jesus is but an exemplar and elder brother] . . .[13]

McConkie obviates that Jesus is but "the great prototype of all saved beings."[14] McConkie goes on to say that praying "through Christ [as a mediator] to the Father . . . is plain sectarian nonsense" and that we "should not strive for a special and personal relationship with Christ . . ."[15] McConkie further states:

> The proper course for all of us is to stay in the mainstream of the Church [the Latter-day Saints]. This is the Lord's Church, and it is led by the spirit of inspiration, and the practice of the Church [which excludes the worship of Jesus] constitutes the interpretation of scripture.
>
> And you have never heard one of the First Presidency or the Twelve, who hold the keys of the kingdom and who are appointed to see that we are not "tossed to and fro, and carried about with every wind of doctrine" (Ephesians 4:14)—you have never heard one of them advocate this excessive zeal that calls for gaining a so-called special and personal relationship with Christ.
>
> . . . never at any time have they taught or endorsed . . . a personal relationship with the Savior.[16]

It should be duly noted that McConkie's statement was never met with a rebuttal from the First Presidency or the Twelve (silence being a vote of ascension).

In his book, *The Divine Center: Why We Need a Life Centered on God and Christ and How We Attain It*, Stephen R. Covey (1932-2012), an American educator and best-selling author (*The 7 Habits of Highly Effective People*), who received a Doctor of Religious Education from Brigham Young University, Provo, Utah, warns his readers against seeking "any kind of 'special' relationship" with Jesus Christ; suggesting that "The Christ-only approach is inappropriate for Latter-day Saints . . ."[17]

Look magazine February 9, 1971 featured a cover article titled, "Today's Kids Turning to Jesus, Turning From Drugs" announcing, "the Jesus movement is upon us. . . . All Christians agree Christ is the great common denominator of the movement. He brings everyone together." In May of 1971, a *Life* periodical summed up the Jesus People Revolution stating, "They feel Christ as an immediate presence." In a twelve-page cover story in *Time* magazine on June 21, 1971 entitled "The Jesus Revolution," the article emphasizes that the "["Jesus People's"] lives revolve around the necessity for an intense relationship with that Jesus and the belief that such a relationship should condition every human life."

Drew Williams, who holds a B.A. from Brigham Young University and has taught LDS doctrine and essential Gospel principles for more than 16 years, explains that, "Latter-day Saints pray to God—Elohim [to the exclusion of Jehovah (Jesus)]— worshipping him [Elohim] and only him."[18] Mormons are taught that "the Father is prior to and pre-exists the Son," as represented in the heretical doctrine promoted by Eusebius of Caesarea (263 AD-339 AD), a historian of Christianity, exegete, and Christian polemicist,[19] and, therefore, should be worshipped to the exclusion of the Son (who is but a subordinate) as a form of henotheism. Henotheism, from the Greek ἑνός θεός (*henos theos*), meaning "one god" is the worship of what is defined as a "single god" while, at the same time, not explicitly denying the existence or the possibility that other deities exist.

Craig L. Blomberg instructs:

> [H]istoric Christianity has always insisted on balancing Christ's *functional* subordination with his ontological equality. In other words, in the very essence of Christ's being he is eternally equal with God, even if in playing certain roles he voluntarily submits himself to his Father . . .[20]

Blomberg further states:

> Christians have usually insisted that a correct formulation of the doctrines of God and Christ is important because the possibility of eternal life depends on it. If Christ was ever less than fully God (even when he assumed a human nature), then he is by definition not the kind of infinite deity necessary

to atone for our sins and to pay the infinite price required for our purification, so that we can live in his presence forever.[21]

Again, Blomberg expresses his misgivings about the LDS understanding of Jesus as God's Son:

> Evangelicals have two basic reservations about the LDS perspective. First, it appears to them that the Father and the Son in the standard Mormon perspective are too separate. Second, it is not clear that either the Father or the Son, especially the Son defined as perpetually subordinate to God, can qualify as fully, eternally God. We [Evangelicals] get the impression . . . that Mormons see Christ as a created being, even if he is the first and highest of all creation. Thus the door at least remains open for polytheism and hence for worshiping created beings.[22]

In the book of *Revelation*, Jesus said, "Behold, I stand at the door, and knock: if any man hear my voice, and open the door, I will come in to him, and will sup with him, and he with me" (*Revelation 3:20 KJV*). This invitation sounds to me like Jesus desires to have a one-on-one "personal relationship" with us that is on a very intimate level! Again, in *John 14:23*, Jesus said, "If a man love me, he will keep my words: and my Father will love him, and we will come unto him, and make our abode with him" (*KJV*). Bruce R. McConkie counters, however:

> And that there will be no doubt as to the meaning of our Lord's words, it is written *in our revelations*: "John 14:23—The appearing of the Father and the Son, in that verse, is a personal appearance; and the idea that the Father and the Son dwell in a man's heart is an old sectarian notion, and is false" (D&C 130:3).[23]

It is of no surprise that *The Song of Solomon*, which expresses the Divine allegorical and reciprocal intimacy between Jehovah and Israel, and Christ and the Church (His bride), was rejected as uninspired by Joseph Smith. In the *Joseph Smith Translation* of the

Bible, there are no revisions to *The Song of Solomon*. It does, however, contain the comment "The Songs of Solomon are not Inspired writings [*sic*]." (See circled comment on the following page.)

The Hebrew title to *The Song of Solomon* is "*Solomon's Song of Songs*." The "*Song of Songs*" has similar construction found among other biblical phrases such as the "king of kings," "The Lord of Lords," and "Holy of Holies," the connotation being that it is the most superlative of all songs. In *1 Kings 4:32 KJV* we read, "And he [Solomon] spake three thousand proverbs: and his songs were a thousand and five." Solomon's choice of words in the opening stanza "The Song of Songs," is a Hebraic superlative construct that is understood as an idiom expressing the "chiefest, greatest, most superlative" of Solomon's songs; the best of the best.

In the "Introduction to the Song of Solomon," *Old Testament Seminary Teacher Manual* (2014) the Church of Jesus Christ of Latter-day Saints, we read:

> When speaking to a group of seminary and institute teachers, Elder Bruce R. McConkie of the Twelve Apostles commented on each of the books in the Old Testament. When he came to the [*The Song of Solomon*] he said, "**The Song of Solomon is biblical trash**—it is not inspired writing."[24]

Yet, in spite of McConkie's stunning disparagement, we find there is a passage (*Song 6:10*) from the *Song of Solomon* that is quoted no less than three times in the *Doctrine and Covenants*! It is found in the 1836 dedicatory prayer for the temple in Kirtland, Ohio (*Doctrine and Covenants* 109:73), and is mentioned in *Doctrine and Covenants* 5:14 and 105:31. You will also notice that this passage in reference to the *Song of Solomon 6:10* is misquoted in *D&C 5:14*, as well as *D&C 105:31*, but is quoted correctly in *D&C 109:73*.

Who *is* she *that* looketh forth as the morning, fair as the moon, clear as the sun, *And* terrible as *an army* with banners? (*Song of Solomon 6:10 KJV*).

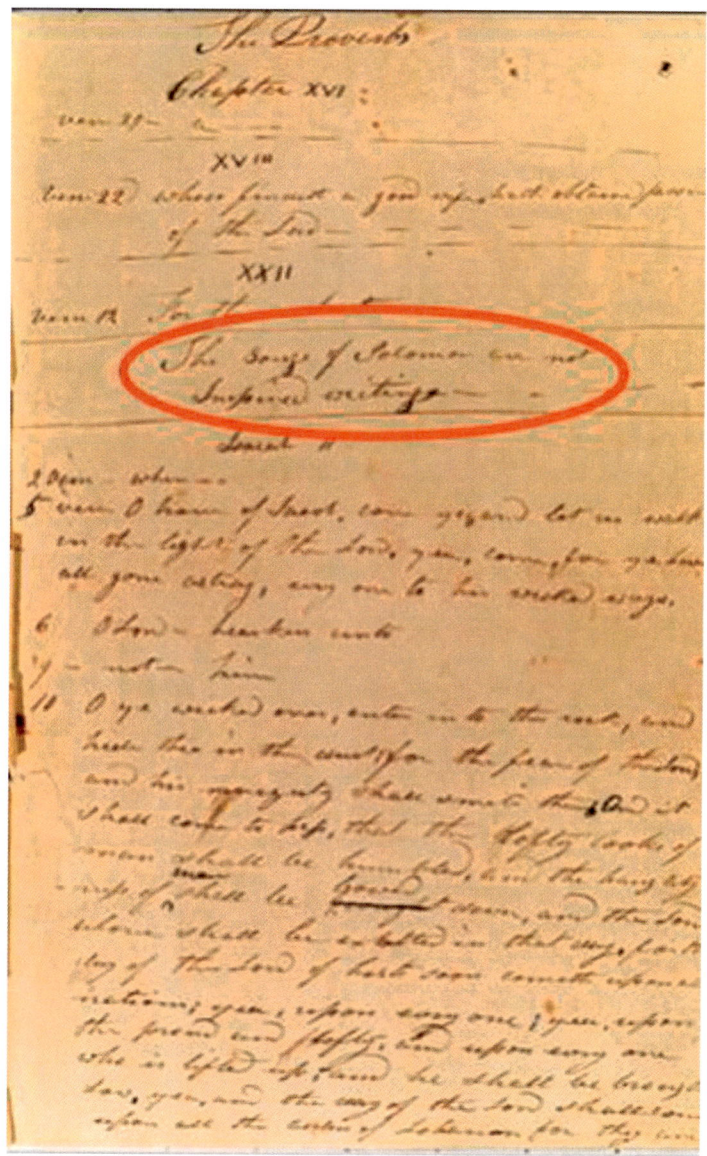

Manuscript page of the *Joseph Smith Translation*. Courtesy of Community of Christ Archives circa 1832.

Solomon and the Shulamite Maiden.

It puzzles me (considering his derogation mentioned above) as to why McConkie would bother to quote this same passage in his book, *The Millennial Messiah* (published in 1983):

> The Church of Jesus Christ of Latter-day Saints, which administers that gospel whereby salvation comes, is now going forth, "clear as the moon and fair as the sun, *And* terrible as *an army* with banners (D&C 5:14)."[25]

Again, on January 6, 1985, in a devotional speech given at BYU Provo, Utah, McConkie addresses the Gospel's "everlasting fulness [*sic*]" stating:

> And so it has gone until the gospel has been restored in its everlasting fulness [*sic*] until the Church of Jesus Christ of Latter-day Saints has been perfected until the kingdom of God [the Mormon church] on earth has been established and is rolling forth, ["]*clear as the sun, fair as the moon, And terrible as an army with banners*["] [See *Song of Solomon 6:10*].[26]

Apostle Orson Pratt apparently had no aversion to using this same "biblical trash" as can be seen in the *Journal of Discourses*:

Will not this produce terror upon all the nations of the earth? Will not armies of this description, though they may not be as numerous as the armies of the world, cause a terror to fall upon the nations? The Lord says the *banners of Zion shall be terrible*? [i.e., "terrible as *an army* with banners"].[27]

Marvin W. Cowan observes:

One of the LDS charges leveled at the Bible used by Protestants and Catholics is that many books have been lost. In the *A[ticles] of F[aith]* on p. 502 Talmage lists 20 "lost books" of the Bible. These are mentioned in the Bible and include such names as: "[*sic*] The Book of the Covenant (Ex. 24:7); Books of Wars of the Lord (Num. 21:14); Book of Jasher (Josh. 10:13) etc. But even if all 20 of these books are mentioned in the Bible, does that prove they were intended to be a part of the Bible? If so, Epicurean and Stoic philosophy should be included also since the Apostle Paul quotes it in Acts 17:18 & 28. But just because some writing is mentioned in the Bible doesn't mean it is scripture! Does the "Inspired Bible" [written by Joseph Smith] solve the problem of these "lost books"? When we check it we find 65 books, not 66! Smith's inspiration and revelation lost another book—The Song of Solomon! But not a single "lost" book has been placed in this "Inspired Bible" or any other LDS book of scripture![28]

Dr. Harry Reeder, III, senior minister of Briarwood Presbyterian Church in Birmingham, Alabama (who is in good company with the majority of biblical commentators on his assessment), observes:

The Song of Solomon obviously has much pastoral use in the issues of marriage and biblical sexuality. Yet, its glorious and ultimate use is to point the people of God as the bride of Christ to our glorious, majestic, and intimate relationship with the Bridegroom, Jesus Christ.[29]

In a number of *King James Bibles*, one can read section headings like those found in *The Song of Solomon* chapter 4: "*Christ setteth forth the graces of the church*" and "*The church prayeth to be made fit for his presence.*" Chapter 4 is a poetic depiction of the marriage act of physical consummation.

To these statements, and many more, that have been leveled, without reservation, against both the theology and praxis of the global network of Christ's Church, the Word of God (without caveat or proviso) must remain the principle line of defense, and preeminent provenance for all Christian apologetics. Even Joseph Smith admitted, "Surely 'facts are stubborn things.' "[30] Again, Joseph Smith asserts, "The *boldness of my plans and measures* can readily be tested by the touchstone of all schemes, . . . *truth*; for truth is a matter of fact . . ."[31] "Light cleaves to light and facts are supported by facts. The truth injures no one . . ."[32] Juanita Brooks (1898-1989), lifelong member of the Church of Jesus Christ of Latter-day Saints, and author of *The Mountain Meadows Massacre*, stated, "I feel sure that nothing but the truth can be good enough for the church to which I belong."[33]

Wilford Woodruff proposed, "If any man has a truth that we have not, we say, 'Let us have it.' I am willing to exchange all the errors and false notions I have for one truth, and should consider that I had made a good bargain."[34] President J. Reuben Clark (1871-1961), an American attorney, civil servant, and a prominent leader in the Church of Jesus Christ of Latter-day Saints, propounded, "If we have the truth it cannot be harmed by investigation. If we have not the truth, it ought to be harmed."[35]

On December 27, 1820 (the year of Joseph Smith's supposed "First Vision"), Thomas Jefferson wrote to William Roscoe (1753-1831), an English historian, and a leading abolitionist, stating, "[W]e are not afraid to follow truth wherever it may lead, nor to tolerate any error so long as reason is left free to combat it." John Stuart Mill (1806-1873), a British philosopher and contemporary of Joseph Smith, said:

> [T]he peculiar evil of silencing the expression of an
> opinion is, robbing the human race; posterity as well
> as the existing generation; those who dissent from the

opinion, still more than those who hold it. If the opinion is right, they are deprived of the opportunity of exchanging error for truth: if wrong they lose what is almost as great a benefit, the clearer perception and livelier impression of truth, produced by its collision with error.[36]

Linus van Pelt (Charlie Brown's best friend). From the Peanuts comic strip by Charles M. Schulz (1922-2000).

Martin Luther boldly stated, "I am not permitted to let my love be so merciful as to tolerate and endure false doctrine." Orson Pratt published this challenge:

> Convince us of our errors of Doctrine, if we have any, by reason, by logical arguments, or by the Word of God and we will ever be grateful for the information and you will ever have the pleasing reflections that you have been instruments in the hands of God of redeeming your fellow beings.[37]

Brigham Young was somewhat self-deprecating in his appraisal of "fanaticism" and the foundation of the Mormon religion:

> I will tell you who the real fanatics are: they are they who adopt false principles and ideas as facts and try to establish a superstructure upon a false foundation. They are the fanatics; and however ardent and zealous they may be, they may reason or argue on false premises till doomsday, and the result will be false. If our religion is of this character we want to know it; we would like to find a philosopher who can prove it to us. We are called ignorant; so we are; but what of it? Are not all ignorant? I rather think so.[38]

Wilford Woodruff offers, "This church has continued to rise. It is the only true church upon the face of the whole earth. Its history is before the world."[39] Joseph Smith said, "Our religious principles are before the world, ready for the investigation of all men."[40] Again, Joseph Smith challenged, "If any man will prove to me, by one passage of Holy Writ, one item I believe to be false, I will renounce and disclaim it as far as I promulgated it."[41]

It is ironic that Joseph Smith gave the following counsel concerning the wayward path that leads to apostasy when he himself was guilty of the same:

> I will give you one of the *Keys* of the mysteries of the Kingdom. It is an eternal principle, that has existed with God from all eternity: That man who rises up to condemn others, finding fault with the Church [i.e., orthodox Christianity], saying that they are out of the way, while he himself is righteous, then know assuredly, that that man is in the high road to apostasy; and if he does not repent, will apostatize, as God lives.[42]

Prior to 1990, the temple endowment ceremony (an esoteric ritual written by Joseph Smith and Brigham Young, and practiced for well over 100 years) depicted a bumbling, befuddled Protestant minister, identified by his clerical collar, who was conveniently recruited by Lucifer as a hireling to serve as Satan's emissary. Having witnessed this putative charade (which can be viewed and read online), it is blatantly obvious that the script was intended to mock and ridicule Orthodox Christianity and its adherents, and, more particularly, its clergy.

This cruel and shameful characterization was only recently done away with, in part, because of negative feedback from a survey issued by the LDS Church. In 1988, a questionnaire was sent out to approximately 3,400 "Temple worthy" (those with a Temple recommend) members of the Church of Jesus Christ of Latter-day Saints in the United States and Canada who were asked to participate in evaluating the endowment ritual. Some of the 92 questions that were addressed are as follows:

- (Question 28): For a person who had been through the endowment ritual, (d) "was the experience unpleasant?", (e) "were you confused by what happened?", (f) "did you feel spiritually uplifted by the experience?"

- (Question 29): "Briefly describe how you felt after receiving your own endowment."

- (Question 35): "What are some of the things that made it difficult for you to go to the temple?"

- (Question 37-k): "Did you find it hard to go to the temple?"

Bruce R. McConkie emphasized that, temples are "sacred sanctuaries set apart from the world, unique and unusual . . . into which only a favored few may enter."

> True it is that if a people know and practice the true law of temple construction and use, they are the Lord's people, and they have the power of God unto salvation which Paul called the gospel. And true it is that if a church is without a knowledge of these mysterious matters, it is not composed of the Lord's people, and in it there is no power to save souls.[43]

10

A "Homely, Wild, Vulgar Fanaticism"

I wish to inform you that I am here and doing what many years ago I resolved to do—the best I can. Watch for the signs of the times. All is right, and the Devil is not dead; for which we have great reason to be thankful. If you do not know whether "Mormonism" is true or untrue, I am perfectly willing that the Devil should assail you until you learn for yourselves (Brigham Young).[1]

Among the Latter-day Saints the preaching of false doctrines disguised as truths of the gospel, may be expected ... (Joseph F. Smith).[2]

It confounds me how so many Mormon authors, previously mentioned (Joseph Smith not excepted), can feign innocence while casting aspersions and dishing out a wholesale diatribe of insolence against what the Latter-day Saints consider sophomoric Christian orthodoxy. One can readily see that Joseph Smith and his faithful devotees have no qualms denigrating mainstream Christianity, but when their doctrine is challenged (as this author intends to do), Mormons quickly cry foul! In addition, they quail when confronted, assuming a "poor me"-martyr's complex. The "Saints" can dish out invective criticisms by the truckload, but God forbid, that one should countermand with a shovel-full of "*I take umbrage with Mormonism*"; for then we are labeled as Mormon haters and bashers, and our literature dismissed as anti-Mormon animus. We are categorized as contentious when "contending for the faith"; we are marked as intolerant when we refuse to embrace what we perceive as heresy. Nietzsche once said, "Truth does not mind being questioned. A lie does not like being challenged."

There is a maxim that "error begets error and heresy begets heresy." Heresy is defined as a belief or opinion contrary to orthodox religious (especially Christian) doctrine; an opinion that is profoundly at odds with what is generally accepted as the beliefs and standards defined within the Orthodox Church's body of creeds. The word heresy comes from the Greek root *"haireisthai"* meaning to choose. It is through the act of one's volition that a choice is made to embrace a heretical teaching, thus straying from the narrow path defined by orthodoxy. Orthodoxy (from Greek ορθοδοξία, *orthodoxía* 'right opinion'), according to *Merriam-Webster*, is a belief or a way of thinking that is "accepted as true or correct, the beliefs, practices, and institution of the Orthodox Church."

Gordon B. Hinckley affirmed: "We [the Church of Jesus Christ of Latter-day Saints] do not accept the Athanasian Creed. We do not accept the Nicene Creed, nor any other creed based on tradition and the conclusions of men."[3] Bruce R. McConkie seethed:

> The Athanasian creed will return to the realm of darkness where it was spawned. The doctrine of salvation by grace alone [*Sola Gratia*] without works shall be anathema. The great and abominable church [both Catholicism and Protestantism] shall tumble to the dust. False worship [Mormons are taught that Christians are worshipping a false, or otherwise "Unknown God"] shall cease."[4]

The Athanasian Creed is a Christian statement of belief emphasizing the Trinitarian doctrine and Christology that has been used by Christian churches since the sixth century. The Athanasian Creed begins by defining each person of the Trinity as uncreated (*Increates*), limitless (*Immensus*), eternal (*Aeternus*), and omnipotent (*Omnipotens*). The Athanasian Creed also declares that those who do not adhere to its decrees "shall be anathema."

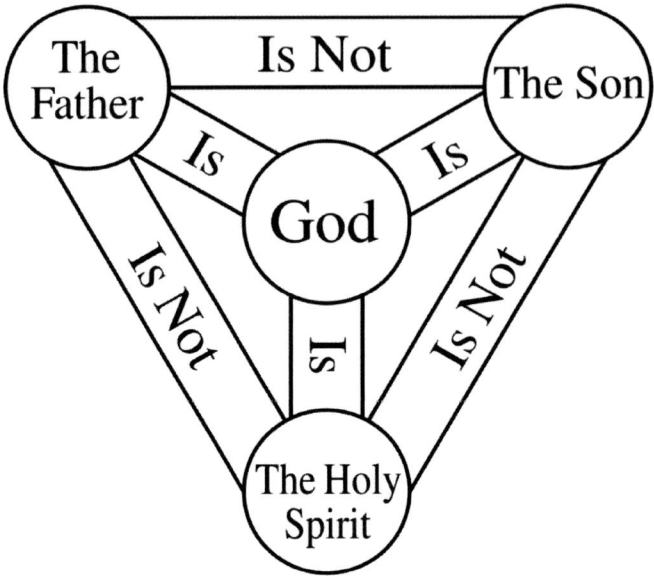

The Shield of the Trinity, a visual representation of the doctrine of the Trinity, derived from the Athanasian Creed.

Creeds are simply formal statements of faith summarizing basic Christian beliefs based on foundational Biblical truths. These "statements of faith" were annunciated as creeds to affirm the standard of truth as the early Church was confronted with false teachings arising within the rank and file of believers. In an article titled "The Importance [And Early Use] Of Creeds," posted on July 12, 2019, J. Warner Wallace notes:

> Christianity has always been *creedal*. From the earliest days right up to (and through) the Post-modern age, Christians have tried to understand and articulate the truth of the Christian Worldview, and their efforts have often taken the form of creeds. . . .
>
> To move away from a creedal form of faith is to move away from the faith altogether. While some within the Christian community may desire an anti-creedal form of Christianity (as they attempt to reconcile the philosophic ideas of the culture with the exclusive truth claims of Christianity) they do so at

their own peril. To deny the role and importance of creeds is to deny the essence and history of Christianity.[5]

Charles Colson, in his book *Against the Night: Living in the New Dark Ages*, writes:

> Christian orthodoxy is properly defined in the context of a tradition determined by the continuity of essential doctrine, traced through a long line of theologians and saints, guaranteed by the work of the Holy Spirit. We cannot approach the Scriptures as though the Council of Nicea [also Nicaea] never met, as though Augustine and Aquinas never wrote, as though Luther never preached. While Scripture is our authoritative source, traditions acts as an authoritative guide to biblical interpretation.
>
> Nor is orthodoxy uniquely Protestant or Catholic—or Orthodox. It is, instead, what C. S. Lewis called "mere Christianity": that which we have received from our fathers; that which was outlined in the earliest creeds and rules of faith; and that which is preserved—if not observed—in every major tradition of the church.[6]

J. Christopher Conkling (born in 1949), author of *A Joseph Smith Chronology*, reports that in a meeting with Justin Butterfield (1790-1855), an attorney, and Governor Ford of Illinois, Joseph Smith replied to Butterfield's comment that "he (Butterfield) is no religionist," stating, "I told him I had no creed to circumscribe my mind; therefore, the people did not like me."[7] Again, J. Christopher Conkling chronicles that in a meeting "with Mr. Butterfield, Judge Stephen A. Douglas, and others," Joseph Smith explained:

> [T]he difference "between the Latter-day Saints and Sectarians was, that the latter were all circumscribed by some peculiar creed, which deprived its members the privilege of believing anything not contained therein, whereas the Latter-day Saints have no creed, but are ready to believe all [so-called] true principles

that exist, as they are made manifest from time to time."[8]

Joseph Fielding Smith observed that "the decisions of the ecumenical councils out of which the creeds of historical Christianity have come" are based on "philosophical speculation" thus defining Mormonism's disputation with, and departure from orthodoxy.[9] Stephen E. Robinson admits that Mormonism lies well outside the bounds of orthodoxy when he states, without equivocation, "the Latter-day Saints reject the doctrines of Nicaea and Chalcedon," in fact, "the Latter-day Saints reject them *all* . . ."[10] Richard Lyman Bushman emphasizes that, "Joseph had an aversion to creeds. Later he criticized the very idea of them. They circumscribed truth when he wanted expansion [i.e., a belief system without boundaries]."[11]

Rex E. Lee notes: "Complete ecumenism would require either that the Church of Jesus Christ of Latter-day Saints deny its divine authority or that others in the ecumenical movement accept it, neither of which is possible."[12] In the Apostle Paul's letter to Titus, the following instruction is given concerning the Church's responsibility toward those who have strayed from the path of orthodoxy: "A man that is a heretic after the first and second admonition reject" (*Titus 3:10 KJV*). The Reverend Martin VanderWal (born August 5, 1964), a graduate of Calvin College in Grand Rapids Michigan, warns that "there will arise false teachers in the church" who will introduce "damnable heresies" to advance their own following. VanderWal again warns that the Church "must identify certain teachings as heretical, and their teachers and followers as heretics" as the Church is sometimes remiss to do. "Even from your own number men will arise and distort the truth in order to draw away disciples after them. So be on your guard!" (*Acts 20:30-31 NIV*). VanderWal emphasizes: "This judgment is part of the work of discipline, necessary for maintaining purity in the church," and is "one of the main purposes of deliberative assemblies in the churches, as Scripture makes clear in Acts 20:28-30, Titus 1:9-11, and 2 John 10."

VanderWal exposits, "the church of Jesus Christ is built by Christ Himself upon the truth of His word" and "upon the foundation of the apostles and prophets, Jesus Christ Himself being the chief cornerstone." VanderWal further implores that "False doctrine, error, heresy, unorthodoxy . . . are not in harmony with [the] truth of God's Word but militate against it" and are "opposed to the church's unity and its very existence." VanderWal contends that those who "confess to these false doctrines" begin to "justify their hold on error" by finding "Scripture that condemns the truth and favors their error." VanderWal notes: "Should those holding" to "false teachings fail to submit" to "discipline" and judgments "made by authoritative deliberative assemblies in the church," they must "become the objects of Christian discipline."[13]

J. Nickols, professor in the division of Biblical Education at Lancaster Bible College, observes: "Augustine once said, in a rather lengthy letter dealing with heresy, that heretics 'prefer their own contentions to the testimonies of Holy writ' and that they consequently 'separate themselves from the true universal church.'"[14]

Under the inspiration of the Spirit, the Apostle John expounded: "They went out from us, but they were not of us; for if they had been of us they would *no doubt* have continued with us: but *they went out* that they might be made manifest that they were not all of us" (*1 John 2:19 KJV*). Not only did the Mormon Church go "out from us," but they, in fact, launched themselves into such fantastic divisive heretical realms that they defy the boundaries of reason! (Although, I will reasonably attempt to define those boundaries.) Stephen E. Robinson writes:

> [I]t has been argued that the diversity tolerated among other Christian denominations is a matter of flexibility within certain broad limits [differences that are yet circumscribed within the sphere of orthodoxy], and that . . . LDS doctrines are so foreign to either the New Testament or traditional Christianity that they violate even these broad limits and cannot therefore be tolerated.[15]

Robinson again suggests: "[T]he claim is made that certain LDS doctrines are so bizarre, so totally foreign to biblical or historical Christianity, that they simply cannot be tolerated."[16] Richard Lyman Bushman wrote that to many observers, "Mormonism appeared to be a bizarre offshoot of mainline Christianity."[17] Hugh Nibley concedes, "The [Mormon] temple and its ordinances seem to be grotesquely out of place and impractical in the present world."[18]

In an article titled "Mormonism and the Heresies" by Brian D. Birch, director of the Religious Studies Program at Utah Valley University and editor of the *Perspectives on Mormon Theology* series (Greg Kofford Books), Birch notes that with the Church of Jesus Christ of Latter-day Saints there is a divergence "from theological positions affirmed by creedal Christianity":

> Latter-day Saints have repeatedly found themselves responding to questions implying that Mormon ideas are too radical to be characterized as legitimately Christian. Importantly, these questions are not coming from strident anti-Mormon voices but from serious, well-respected, and friendly interlocutors.[19]

Drew Williams asked:

> How can a religious organization [the LDS Church] claim to be associated with the restoration of the ancient church of Christ and still be so different from mainstream Christianity?
>
> . . . In many ways, the claims made by Latter-day Saints, which are based on LDS doctrine, are outrageous compared to what has been traditionally accepted as "Truth."[20]

Neal A. Maxwell concedes: "As we review these several [LDS] doctrines, bear in mind President [Brigham] Young's caution that the restored gospel is not 'comely.' In fact, in its comparative strangeness it is a stumbling block to many."[21] Abner Cole (1783-1835), also known by his pen name, Obadiah Dogberry, Esq., who was a 19th-century American newspaper editor, and one of the earliest critics of the spiritual claims of Joseph Smith, articulated:

> The page of history informs us, that from time immemorial, MAN has more or less been the dupe of superstitious error and imposition; so much so, that some writers in derision have called [Joseph Smith] "a religious animal," and it often happens that the

more absurd the *dogma*, the more greedily will it be swallowed.[22]

Richard Lyman Bushman discloses:

> [Nancy Towle (1796-1876), who was] a thirty-five-year-old itinerant, [and] was one of a corps of female evangelists who helped to satisfy the nation's hunger for preaching in the 1830s. . . . concluded "that [Mormonism] was one of the most deep-concerted-plots of Hell, to deceive the hearts of the simple that had ever come, within the limits of my acquaintance."[23]

Charles Dickens (1812-1870), regarded by many as the greatest novelist of the Victorian era, gave his editorial approval to an article James Hannay (1827-1873), a Scottish novelist, journalist and diplomat, contributed in Dickens' weekly journal, *Household Words*, when he penned, "[Mormonism] exhibits fanaticism in its newest garb—homely, wild, vulgar fanaticism . . ." Hannay further appraised Mormonism as "marked" by "industry, and pitiable superstitious delusion. What the Mormons do, seems to be excellent; what they say, is mostly nonsense."[24]

Richard J. Dunn, Professor Emeritus Department of English at the University of Washington, Seattle, observed, "Except for the approval of Mormon practicality, [Charles] Dickens shared his ages prejudices and extended his disgust with Nonconformists to the Mormons."[25] Leo Tolstoy (1828-1910), a Russian writer regarded as one of the greatest authors of all time, decried that Mormonism was "two-thirds deception and one third devotion," and thus similar to other religious institutions "the product of deception [and] lies for a good purpose."[26]

James R. Spencer (1942-2016), Christian author, lecturer, newspaper journalist and businessman, offers his appraisal of the LDS Church:

> Mormonism is wrong in so many important ways that the best minds of Bible-centered Christianity have declared its doctrine heretical. . . . The Church at

large has made a broad-based, reluctant, and solemn declaration that Mormonism is heretical.[27]

Brian D. Birch notes:

[B]etween 1995 and 2001, five major denominations formally rejected Mormonism as part of the Christian community of faith. In addition to the Roman Catholic Church, the United Methodist Church, the Presbyterian Church USA, the Southern Baptist Convention, and the Missouri Synod of the Lutheran Church all offered similar rulings on the status of Mormonism.[28]

After freely and profusely adding to the Scriptural canon, Mormonism implicitly demands that those of us who hold to the norm of commonly held beliefs, reshuffle the deck of orthodox Christianity, which Joseph Smith shamelessly exploited and redefined "with deceptive words" (*2 Peter 2:3 NKJV*), and commit ourselves to a totally new paradigm of who God is and how it is that God saves. *Barnes' Notes on the Bible* states: "One of the most successful arts of the adversary of souls has been to mingle fable with truth; and when he cannot overthrow the truth by direct opposition, to neutralize it by mingling with it much that is false and frivolous."[29]

The Apostle Paul lamented: "I know this, that after my departing shall grievous wolves enter in among you, not sparing the flock. Also of your own selves shall men arise, speaking perverse things, to draw away disciples after them" (*Acts 20:29-30 KJV*). Carl Moser ascertained:

Almost all converts to Mormonism come from a nominally Christian background. . . . [Moreover] according to several "eyeball" estimates I have seen or heard reported, 75-80 percent of Mormon converts come from specifically Protestant backgrounds. . . . Mormon missionaries don't evangelize, they proselytize.[30]

Richard Lyman Bushman observes that Mormonism is an "amorphous religious culture flourishing along the margins of the standard Christian denominations."[31] John G. Turner acknowledges that the Mormon Church "primarily consisted of converts reared in Protestant Bible-drenched societies."[32] In 1980, 40 percent of Mormonism's 217,000 converts came from Baptist backgrounds. The proselytizing of Southern Baptist was further implemented when the Mormon Church built temples in Atlanta, Georgia and Dallas, Texas, two of the Southern Baptists' most important hubs where they had previously enjoyed a *de facto* religious presence.

The Reverend Benjamin Franklin Morris (1810-1867), an historian and minister of the Congregational Church, wrote:

> I wish to state . . . one interesting fact. It is this. The great body of the Mormons are from those churches where the great cardinal doctrines of the Bible are kept rather in the *back ground*. Comparatively few have had the privilege of sitting under a thoroughly educated ministry, and thus of being fully indoctrinated into the prime truths and doctrines of the Bible.[33]

Richard Ostling, an American author and journalist, and his wife, the late Joan Ostling, reveal that the bulk of Mormon converts are proselytized Christians who have had some nominally religious experience:

> Mormonism succeeds by building on a preexisting Christian culture and by being seen as an add-on [offering something "better," or what some refer to as the so-called "more" of Mormonism], drawing converts through a form of syncretism. Mormonism flourishes best in settings with some prior Christianization.[34]

Syncretism is defined as "the combination of different forms of belief or practice" and "to unite and harmonize especially without critical examination or logical unity" (*Merriam-Webster*). The bottom line is that syncretism is not reconcilable to true Christianity. The reality is, any addendum or modification to creedal orthodoxy (well-entrenched biblical laws and principles embraced by mainstream Christianity) to accommodate a "better" religion is heresy (see *Revelation 22:18-20*).

Leonard J. Arrington and Davis Bitton observe:

> Analyzing the thirty-four men who were in the First Presidency and Quorum of the Twelve—the top echelon of Mormon leaders—between 1832 and 1849, one scholar has found that ten had been Methodist, one Baptist, five Disciples of Christ, two Presbyterian, three Congregationalist, one Shaker, eight unaffiliated, . . . and four unknown, with several having affiliated with more than one religious group before Mormonism.[35]

Milton V. Backman. Jr. (1927-2016) who was a historian of American religions with particular emphasis on the early history of the Latter-day Saint movement, stated:

> Before uniting with the restoration movement [the Mormon Church], the Whitmers were active members of a German Reformed church. Joseph Smith, Sr., helped organize a Universalist church in Vermont, and Hyrum and Samuel Smith belonged to the Presbyterian church during the 1820s.[36]

Rollin Lynde Hartt remarked:

> The [Mormon religion] is a huge maw, gulping a dozen denominations. Are you a Baptist? The Mormon believes in immersion. A Methodist? The Mormon obeys his bishop. A Campbellite [now Disciples of Christ]? The Mormon claims a yet closer return to apostolic ordinance. A Theosophist? The Mormon holds to preexistence. A Spiritualist? The Mormon hears voices from the dead. A Faith Healer? The Mormon heals by the laying on of hands. A Second Adventt [sic]? The Mormon awaits the Messiah. A Universalist? The Mormon says all will be saved.[37]

Again, the Apostle Paul warns, "Also of your own selves shall men arise, speaking perverse things, to draw away disciples [from the common fold of believers] after them" (*Acts 20:30 KJV*). Joseph Smith conceded:

> One great evil is that men are ignorant of the nature of spirits; their power, laws, government, intelligence, etc., and imagine that when there is anything like power, revelation, or vision manifested [i.e., the "Restored Church" founded by the Prophet, Seer and Revelator, Joseph Smith], that it must be of God.[38]

> I advise all of you to be careful what you do, or you may by-and-by find out that you have been deceived.[39]

Joseph Smith rightly asserted: "[N]othing is a greater injury to the children of men than to be under the influence of a false spirit when they think they have the Spirit of God."[40] President John Taylor warned: "It is not every revelation that is of God, for Satan has the power to transform himself in to an angel of light; he can give visions and revelations as well as spiritual manifestations . . ."[41]

Joseph Smith propounds, "Satan hath sought to deceive you, that he might overthrow you . . . Behold, I, the Lord, have looked upon you [the Latter-day Saints], and have seen abominations in the church that profess my name."[42] George A. Smith relates that, "there was a prevalent [counterfeit] spirit all through the early history of this Church [the Church of Jesus Christ of Latter-day Saints]."[43] Ivan J. Barrett reports:

> Those who claimed to be ministering angels for the Church . . . were of Satan appearing as angels of light. Many of the Saints were bewildered by the different voices and consequent confusion. . . .

> Nearly every quorum of the priesthood was infested with this corrupting spirit. Many who had been humble and faithful in the performance of duty in the Church had become haughty in spirit and lifted up in pride.[44]

Alvin R. Dyer addresses the Church's "Dark Hours":

> It mattered not what station a man held in the Church, whether he was of the Presidency, the Quorum of the Twelve, the First Council of Seventy, with other

leaders, or a member at large. For, as the gospel net gathers all types of potential leadership, so also do the seeds of rebellion and apostasy spring up in various places.[45]

On January 1, 1836, Joseph Smith made the following entry in his personal journal:

[I]ndeed the adversary is bringing into requisition all his subtlety to prevent the Saints from being endowed, by causing a division among the Twelve, also among the Seventy, and bickering and jealousies among the Elders and the official members of the Church; and so the leaven of iniquity ferments and spreads among the members of the Church.[46]

On January 1838, Joseph Smith recorded:

[T]he spirit of apostate mobocracy . . . continued to rage and grow hotter and hotter, until ["On the evening of the 12th"] Elder Rigdon and myself were obligated to flee from its deadly influence . . . and on the 16th we pursued our journey with our families, in covered wagons towards the city of Far West, in Missouri.[47]

Again, in 1843, Joseph Smith made a journal entry stating:

Of the Twelve Apostles chosen in Kirtland, and ordained under the hands of Oliver Cowdery, David Whitmer and myself, there have been but two but what have lifted their heel against me—namely Brigham Young and Heber C. Kimball.[48]

The Church of Jesus Christ of Latter-day Saints that was founded on the ambiguous doctrine of the "Great Apostasy" was rife with its own factious dissenters and apostates! who believed that Joseph Smith was a fallen prophet and wanted to return to the "Old School" of the more familiar "First Principles" that anchored and defined the early history and foundation of "true" Mormonism.

Elder Sidney Rigdon

Joseph Smith, who taught that, "Lying spirits are going forth in the earth [and that] There will be great manifestations of spirits, both false and true," admitted, "There have also been ministering angels in the [LDS] Church which were of Satan appearing as an angel of light."[49] Smith conceded, "The Church of Jesus Christ of Latter-day Saints has also had its false spirits . . . it is not to be wondered at if there should be found among us false spirits."[50] Joseph Smith coyly stated, "All organized bodies have their peculiar evils, weaknesses and difficulties."[51]

John Corrill (1794-1842), an early member and leader of the Church of Jesus Christ of Latter-day Saints, and an elected representative in the Missouri State Legislature, and was prominently involved in the Mormon conflicts in Missouri before leaving the church in 1839, observed: "Many improprieties and visionary notions crept into the church, which tried the feelings of the more sound minded . . ."[52] Corrill further reports: "[T]hose visionaries spirits spoken of before continued in the church, and rose to such a height that the elders became so dissatisfied with them that they determined to have something done about it."[53]

Richard Lyman Bushman adds:

> Visiting branches outside of Kirtland, Parley Pratt came across "strange spiritual operations" that were "disgusting, rather than edifying." People would swoon, make unseemly gestures, fall into ecstasies and cramps. Pratt felt that "a false and lying spirit seemed to be creeping into the Church."[54]

On August 2, 1913, the First Presidency issued a warning to its members: "[F]alse spirits . . . exercise an influence so imitative of that which proceeds from a Divine source that even these persons, who think they are 'the very elect,' find it difficult to discern the difference."[55] Joseph F. Smith enjoins:

> From the days of Hiram Page [an early member of the Latter Day Saint movement and one of the Eight Witnesses to the *Book of Mormon*'s golden plates] (Doc. and Cov., Sec. 28), at different periods there have been manifestations from delusive spirits to members of the Church. . . . [Members] of the Church [of Jesus Christ of Latter-day Saints] are [being] led astray by false spirits . . .[56]

Roy W. Doxey notes, "In 1946, President J. Reuben Clark, Jr. of the First Presidency [of the Mormon Church], told the people attending the April general conference of false teachings which were being entertained by some members of the Church":

> I have said on other occasions, and I repeat now that there are being taught amongst us, unfortunately, doctrines which are utterly destructive, not only of Jesus the Christ, but even of God himself, and we must be on our watch that neither we nor our children be influenced, debauched, or polluted by such doctrines.[57]

J. Reuben Clark mentions the following that are but a few (from a list of 10) of the so-called "false" doctrines at issue:

- God is not an anthropomorphic being.

- Joseph Smith did not see God nor really experience any supernatural phenomena [i.e., the "First

Vision"]. He wrote the Book of Mormon without divine assistance. He also gave revelations to suit his purpose and the situation without divine assistance.

- The value of Mormonism is in its practice and in its system. Its origin need not be basic to one's belief in or acceptance of Mormonism for its value.

- The three-degrees-of-glory story is a myth.

- Temple work . . . is absurd and foolish in its objectives.

- The Belief that man might become as God is equally foolish.

- Practically every theological idea advanced by Joseph Smith can be found in some ancient religion or in some current beliefs contemporary with his time.[58]

NOTE: I will address each of these issues at length in the volumes to follow.

When one enters the fray of spiritual warfare and the penumbra of Christian controversy, he should be well advised ("in the multitude of counsellors *there is* safety"—see *Proverbs 11:14 KJV*), and thoroughly equipped to give a defense for the hope that lies within the fair jurisprudence of Christian orthodoxy. One should take the utmost care so as not to become entangled in the feud for which he has so valiantly chosen to redress. The enemy (Satan, the true author/father of all lies) is shrewd and battle hardened and is "indefatigable . . . in tempting and laying snares."[59] Nor will he give up easily. (After all, he took on God Himself in "The Temptation of Christ.") The Apostle Paul wrote: "Lest Satan should get an advantage of us: for we are not ignorant of his devices" (*2 Corinthians 2:11 KJV*).

Apostle Dallin H. Oaks said, "Satan can even use truth to promote his purposes. Facts severed from their context, can convey an erroneous impression."[60] Joseph F. Smith adds:

Satan . . . seeks by imitation-miracles to blind and deceive the children of God. . . .

The danger and power for evil in witchcraft is not so much in the witchcraft itself as in the foolish credulence that superstitious people give to the claims made in its behalf.[61]

The First Presidency of the LDS Church (Heber J. Grant, J. Reuben Clark, Jr., and David O. McKay) acknowledged:

Satan is making war against all the wisdom that has come to men through their ages of experience. He is seeking to overturn and destroy the very foundations upon which society, government and religion rest. . .
.

He is working under such perfect disguise that many do not recognize either him or his methods. . .
.

Without their knowing it, the people are being urged down paths that lead only to destruction.[62]

Joseph Smith proclaimed: "Every spirit, or vision . . . is not of God. The devil is an orator; he is powerful; he took our Savior on to a pinnacle of the temple, and kept him in the wilderness for forty days."[63] Abraham Kaplan (1918-1993), Professor of Philosophy and Sociology at the University of Haifa observed, "The Devil not only quotes Scripture; he can also wear a prayer shawl and phylacteries."[64] Spencer W. Kimball cautioned:

The evil one is alert. He is always ready to deceive and claim as his victims every unwary one, every careless one, every rebellious one. . . . He is undeviating in his purposes and is clever and relentless in his pursuit of them. . . . [Lucifer] will use his logic to confuse and his rationalizations to destroy. . . . The arch deceiver has studied every way possible to achieve his ends, using every tool, every device possible. . . . He never sleeps—he is diligent and persevering. He analyzes carefully his problem and then moves forward diligently, methodically to reach that objective. . . . He uses every teaching art to subvert man. . . . The adversary is subtle. He is cunning. . . . whispering half-truths until he has his intended captives following him.[65]

Wilford Woodruff warned that, "We are surrounded by . . . evil spirits that are at war against God and against everything looking to the building up of the kingdom of God . . . We are in the midst of darkness and temptation."[66] Brigham Young implored: "People are liable in many ways to be led astray by the power of the adversary, for they do not fully understand that it is a hard matter for them to always distinguish the things of God from the things of the devil."[67] Joseph Smith mused:

> The work in which we are unitedly engaged is one of no ordinary kind. The enemies we have to contend against are subtle and well skilled in maneuvering . . .
>
> [T]he angelic form, the sanctified look and gesture, and the zeal that is frequently manifested by him for the glory of God, together with the prophetic spirit, the gracious influence, the godly appearance, and the holy garb, which are so characteristic of his proceedings and his mysterious windings.[68]

Joseph F. Smith admonished:

> Let it not be forgotten that the evil one has great power in the earth and that by every possible means he seeks to darken the minds of men and then offers them falsehood and deception in the guise of truth. Satan is a skillful imitator, and as genuine gospel truth is given the world in ever-increasing abundance, so he spreads the counterfeit coin of false doctrine. Beware of his spurious currency, it will purchase for you nothing but disappointment, misery and spiritual death. The "Father of lies" he has been called, and such an adept has he become, through the ages of practice in his nefarious work, that were it possible he would deceive the very elect.[69]

Joseph Fielding McConkie exposits:

The greatest truths are always opposed by the greatest heresies. The greater the outpouring of the spirit of truth, the greater the deluge of falsehoods that will follow. The legions of the adversary are seasoned warriors and are not about to retreat simply because the banners of truth have been unfolded. . . . Every truth of salvation will have its counterfeit, every principle of righteousness its impostor, every good cause its cortege of opportunists. False Christs, false prophets, false revelations, and false doctrines abound and "if possible, they shall deceive the very elect, who are the elect according to the covenant" (Joseph Smith—Matthew 1:22).[70]

Elder Boyd K. Packer (1924-2015), an American religious leader and former educator, who served as president of the Quorum of the Twelve Apostles of The Church of Jesus Christ of Latter-day Saints from 2008 until his death, commented:

All inspiration does not come from God. (See D&C 46:7.) The evil one has the power to tap into those channels of revelation and send conflicting signals which can mislead and confuse us. There are promptings from evil sources which are so carefully counterfeited as to deceive even the very elect [members of the LDS Church]. (See Matt. 24:24.)[71]

Joseph Fielding McConkie observed: "Many in this life seek to avoid the fight. They act as if a truce had been declared between the forces of light and darkness. Indeed, their perception of the gospel is that it must be lived and taught in such a manner that offense is never given."[72] A. W. Tozer (1897-1963), an American Christian pastor, author, magazine editor, and spiritual mentor, argued:

There is a notion abroad that to win a man we must agree with him. Actually, the opposite is true. G. K. Chesterton remarked that each generation has had to be converted by the man who contradicted it most. The man who is going in a wrong direction will never be set right by the affable religionist who falls into step beside him and goes the same way. Someone must place himself across the path and insist that the straying man turn around and go in the right direction.[73]

Satan has counted the cost of yielding hard-fought ground wherein he has blinded and enslaved a myriad of untold thousands.

The Temptation of Christ.

Wilford Woodruff wrote of the height of the apostasy of the Mormon Church in Kirtland, Ohio, stating: "Here . . . was a manifestation—and a very strange one, too—of the power that the devil had over the leading men whom God raised up to assist in laying the foundation of this Church and in bringing forth the Book of Mormon."[74] Heber C. Kimball recalled, "Joseph [Smith] . . . told me that he had contests with the devil, face to face. He also told me how he was handled and afflicted by the devil."[75] John MacArthur wrote:

> [F]alse teaching is the deadliest and most abhorrent of evils, because it is always an expression of

unbelief, which is the distillation of pure evil. . . .
heresy that undermines the gospel . . . places souls in
eternal peril under the darkness of the kind of lies that
keep people in permanent bondage to their sin.

That is why there is no more serious
abomination than heresy. It is the worst and most
loathsome kind of spiritual filth.[76]

NOTES

Introduction:

1. William Shakespeare, *The Tempest* Act 2 Scene 1.

2. "Chronological Snobbery" First coined by C. S. Lewis in 1955 in *Surprised by Joy: the Shape of My Early Life*, Geoffrey Bles (UK), Harcourt Brace (US), New York, 1955, Chapter 13, pp. 201-208.

3. Fiona and Terryl Givens, *All Things New: Rethinking Sin, Salvation, and Everything in Between*, Faith Matters Publishing, Meridian, Idaho 2020, pp. 21, 22, 28, 79, & 174.

4. Brigham Young (March 8, 1863) *Journal of Discourses* Vol. 10, p. 110.

5. John J. Stewart, *Mormonism and the Negro*, Bookmark, a division of Community Press Publishing Company 1960, Orem, Utah, pp. 46-47. Letter of LDS First Presidency to Dr. Lowry Nelson, a nationally prominent sociologist, and member of the LDS Church, July 17, 1947, in response to Lowry's letter to the First Presidency.

6. *Ibid.*, p. 53.

7. Joanna Brooks, *Mormonism and White Supremacy: American Religion and the Problem of Racial Innocence*, Oxford University Press 2020, pp. 12, & 16.

8. "The Case of the Mormon Historian: What Happened when Michael Quinn Challenged the History of the Church he Loved," David Haglund, November 01, 2012.

9. *D. Michael Quinn, The Mormon Hierarchy: Origins of Power*, Signature Books, Salt Lake City, Utah, 1994, p. 112.

10. *The Seventh East Press, An Independent Student Weekly*, Provo, Utah, November 18, 1981.

11. The Jaunita Brooks Lecture Series, The 34th Annual Lecture; Leonard Arrington, Church Historian: Lessons Learned, by Gregory A. Prince, Ph.D., February 16, 2017.

12. Gregory A. Prince, *Leonard Arrington and The Writing of Mormon History*, Salt Lake City: University Press 2016, p. 303.

13. *Ibid.*, p. 285.

14. As reported by Bob Mins in an article published in the *Salt Lake Tribune*, May 9, 2018, titled "Leonard Arrington's vast journals shows battles the Mormon historian had with the church's past."

15. "Why Leonard Arrington was removed as Church Historian," from "Today is Mormon History", Reddit: r/Mormon, July 6, 1981.

16. Clara V. Dobay, in an article titled "Intellect and Faith: The Controversy Over Revisionist History," *Dialogue: A Journal of Mormon Thought*, Volume 27, No. 1, Spring of 1994, pp. 91-105.

17. *Ibid.*

18. First issue of *Dialogue: A Journal of Mormon Thought*, Spring of 1966.

19. *Joseph Smith Papers: Council of Fifty, Minutes*, Church Historian's Press, Salt Lake City, Utah, 2016, p. 42; underlining in original.

20. *FAIR* (*"Faithful Answers, Informed Response"*) "Mormonism and Government/The Council of Fifty."

21. J. Keith Melville, "Theory and Practice of the Church and State During the Brigham Young Era," *BYU Studies Quarterly: Vol. 3: Iss. 1, Article 5,* Autumn 1960, p. 33.

275

22. *Times and Seasons* "Book Review: *The Council of Fifty: A Documentary History*" by David Banack, December 15, 2014.

23. Boyd K. Packer, *Faithful History: Essay on Writing Mormon History*, Signature Books, Salt Lake City 1992, p. 103 footnote.

24. Richard Lyman Bushman in an interview with *Wheat & Tares*' blogger Rick Bennett, in a "Gospel Tangents" podcast May 23, 2022.

25. Preface to the 1958 edition of *Mormon Doctrine*, Bookcraft, Salt Lake City, Utah.

26. *The Religious Educator* Volume 4 No. 3, 2003, p. 92.

27. In an article published in *Mormon Matters*: An Open Stories Foundation Podcast, "The Death of McConkie's *Mormon Doctrine*," May 20, 2010.

28. *Teachings of the Prophet Joseph Smith*, sel. Joseph Fielding Smith, Deseret Book Co., Salt Lake City, Utah 1976, pp. 345-346.

29. Robert L. Millet, *A Different Jesus? The Christ of the Latter-day Saints*, Grand Rapids: Eerdmans, 2005, p. 144.

30. Andrew C. Skinner, *To Become Like God: Witnesses of Our Divine Potential*, Deseret Book, Salt Lake City, Utah 2016, p. 121; Gordon B. Hinckley, "Don't Drop the Ball," *Ensign*, November 1994, p. 48.

31. *Ibid.*, p. 136.

32. Joanna Brooks, *Mormonism and White Supremacy, op. cit.*, p. 12.

33. Tim Keesee, *A Company of Heroes: Portraits from the Gospel's Global Advance*, Crossway, Wheaton, Illinois 2019, p. 119.

34. Richard Lyman Bushman, "Joseph Smith's Many Histories," in *The Worlds of Joseph Smith: A Bicentennial Conference at the Library of Congress*, edited by John W. Welch, Provo, Utah: Brigham Young University Press, 2006, p. 4.

35. Davis Bitton, in an article titled "I Don't Have a Testimony of the History of the Church" published by FAIR from the 2004 FairMormon Conference.

36. "Alternate Interpretations of History"—Study.com, by Nate Sullivan.

37. 123saltlakecitymessenger.pdf; Marlin K. Jensen, "Q & A," John A. Widtsoe Association for Mormon Studies, Utah State University (November 11, 2011); online at http://mormon-chronicles.blogspot.com/2012/01/rescue-plan-to-address-difficulties-of.html.

38. Jon Butler, "The American Experience" interview with Jon Butler, May 2006.

39. Terryl L. Givens, *By the Hand of Mormon: The American Scripture that Launched a New World Religion*, Oxford University Press 2002, p. 175; italics in original.

40. B. H. Roberts, *Studies of the Book of Mormon*, University of Illinois Press, 2nd edition, 1992, p. 115.

41. Mark Twain, Autobiographical dictation, December 2, 1906. Published in *Autobiography of Mark Twain, Volume 2*, University of California Press, 2010, p. 302.

Chapter 1:

1. Lance S. Owens, "Joseph Smith: America's Hermetic Prophet," in *The Prophet Puzzle: Interpretive Essays on Joseph Smith*, ed. Bryan Walterman, Signature Books, Salt Lake City, Utah, 1999, p. 164.

2. Josiah Quincy, *Figures of the Past from the Leaves of Old Journals* (Boston: Roberts Brothers, 1883), pp. 378-379.

3. John Taylor, *Journal of Discourses*, 15:25.

4. *Matthew 13:47-50 KJV.*

5. *Matthew 13:52 KJV.*

6. Will Durant, *The Story of Philosophy*, Chapter 2, Aristotle and Greek Science, Part 3, The Foundation of Logic.

7. Joseph F. Smith, *Gospel Doctrine Volume I*, Deseret Book Company, Salt Lake City, Utah, 1970-71, p. 356.

8. Borrowed from a Devotional Address titled "Our Relationship with the Lord," delivered at Brigham Young University, Provo, Utah, on March 2, 1982.

9. Drew Williams, *The Complete Idiot's Guide to Understanding Mormonism*, Alpha Books, Indianapolis, Indiana, 2003, p. 101.

10. Benjamin E. Park, *Kingdom of Nauvoo: The Rise and Fall of a Religious Empire on the American Frontier*, Liveright Publishing Corporation, 2020, p. 4.

11. McKay Coppins, in an article titled "The Most American Religion," published in *The Atlantic*, January/February 2021.

12. Everett L. Cooley, in his preface to *Studies of the Book of Mormon*, University of Illinois Press, 2nd edition, 1992, p. vii.

13. B. H. Roberts, *Studies of the Book of Mormon*, *op, cit.*, p. 283.

14. *A Comprehensive History of The Church of Jesus Christ of Latter-day Saints*, Century I, Vol. I, Brigham Young University Press, Provo, Utah, 1976, pp. 266-67.

15. Mormonism by G. K. Chesterton, from *Uses of Diversity*, 1921.

16. Thomas Ford, *History of Illinois*, Chicago: S. C. Griggs & Co. 1845, p. 359. See also *History of the Church of Jesus Christ of Latter-day Saints*, Period II Volume VII, published by the Church, Salt Lake City, Utah 1932, pp. 39-40.

17. "The Father and the Son: A Doctrinal Exposition by the First Presidency and the Twelve," *Improvement Era*, August 1916, pp. 936-39; note: the *Improvement Era* preceded the *Ensign* magazine.

18. *Gospel Doctrine Sermons and Writings of Joseph F. Smith*, 5th ed., Deseret Book 1939, Salt Lake City, Utah, p. 68.

19. Alex Beam, *American Crucifixion: The Murder of Joseph Smith and the Fate of the Mormon Church*, PublicAffairs, New York 2014, p. 29.

20. *Ibid.*, p. 439.

21. *John 4:14 NIV.*

22. Francis J. Beckwith and Stephen E. Parrish, *The Mormon Concept of God: A Philosophical Analysis*, The Edwin Mellen Press, Lewiston, New York 1991, pp. 675, & 676.

23. Spencer W. Kimball, *The Miracle of Forgiveness*, Bookcraft, Salt Lake City, Utah 1969, pp. 2, & 173.

24. *Joseph Smith: Rough Stone Rolling*, Vintage Books, a Division of Random House, Inc., New York, 2007, p. 201.

25. *Ibid.*, p. 196.

26. *The Millennial Messiah*, Deseret Book Company, Salt Lake City, Utah, 1983, p. 675.

27. "The New and Everlasting Covenant," *Ensign* magazine, December 2015, pp. 40-47.

28. Joseph Fielding Smith, *Doctrines of Salvation: Sermons and Writings of Joseph Fielding Smith*, Compiled by Bruce R. McConkie, Bookcraft, Salt Lake City, Utah, 1954-56, 1:156.

29. *Doctrine and Covenants* 132:4, & 6: italics and emphasis added.

30. Rex E. Lee, *What Do Mormons Believe?*, Deseret Book Company, Salt Lake City, Utah, 1992, pp. 13, & 40-41.

31. "The Mormons," *The Atlantic*, February 1900.

32. In an introductory essay to *Reflections on Mormonism: Judaeo-Christian Parallels*, Bookcraft, Salt Lake City, Utah, 1978, p. xvi; emphasis added.

33. *The Doctrine and Covenants of The Church of Jesus Christ of Latter-Day Saints*, published by the Deseret Book Company, Salt Lake City, Utah, 1973, p. iii; emphasis added.

34. *The Biblical Roots of Mormonism*, Published by CFI, an imprint of Cedar Fort, Inc., Springville, Utah 2010, p. 143.

35. *Millennial Star* 64:1; emphasis added.

36. *Gospel Doctrine*, 5th ed. 1939, *op. cit.*, p. 489; emphasis added.

37. *Hearken O Ye People: Discourses on the Doctrine and Covenants*, Randall Book Co., Sandy, Utah, 1984, pp. 154-155; emphasis added.

38. *Blood of the Prophets: Brigham Young and the Massacre at Mountain Meadows*, University of Oklahoma Press, paperback 2004, p. 7.

39. *The Millennial* Messiah, *op. cit.*, p. 161; italics added to the conditional *ifs*.

40. Bruce R. McConkie, in Conference Report, October 1983, p. 104; italics added to conditional *ifs*.

41. *The Millennial* Messiah, *op. cit.*, p. 179.

42. Bruce R. McConkie, in *Conference Report*, October 1983, pp. 105-106.

43. *The Essential Nibley: Excerpts From The Writings of Hugh Nibley*, Deseret Book Company, Salt Lake City, Utah, 2014, p. 105.

44. *Ibid.*, p. 229.

Chapter 2:

1. Richard Lyman Bushman, *Joseph Smith: Rough Stone Rolling*, *op. cit.*, p. 58.

2. Brigham D. Madsen, "Reflections on LDS Disbelief in the Book of Mormon as History," the Fall issue of *Dialogue: A Journal of Mormon Thought*, vol. 30, No. 3, p. 95.

3. *Ibid.* p. 95.

4. Dallin H. Oaks, "The Historicity of the Book of Mormon" in *Historicity and the Latter-day Saints Scriptures*, ed. Paul Y. Hoskisson, Provo, Utah: Religious Studies Center, Brigham Young University, 2001, pp. 237-48.

5. Don Bradly, *The Lost 116 Pages: Reconstructing the Book of Mormon's Missing Stories*, Greg Kofford Books, Salt Lake City, 2019, p. 5.

6. Joseph Smith "Church History," *Times and Seasons*, 1 March 1842, 3:706-707.

7. *Bruce R. McConkie, Mormon Doctrine*, Salt Lake City, Utah, Bookcraft, 1966, p. 327.

8. John A. Widtsoe and Franklin S. Harris, Jr., *Seven Claims of the Book of Mormon*, Deseret News Press, Salt Lake City 1937, p. 37.

9. See FARMS UPDATE for October 1984 revised February 1985, quoting the *Saint's Herald*, 4 October 1884, 31:644; William Smith on Mormonism: 12; and *Tiffany's Monthly*, May 1859: 165-166.

10. *History of Joseph Smith: By His Mother, Lucy Mack Smith*, Bookcraft, Salt Lake City, Utah, 1958, p. 107.

11. *Why I Believe*, Bookcraft, Salt Lake City, Utah 2002, p. 80.

12. *American Massacre: The Tragedy at Mountain Meadows, September 1857*, Vintage Books, New York, 2003, p. 5.

13. Joseph Smith, *Elders' Journal* 1:42-43.

14. Lavina Fielding Anderson, *Lucy's Book: A Critical Edition of Lucy Mack Smith's Family Memoir*, Signature Books 2001, Salt Lake City, Utah, p. 379.

15. "Golden Bible," *Painesville Telegraph*, 22 September 1829.

16. Philanthropies: Church History, Richard Oman in "Martin Harris' Wallet is Donated to the LDS Church."

17. Betsy Gaines Quammen, *American Zion: Cliven Bundy, God & Public Lands in the West*, Torrey House Press, Salt Lake City, Utah 2020, p. 25.

18. Terryl and Fiona Givens, *The Crucible of Doubt: Reflections on the Quest for Faith*, Deseret Book, Salt Lake City, Utah 2014, p. 82.

19. Don Bradley, *The Lost 116 Pages: Reconstructing the Book of Mormon's Missing Stories*, Greg Kofford Books, Salt Lake City, Utah 2019, pp. 40, & 42.

20. Excerpt from *Opening the Heavens: Accounts of Divine Manifestations 1820-1844*, LDS Living.

21. William L. Davis, *Visions in a Seer Stone: Joseph Smith and the Making of the Book of Mormon*, the University of North Carolina Press *Chapel Hill* 2020, p. 172.

22. David Whitmer, *An Address to All Believers in Christ*, Richmond, Mo.: n.p., 1887, p. 12.

23. David Whitmer interview given to *Kansas City Journal*, June 5, 1881, reprinted in the Reorganized Church of Jesus Christ of Latter-Day Saints *Journal of History*, Vol. 8 (1910), pp. 299-300.

24. *An Insider's View of Mormon Origins*, Signature Books, Salt Lake City, Utah, 2002, pp. 3-4.

25. *Joseph Smith: Rough Stone Rolling, op. cit.*, pp. 71-72.

26. Emma Smith Bidamon Interview with Joseph Smith III, February 1879 Published as "Last testimony of Sister Emma," *Saints' Herald* 26 (1 October 1879): pp. 289-90.

27. *Oliver Cowdery Scribe, Elder, Witness*, Edited by John W. Welch and Larry E Morris, The Neal A. Maxwell Institute for Religious Scholarship, Brigham Young University, Provo, Utah 2006, pp. 76, & 77.

28. Cowdery, *Messenger and Advocate*, October 1834; Richard Bushman in his *Notes to Pages 96-98, Joseph and the*

Beginnings of Mormonism, University of Illinois Press, Urbana, 1984, p. 222.

29. *Mormon Doctrine, op. cit.*, p. 818; italics in original.

30. *An Insider's View of Mormon Origins, op. cit.*, p. 259.

31. *Documentary History of the Church*, Vol. III, p. 18.

32. "All My Endeavors to Preserve Them," *Journal of Book of Mormon Studies*, Volume 8, Number 2, 1999, p. 16.

33. Lucy Mack Smith, "Lucy Mack Smith, History, 1845," pp. 103-104, josephsmithpapers.org; spelling, capitalization, and punctuation standardized.

34. Dean C. Jessee, ed., *The Personal Writings of Joseph Smith*, Salt Lake City: Deseret Book, 1984, 1:6–7.

35. High Priest Martin Harris, one of the Three Witnesses; see William E Berrett and Alma P. Burton, eds., *Readings in L.D.S. Church History from Original Manuscripts*, Volume 1, p. 63.

36. Quoted in *The Complete Discourses of Brigham Young*, edited by Richard S. Van Wagoner, Salt Lake City, Utah, Signature Books, 2009, pp. 3136-37.

37. *American Massacre, op. cit.*, p. 8.

38. *The Millennial Messiah, op. cit.*, p. 155; *2 Nephi* 27:22.

39. Brigham Young, *Journal of Discourses*, 19:38.

40. *Chicago Times*, October 17, 1881; cited in Cook, ed., *David Whitmer Interviews*, pp. 74-76.

41. David Whitmer, found in P. Wilhelm Poulson, "Interview with David Whitmer," *Deseret Evening News,* 16 August 1878, p. 2; emphasis added.

42. *Doctrine and Covenants* 128:19-20.

43. Robert Boylan, "Psalm 85:11: A Prophecy of the Book of Mormon?" Posted February 18, 2017.

44. Amanda Colleen Brown, in an article titled "Out of the Dust: An Examination of Necromancy as a Literary

Construct in the Book of Mormon," Studia Antiqua 14.2 Fall 2015, p. 34.

45. *The Millennial Messiah, op. cit.*, p. 152; italics added.

46. Emma Wilby, *Cunning Folk and Familiar Spirits: Shamanistic Visionary Traditions in Early Modern British Witchcraft and Magic*, Sussex Academic Press; 1st edition (April 1, 2006), pp. 59-61.

47. *The Millennial Messiah, op. cit.*, p. 83.

48. General Conference, April 1986, "The Question of a Mission."

49. See *1 Timothy 4:1 KJV.*

50. *Doctrines of Salvation*, Volume 3, p. 213.

51. *Religious Truths Defined*, Bookcraft, Inc., Salt Lake City, Utah, 1959, p. 324.

52. *"This is My Doctrine": The Development of Mormon Theology*, Greg Kofford Books, Draper, Utah, 2011, p. 51.

53. Amanda Colleen Brown, *op. cit.*, pp. 27, & 33.

54. Le Grand Richards, *A Marvelous Work and a Wonder*, Deseret Book Company, Salt Lake City, Utah, 1950, p. 69.

55. *Mormon Claims Answered*, by Marvin W. Cowan, 6th Revision and Printing 1984, p. 30; italics in original.

56. Fiona and Terryl Givens, *All Things New: Rethinking Sin, Salvation, and Everything in Between*, Faith Matters Publishing, Meridian, Idaho 2020, pp. 47, & 59.

57. Parley P. Pratt, as quoted in *Journal of Discourses* Volume 2, pp. 44, 45, & 46.

58. *Ibid.*, p. 44.

Chapter 3:

1. *View of the Hebrews; Or the Tribes of Israel in America*, Second edition, published and printed by Smith and Shute, Poultney, (VT.) 1825, p. 173.

2. *The Power of the Word: Saving Doctrines from the Book of Mormon*, Deseret Book Company, Salt Lake City, Utah, 1994, pp. 291-292, & 294.

3. Church Radio, Publicity, and Missionary literature Committee, *A Short History of the Church of Jesus Christ of Latter-day Saints*, Salt Lake City: Church of Jesus Christ of Latter-day Saints, 1938, p. 20.

4. *Studies of the Book of Mormon*, 2nd edition, Signature Books, Salt Lake City, Utah, 1992, paperback, pp. xv-xvi.

5. *Ibid.*, p. xvi.

6. *An Insider's View of Mormonism*, Signature Books, Salt Lake City, Utah, 2002, *Preface* pp. xii-xii.

7. In the Introduction to *Studies of the Book of Mormon, op. cit.*, p. 23.

8. *Ibid.*, p. 30.

9. *Improvement Era*, Volume 6, issue 2, p. 790.

10. *Studies of the Book of Mormon, op. cit.*, p. 240.

11. Lucy Mack Smith, *Biographical Sketches*, p. 85.

12. Fawn Brodie, No Man Knows My History, Alfred A. Knopf, New York, New York 1946, p. 48.

13. *Studies of the Book of Mormon, op. cit.*, p. xvii.

14. *Ibid.*, p. 59.

15. *Ibid.*, p. 60.

16. Thomas Ferguson to Ronald Barney, January 10, 1983, Ferguson Collection, University of Utah; see *Mormon Mavericks: Essays on Dissenters*, pp. 270-271.

17. *Studies of the Book of Mormon, op. cit.*, p. 155.

18. Terryl L. Givens, *By the Hand of Mormon: The American Scripture that Launched a New World Religion*, Oxford University Press 2002, p. 94.

19. *Under the Banner of Heaven*, Anchor Books, New York, 2003, p. 71.

20. *An Insider's View of Mormon Origins, op. cit.*, pp. 56-57.

21. Paul C. Gutjahr, *The Book of Mormon: A Biography, op. cit.*, pp. 144-145.

22. U.S. Bureau of the Census, *Historical Statistics of the United States: From: the Colonial Times to the Present* (1976), pp. 8, & 392.

23. Alex Beam, *American Crucifixion, op. cit.*, p. xiv Introduction.

24. Betsy Gaines Quammen, *American Zion: Cliven Bundy, God & Public Lands in the West*, Torrey House Press, Salt Lake City, Utah 2020, pp. 21, & 22.

25. Benjamin E. Park, *Kingdom of Nauvoo, op. cit.*, p. 51.

26. *Ibid.*, pp. 112-113.

27. *Reflections on Mormonism: Judaeo-Christian Parallels, op. cit.*, p. 91.

28. *Devil's Gate: Brigham Young and the Great Mormon Handcart Tragedy*, Simon & Schuster Paperbacks, New York, NY, 2008, p. 33.

29. from an article titled "The Mormons" in *The Atlantic*, February 1900.

30. *Under the Banner of Heaven, op. cit.*, p. 114.

31. Richard Lymann Bushman, "The Visionary World of Joseph Smith," *BYU Studies* (1997-98), p. 211.

32. Alex Beam, *American Crucifixion, op. cit.*, p. 16.

33. Painesville, Ohio *Telegraph*, 15 March 1831, as cited in Hill, "Role of Christian Primitivism," p. 101.

34. Blake Ostler, *Dialogue: A Journal of Mormon Thought*, Spring 1987, p. 80.

35. Ross Anderson, *Understanding the Book of Mormon*, Zondervan Academic, Nashville, TN, 2009, pp. 76-77.

36. *Ibid.*, p. 77.

37. *The Mormon Experience: A History of the Latter-day Saints*, University of Illinois Press, Urbana and Chicago, second edition 1992, p. 15.

38. *Ibid.*, pp. 31, & 32.

39. In an article titled "The Case for Historicity: Discerning the Book of Mormon's Production," FAIR conference 2004.

40. William L. Davis, *Visions in a Seer Stone, op. cit.*, p. 113.

41. *Ibid.*, p. 115.

42. *Ibid.*, p. 115.

43. *Ibid.*, pp. 116, & 119.

44. *Ibid.*, p. 120.

45. *Journal of the Book of Mormon Studies (1992-2007)*, Vol. 2, No. 2, Fall 1993, p. 2.

46. *The Story of the Latter-day Saints, op. cit.*, p. 21.

47. *Joseph Smith: Rough Stone Rolling, op. cit.*, p. 91.

48. *How Wide the Divide?: A Mormon & an Evangelical in Conversation*, InterVarsity Press, Downers Grove, Illinois, 1997, *op. cit.*, p. 48.

49. *Ibid.*, p. 49-50; italics in original.

50. Terryl L. Givens, *By the Hand of Mormon: The American Scripture that Launched a New World Religion*, Oxford University Press 2002, pp. 46-47.

51. *Ibid.*, p. 199.

52. Terryl and Fiona Givens, *The Crucible of Doubt, op. cit.*, p.39; Robert B. Thompson, 5 Oct. 1840, in Andrew F. Ehat and Lyndon W. Cook, eds. *The Words of Joseph Smith: the Contemporary Accounts of the Nauvoo Discourses of the Prophet Joseph Smith*, Orem, Utah, Granden 1994, p. 48.

53. *Mormon Doctrine, op. cit.*, p. 132.

54. Stephen E. Robinson in an article titled " 'Expanded' Book of Mormon?" in *The Book of Mormon: Second Nephi, the Doctrinal Structure*, published by Brigham Young

University, Provo, Utah: Religious Studies Center 1989, p. 414.

55. *How Wide the* Divide, *op. cit.*, p. 105.

56. Richard Lloyd Anderson, "By the Gift and Power of God," *Ensign*, September 1977.

57. *An Insider's View of Mormon Origins, op. cit.*, pp. 3-4.

58. *The Book of Mormon and its Relationship with the Bible,* published by David J. Richards, 2017, p. 273.

59. B. H. Roberts, Studies of the Book of Mormon, op. cit., pp. 91-92.

60. Ibid., p. 46; B. H. Roberts to Heber Grant, *et al.*, 29 December 1921.

61. Lyle Campbell. 1997. *American Indian Languages: The Historical Linguistics of Native America.* Oxford University Press.; Ives Goddard. 1996. "Introduction," *Handbook of North American Indians, Volume 17, Languages.* Ed. Ives Goddard. Washington: Smithsonian Institution; Marianne Mithun. 1999. *The Languages of Native North America.* Cambridge University Press.

62. Terryl and Fiona Givens, *The Crucible of Doubt, op. cit.*, p. 7.

63. See Ronald W. Walker, "Seeking the 'Remnant': The Native American during the Joseph Smith Period," *Journal of Mormon History*, vol. 19, no. 1 Spring 1993, pp. 1-33.

64. *An Insider's View of Mormon Origins, op. cit.*, p. 57.

65. Rodney L. Meldrum, in an article in Book of Mormon Evidence .org under the heading "Hebrew Language/Culture in N. America at 8 Sites!" May 17, 2018.

66. *Joseph Smith: Rough Stone Rolling, op. cit.*, p. 92.

67. *Reflections on Mormonism: Judaeo-Christian Parallels, op. cit.*, pp. 90, & 94.

68. *Ibid.*, p. 152.

69. *Ibid.*, pp. 152-153.

70. *The Crucible of Doubt, op. cit.*, p. 25.

71. Edwin O. Haroldsen, "Good and Evil Spoken Of," *Ensign*, August 1995, p. 8.

72. Wesley P. Walters, *The Use of the Old Testament in the Book of Mormon*, 1990, p. 30; see also the strange use of words like "methought" as in *1 Nephi* 8:4.

73. *Answers: Straightforward Answers to Tough Gospel Questions, op. cit.*, pp. 204-205.

74. *The Story of the Latter-day Saints, op. cit.*, p. 40.

75. *A Comprehensive History of The Church of Jesus Christ of Latter-day Saints*, Century I, Vol. I, *op. cit.*, p. 133.

76. Mark Twain, *Roughing It*, Hartford, 1872, p. 107.

77. Mark Twain's review of the *Book of Mormon*, Chapter XVI of *Roughing It*.

78. *The Essential Nibley, op. cit.*, p. 145.

79. M. T. Lamb, *The Golden Bible: Or, The Book of Mormon. Is it from God?* Published by Ward and Drummund, New York 1887, p. 27.

80. *Ibid.*, pp. 38, 47, 48, 49, 51, 53, 54, & 57.

81. Bernard DeVoto, "The Centennial of Mormonism," *American Mercury*, 1930, p. 5.

82. Harold Bloom, *The American Religion: The Emergence of the Post-Christian Nation*, New York: Simon & Schuster, 1992, pp. 85, & 86.

83. Terryl L. Givens, *By the Hand of Mormon, op. cit.*, p. 12.

84. In a sermon titled "Our Manifesto" April 25, 1891.

85. *Joseph Smith: Rough Stone Rolling, op. cit.*, p. 84.

86. *An Insider's View of Mormonism, op. cit.*, p. 89.

87. Mormon Think, "Could Joseph Smith have written the Book of Mormon?" Search at www.mormonthink .com/ josephweb.htm#.

88. *Reflections on Mormonism: Judaeo-Christian Parallels*, *op. cit.*, pp. 147, & 148.

89. "Making Sense of the 'Lost' ending of Mark 16:9-20".

90. *A Textual Commentary on the Greek New Testament*, Stuttgart, 1971, pp. 122-126.

91. Richard Carrier Blogs, *Mark 16:9-20*, Wednesday, May 11, 2011.

92. "A Textual and Structural Analysis of Mark 16:9-20," in Filologia Newtestamentarea Vol. 17 *Biblical Studies on the Web* (2004) p. 27.

93. Quoted by Louis Midgly in "The Current Battle over the Book of Mormon: 'Is Modernity Itself Somehow Canonical?' " *Review of Books on the Book of Mormon 6*, No. 1 (1994); p. 204.

94. Terryl L. Givens, *By the Hand of Mormon, op. cit.*, p. 156.

95. *Ibid.*, p. 183.

96. Terryl and Fiona Givens, *The Crucible of Doubt, op. cit.*, p.140.

97. "Archaeological Trends and the Book of Mormon Origins"—*BYU Studies*.

Chapter 4:

1. George Albert Smith, *Conference Report*, p. 30, April, 1929.

2. Brigham Young, *Journal of Discourses*, 15:41, May 26, 1872.

3. *The Latter-day Saints: The Mormons Yesterday and Today*, Doubleday & Company, Inc., Garden City, New York, 1966, p. 18.

4. *Deseret News: Semi-Weekly*, October 2, 1883, p. 1.

5. Section 84:42.

6. Joseph Fielding Smith, *Selections from Answers to Gospel Questions*, Deseret News Press, Salt Lake City, Utah, 1972-73, pp. 48-49, 33, & 34.

7. The Great Apostasy, Deseret Book Company, Salt Lake City, Utah, 1968, Preface p. iiv; emphasis added.

8. Bruce R. McConkie, *A New Witness for the Articles of Faith*, Deseret Book Company, Salt Lake City, Utah, 1985, pp. 141-142.

9. *The Millennial Messiah, op. cit.*, p. 693.

10. *The Essential Nibley, op. cit.*, p. 215.

11. *Ibid.*, p. 215.

12. Article posted by Robert M. Bowman Jr. on IRR.org Institute for Religious Research, "The Great Apostasy: Did the Church Disappear?", March 14, 2012.

13. Craig L. Blomberg & Stephen E. Robinson, *How Wide the Divide?, op. cit.,* pp. 45, & 36.

14. Joseph Smith's Account of the First Vision, *The Joseph Smith Papers*, History, circa Summer 1832, p. 2.

15. *Selections from Answers to Gospel Questions, op. cit.*, p. 221.

16. *Answers to Gospel Questions* Vol. V, Deseret Book Company, Salt Lake City, Utah, 1975, p. 177.

17. *Deseret News*, January 6, 1858, p. 350; *Journal of Discourses*, Vol. VI, p. 137.

18. *Are Mormons Christians?*, Bookcraft, Salt Lake City, Utah, 1991, p. 34; italics in original.

19. *The Millennial Messiah, op. cit.*, p. 202.

20. *Mormon Doctrine, op. cit.*, p. 411.

21. *Improvement Era* 4:230.

22. *Are Mormons Christians?, op. cit.*, p. 35.

23. *Joseph Smith: Rough Stone Rolling, op. cit.*, p. 159.

24. *Doctrine and Covenants* 33:4; see also *2 Nephi* 26:29.

25. *Doctrine and Covenants* 60:8, 13.

26. *The Millennial Messiah, op. cit.*, p. 73.

27. *Documentary History of the Church*, Vol. V, p. 389.

28. Prophet Joseph Smith, The *Elder's Journal*, Joseph Smith, Jr., editor, Vol. I, No. 4, p. 60.

29. *Answers: Straightforward Answers to Tough Gospel Questions*, Deseret Book Company, Salt Lake City, Utah, 1998, pp. 57, & 58.

30. *Improvement Era* 21:639, April 6, 1918; italics in original.

31. *Teachings of Presidents of the Church, Spencer W. Kimball*, published by The Church of Jesus Christ of Latter-day Saints, 2006, p. 5; italics in original.

32. *Answers: Straightforward Answers to Tough Gospel Questions, op. cit.*, pp. 196-197, & 198.

33. *The Meaning of Truth*, Deseret Book Company, Salt Lake City, Utah, 1970, pp. 83, 124 & 131; Bruce R. McConkie, *The Millennial Messiah, op. cit.*, p. 112; Joseph Fielding Smith, *Answers to Gospel Questions, op. cit.*, Volume 1, p. 97.

34. *Mormon Doctrine, op. cit.*, pp. 269, & 525.

35. *A New Witness for the Articles of Faith*, Deseret Book Company, 1985, p. 55.

36. Hyrum M. Smith, *Conference Report*, October 1916, p. 43; emphasis added.

37. *Joseph Smith and the Restoration: A History of the LDS Church to 1846*, Young House: Brigham Young University Press, Provo, Utah, 1973, pp. 455, 462, & 464; the *Millennial Star*, 1:5.

38. *Teachings of Presidents of the Church: Joseph F. Smith*, Published by The Church of Jesus Christ of Latter-day Saints, Salt Lake City, Utah, 1998, p. 389.

39. Joseph F. Smith, *Conference Report*, p. 5, April 1915.

40. Neal A. Maxwell, *Things as They Really Are*, Salt Lake City, Deseret Book, 1978, p. 45; italics in original.

41. *Ibid.*, p. 46.

42. *The Millennial Messiah, op. cit.*, p. 262.

43. *Ibid.*, p. 164.

44. *Ibid.*, p. 162.

45. *Brigham Young: Pioneer Prophet*, The Belknap Press of Harvard University Press, Cambridge, Massachusetts, and London, England, 2012, p. 99.

46. Brigham Young, *Journal of Discourses*, Volume 8, p. 199.

47. Orson Pratt, *The Seer, op. cit.*, p. 255.

48. *The Mormon* Experience, *op. cit.*, pp. 23-24.

49. *1 Nephi* 14:1.

50. *Teachings of the Prophet Joseph Smith*, Compiled by Joseph Fielding Smith, Deseret Book Company, Salt Lake City, Utah, 1984, p. 345.

51. *Joseph Smith: Rough Stone Rolling, op. cit.*, p. 285.

52. *Teachings of the Prophet Joseph Smith, op. cit.*, p. 327.

53. *Ibid.*, p. 310.

54. *Ibid.*, p. 290.

55. *Isaiah 66:2 KJV.*

56. *Joseph Smith: Rough Stone Rolling, op. cit.*, pp. 99, & 100.

57. *The Mormon Experience, op. cit.*, p. 31.

58. *Joseph Smith: Rough Stone Rolling, op. cit.*, pp. 132-133.

59. *Ibid.*, p. 274.

60. *Ibid.*, pp. 387, 436, 458 & 527.

61. *Studies of the Book of Mormon, op. cit.*, p. xiv.

62. *Brigham Young: Pioneer Prophet, op. cit.*, pp. 23-24.

63. *Teachings of Presidents of the Church: Joseph F. Smith, op. cit.*, p. 204.

64. Godbodied The Matter of the Latter-Day Saints—reprint from his book *Jesus Christ, Eternal God: Heavenly Flesh and the Metaphysics of Matter*, Oxford University Press, 2012 *Brigham Young University Studies* 50 no. 3, 2011.

65. *The Doctrine and Covenants Speaks Vol. I*, Deseret Book Company, Salt Lake City, Utah, 1976, p. 8; *Documentary History of the Church*, Vol. II, p. 52.

66. *Joseph Smith: Rough Stone Rolling, op. cit.*, p. 108.

67. Benjamin E. Park, *Kingdom of* Nauvoo, *op. cit.*, p. 16.

68. Alex Beam, *American Crucifixion, op. cit.*, pp. 28, & 29.

69. *Brigham Young: Pioneer Prophet, op. cit.*, p. 104.

70. Leonard J. Arrington, *Brigham Young: American Moses*, Vintage Books, New York, 2012, pp. 204-205.

71. https://www.ligonier.org/learn/devotionals/denying-gods-transcendence/

72. *How Wide the Divide?, op. cit.*, p. 107; italics in original.

73. *Doctrines of Salvation, op. cit.*, pp. 14-25; italics in original; emphasis added.

74. *Conference Report*, October 1917, p. 3.

75. Henry David Thoreau's *Walden*, chapter 2 "Where I Lived and what I Lived for."

76. Fiona and Terryl Givens, *All Things New: Rethinking Sin, Salvation, and Everything in Between*, Faith Matters Publishing, Meridian, Idaho 2020, p. 63.

77. *The Kingdom of God Restored*, Deseret Book Company, Salt Lake City, Utah, second edition 1957, p. 97; emphasis added.

78. *Joseph Smith: Rough Stone Rolling, op. cit.*, p. 122.

79. *Life of Heber C. Kimball*, Orson F. Whitney, 1888 edition, pp. 332-333; emphasis added.

80. Mark E. Petersen, *For Righteousness Sake*, Bookcraft, Salt Lake City, Utah, 1972, p. 101.

81. *2 Timothy 4:3-4 KJV*; emphasis added.

82. *For Righteousness Sake, op. cit.*, p. 76.

83. *Your Faith and You*, Bookcraft, Salt Lake City, Utah, 1953, p. 40.

84. Benjamin F. Johnson, *My Life's Review*, Zion's Press, Independence, Missouri, 1947, p. 96.

85. Remarks made in the Bowery, Great Salt Lake City, August 26, 1860.

86. The *Nephi L. Morris Papers*.

87. *Deseret News*, June 8, 1935.

88. Jana Riess, "Mormon Apostle Criticized for Anti-Catholic Remarks," *Religion News Service (RNS)*, October 23, 2015.

89. *Ibid.*

90. *Presbyterian Banner*, February 12, 1879.

91. B. H. Roberts, *Life of John Taylor*, Bookcraft, Salt Lake City, Utah, 1963, pp. 40-44.

92. Prophet Brigham Young, *Journal of Discourses*, 8:171.

93. *Teachings of Presidents of the Church: Wilford Woodruff*, published by The Church of Jesus Christ of Latter-day Saints, 2004, p. 10.

94. *Journal of Discourses*, 12:205; *Discourses of Brigham Young*, 1941 edition, edited by John A. Widtsoe, p. 4.

95. *Journal of Discourses*, 12:313; *Discourses of Brigham Young, op. cit.*, p. 5; italics added.

96. In *Conference Report*, April 1880, pp. 84-85.

97. Wilford Woodruff, *Millennial Star* 52:162, February 11, 1890.

98. *Doctrine and Covenants* 1:30.

99. *The Millennial Messiah, op. cit.*, p. 126.

100. Melvin J. Ballard, *Conference Report*, October 1938, pp. 106-107.

101. *The Doctrine and Covenants Speaks Vol. 1, op. cit.*, p. 208.

102. *John 1:12 KJV.*

103. *The Millennial Messiah, op. cit.*, p. 334.

104. *1 Timothy 2:5 KJV.*

105. *Acts 4:12 KJV.*

106. "The Great Apostasy: Did the Church Disappear?", *op. cit.*

107. John MacArthur, *The Truth War, op. cit.*, pp. 160, & 163.

108. *The Doctrine and Covenants Speaks Vol. 1, op. cit.*, p. 208.

109. *Ibid.*, p. 78.

110. *Answers to Gospel Questions Vol. V, op. cit.*, p. 179.

111. *The Journal of Joseph, The Personal Diary of a Modern Prophet by Joseph Smith, Jr.* compiled by Leland R. Nelson, Council Press, Provo, Utah, 1979, p. 110.

112. *Answers: Straightforward Answers to Tough Gospel Questions, op. cit.*, p. 140.

113. *The Essential Nibley, op. cit.*, p. 211.

114. *Gospel Doctrine*, 5th ed., 1939, *op. cit.*, pp. 43-44; emphasis added.

115. Patrick Q. Mason, "God and the People Reconsidered: Further Reflections on Theodemocracy in Early Mormonism," BYU Religious Studies Center, *The Council of Fifty*, p. 37.

116. *Doctrines of Salvation: Sermons and Writings of Joseph Fielding Smith Vol. II, op. cit.*, pp. 14, 15, & 25; italics in original.

117. *Teachings of the Prophet Joseph Smith, op. cit.*, p. 119.

118. *Doctrines of Salvation*, Volume 2, *op. cit.*, p. 138.

119. *Selections from Answers to Gospel Questions, op. cit.*, p. 317.

120. *Mormonism Unveiled*, New York: O. Pratt and Fordham, 1838, p. 15.

121. *The Doctrine and Covenants Speaks Vol. I, op. cit.*, p. 111.

122. *Journal of Discourses*, 22:335.

123. *History of the Church*, Volume VII, 1932, *op. cit.*, p. 287.

124. *The Millennial Messiah, op. cit.*, p. 147.

125. *Ibid.*, p. 146.

126. *Ibid.*, p. 144.

127. *Ibid.*, p. 162.

128. *Ibid.*, p. 166.

129. *Ibid.*, pp. 176-177.

130. *Ibid.*, p. 194.

131. *Documentary History of the Church*, Vol. V, p. 257.

132. Bruce R. McConkie, "The Caravan Moves On," *Ensign* (Conference Edition), November 1984, p. 82.

133. *Answers: Straightforward Answers to Tough Gospel Questions, op. cit.*, pp. 138, & 139.

134. *Ibid.*, p. 199.

135. *Documentary History of the Church*, Vol. I, p. 105.

136. James E. Talmage, *Conference Report* 1913, p. 118.

137. Wayne Jackson, in an article published in the *Christian Courier* titled "Did Jesus Christ Exist in the Form of God on Earth?"

138. In an article posted in *Faith Matters*, "The Only True and Living Church?" by Philip Barlow, April 12, 2020; italics in original.

Chapter 5:

1. Joseph Smith to James Arlington Barnet, Nov. 13, 1843, in Joseph Smith *et al. History of the Church of Jesus Christ of Latter-day Saints*, ed. B. H. Roberts 2nd ed. rev., 7 Vols., Salt Lake City, Utah: Deseret Book, 1963, 6:78.

2. *The Story of the Latter-day Saints*, Deseret Book Company, Salt Lake City, Utah, 1986, pp. 65-66.

3. *Ibid.*, p. 5.

4. *Gospel Doctrine*, 5th ed. 1939, *op. cit.*, p. 38.

5. *The Doctrine and Covenants Speaks Vol. I, op. cit.*, p. 534.

6. *Teachings of Presidents of the Church: George Albert Smith*, published by The Church of Jesus Christ of Latter-day Saints, 2011, pp. 51, & 52.

7. *George Albert Smith, Conference Report*, p. 28, April 1934.

8. Jeffrey R. Holland, "Our Most Distinguishing Feature," *Ensign*, May 2005, p. 43.

9. *Ibid.*, p. 364.

10. *Teachings of the Prophet Joseph Smith, op. cit.*, p. 364.

11. *Teachings of Presidents of the Church: Wilford Woodruff, op. cit.*, pp. 38, 39 & 42.

12. Joseph Fielding Smith, *Conference Report*, April 1967, pp. 97-98.

13. *Teachings of Presidents of the Church: Joseph F. Smith, op. cit.*, p. 297.

14. *Documentary History of the Church*, Vol. V, p. 424.

15. *The Story of the Latter-day Saints, op. cit.*, p. 45.

16. *A Comprehensive History of the Church of Jesus Christ of Latter-day Saints*, Volume 2, *op. cit.*, p. 361.

17. *The Mormon Experience, op. cit.*, p. 28.

18. *The Mediation and the Atonement*, published in 1892, p. 157.

19. "The Great Apostasy: Did the Church Disappear?", *op. cit.*

20. *Doctrine and Covenants* 115:5.

21. "The Certain Sounds," *Church News*, October 9, 1983, p. 24.

22. *Blood of the Prophets, op. cit.*, p. 13; italics in original.

23. *The Biblical Roots of Mormonism, op. cit.*, p. 111.

24. *Brigham Young: Pioneer Prophet, op. cit.*, p. 235.

25. *The Millennial Messiah, op. cit.*, p. 294.

26. *Ibid.*, p. 595.

27. *How Wide the Divide?, op. cit.*, p. 57.

28. *Answers: Straightforward Answers to Tough Gospel Questions, op. cit.*, p. 214; italics in original.

29. *Ibid.*, p. 11.

30. Joseph Fielding McConkie, *Prophets & Prophecy*, Bookcraft, Salt Lake City, Utah 1988, pp. 16, & 17.

31. *Joseph Smith: Rough Stone Rolling, op. cit.*, pp. 129, & 121.

32. *Teachings of the Prophet Joseph Smith, op. cit.*, p. 274; *Documentary History of the Church*, Vol. V, p. 258.

33. *Selections from Answers to Gospel Questions, op. cit.*, Appendix p. 45.

34. *Answers to Gospel Questions* Volume I, Deseret Book Company, Salt Lake City, Utah, eighth printing 1966, p. 97.

35. *A Sure Foundation, Answers to Difficult Gospel Questions*, Deseret Book Company, Salt Lake City, Utah, 1988, p. 215.

36. *Ibid.*, p. 216; italics added.

37. *Doctrinal New Testament Commentary*, 3 Volumes, Bookcraft, Salt Lake City, Utah, 1965-73, 1:133.

38. *Essentials in Church History, op. cit.*, p. 335.

39. See *Doctrine and Covenants* 130:6–9.

40. Orson F. Whitney, *Conference Report*, October 5, 1925, p. 105; emphasis added.

41. *Conference Reports of the General Conference of the Church of Jesus Christ of Latter-day Saints*, October 1916, p. 55.

42. Quote and reference found in *Are Mormons Christians?, op. cit.*, Notes #19, p. 117.

43. *Ibid.*, p. 17.

44. Wilford Woodruff, in *Conference Report*, October 1897, p. 23.

45. *The Biblical Roots of Mormonism, op. cit.*, p. 101; italics in original; emphasis added.

46. *Teachings of Presidents of the Church: Joseph F. Smith, op. cit.*, p. 138.

47. *The Biblical Roots of Mormonism, op. cit.*, pp. 135-136.

48. The Mormon Olympians website, "Priesthood in Mormonism."

49. *Mormon Doctrine, op. cit.*, p. 594.

50. *Ibid.*, p. 499.

51. *Teachings of Presidents of the Church: Joseph F. Smith, op. cit.*, p. 139.

52. *The Complete Idiot's Guide to Understanding Mormonism, op. cit.*, p. 179.

53. *Ibid.*, p. 178.

54. *Teachings of Presidents of the Church: George Albert Smith, op. cit.*, p. 115.

55. *Deseret News: Semi-Weekly*, December 2, 1879, p. 1.

56. *Teachings of the Prophet Joseph Smith, op. cit.*, p. 375.

57. *Ibid.*, p. 311.

58. *Ibid.*, p. 305.

59. *Selections from Answers to Gospel Questions, op. cit.*, p. 191; *Doctrine and Covenants* 68: 1-5.

60. *Reflections on Mormonism: Judeo-Christian Parallels, op. cit.*, p. xv *Introductory Essay*.

61. *History of the Church of Jesus Christ of Latter-day Saints, op. cit.*, pp. 256-259.

62. *The Millennial Messiah, op. cit.*, p. 123.

63. *Selections from Answers to Gospel Questions, op. cit.*, Appendix p. 20.

64. *Essentials in Church History*, Deseret News Press, Salt Lake City, Utah, 1953, p. 144.

65. *Ibid.*, p. 133; *Isaiah 2:1 KJV.*

66. *Brigham Young: Pioneer Prophet, op. cit.*, p. 87.

67. *Joseph Smith: Rough Stone Rolling, op. cit.*, Preface, p. xxi; italics in original.

68. "Three Levels of Heaven?" Article ID: JAM523 by: James R. White.

Chapter 6:

1. Lowell L. Bennion, *An Introduction to the Gospel*, The Utah Printing Company, Salt Lake City, Utah, 1959, p. 111.

2. Heber J. Grant, *Conference Report* April 1929, p. 129.

3. Eric Shuster and Charles Sale, *The Biblical Roots of Mormonism, op. cit.*, p. 127.

4. Boyd K. Packer, *The Holy Temple*, Bookcraft, Salt Lake City, Utah, 3rd printing 1981, pp. 83-84.

5. *Church News*, "From Copenhagen to Carrara to Rome: The Modern-day Travels of Ancient-Apostle Statues," January 17, 2019.

6. *The Millennial Messiah, op. cit.*, p. 322.

7. *LDS Living*, "5 Things You Never Knew About the *Christus* Statue" adapted from "The *Christus* Legacy," by Matthew O. Richardson, January 19, 2019.

8. *Deception by Design: The Mormon Story*, WestBow Press, 2011, p. 143.

9. *Documentary History of the Church*, Vol. IV, p. 572.

10. *Teachings of the Prophet Joseph Smith, op. cit.*, p. 292.

11. *Ibid.*, pp. 365, & 366; *Documentary History of the Church*, Vol. VI, p. 78.

12. As related by Wilford Woodruff, *Conference Report* 1898, p. 89.

13. *Documentary History of the Church*, Vol. VI, pp. 478-479.

14. Related by Lorenzo Brown in 1880, "Sayings of Joseph, by Those Who Heard Him at Different Times," *Joseph Smith,*

Jr., Papers, Salt Lake City, Utah: Church Historical Library, Manuscript Section.

15. *Documentary History of the Church*, Vol. V, p. 139.

16. *Ibid.*, p. 362.

17. *Essentials in Church History, op. cit.*, p. 360; *Documentary History of the Church*, Vol. VI, p. 58.

18. Joseph Smith's "Sermon on Plurality of Gods" as printed in *Documentary History of the Church*, Vol. VI, pp. 473-479.

19. *Documentary History of the Church*, Vol. V, pp. 139-140.

20. *Teachings of the Prophet Joseph Smith, op. cit.*, p. 350; taken from the *King Follett Discourse*.

21. *Documentary History of the Church*, Vol. VI, pp. 308-309, April 7, 1844; taken from the *King Follett Discourse*.

22. *Documentary History of the Church*, Vol. V, p. 401.

23. *Documentary History of the Church*, Vol. VI, pp. 305-306.

24. *Ibid.*, p. 368; *Documentary History of the Church*, Vol. VI, pp. 366-67.

25. *Documentary History of the Church*, Vol. IV, p. 445.

26. *Documentary History of the Church*, Vol. V, p. 21.

27. *Improvement Era*, Volume 12, p. 187; taken from the *King Follett Discourse*.

28. Joseph Smith quoted by Wilford Woodruff in a *Conference Report*, p. 57, April 8, 1898.

29. *Teachings of the Prophet Joseph Smith, op. cit.*, p. 279.

30. *Ibid.*, p. 339.

31. Joseph Smith, Jr., Journal, May 26, 1844, in *An American Prophet's Record: The Diaries and Journals of Joseph Smith*. Edited by Scott H. Faulring, Salt Lake City, Utah: Signature Books in association with Smith Research Associates, 1989, p. 484.

32. *Ibid.*, p. 361; *Documentary History of the Church*, Vol. VI, p. 317.

33. *Documentary History of the Church*, Vol. VI, p. 366.

34. *Ibid.*, pp. 273-274.

35. *History of the Church*, 5:554, from a discourse given by Joseph Smith on August 27, 1843 in Nauvoo, Illinois; reported by Willard Richards and William Clayton.

36. *Documentary History of the Church,* Vol. VI, pp. 72, & 78.

37. Josiah Quincy, *Figures of the Past: From the Leaves of Old Journals* (Class of 1821, Harvard College), Boston: Roberts Brothers, 1883, p. 397.

38. *History of the Church*, 6:364-65; May 12, 1844.

39. *History of the Church*, 4:445, November 7, 1841.

40. Lucy Mack Smith, "The History of Lucy Smith, Mother of the Prophet," 1844-45 manuscript, book 13, p. 5, Church Archives.

41. George Q. Cannon, *Life of Joseph Smith the Prophet*, The Deseret News, Salt Lake City, Utah 1907, p. 432.

42. *American Massacre, op. cit.*, p. 13.

43. *Joseph Smith: Rough Stone Rolling, op. cit.*, p. 173.

44. *Ibid.*, p. 553.

45. *Selections from Answers to Gospel Questions, op. cit.*, p. 297.

46. *Gospel Doctrine*, 5th edition 1939, *op. cit.*, p. 373; *Juvenile Instructor* Vol. 41, March 1986, p. 178.

47. *Journal of Discourses*, 24:268, June 24, 1833.

48. Quote is from "What Does It Mean to Have a Testimony?" *Improvement Era*, May 1945, p. 280.

49. *Selections from Answers to Gospel Questions, op. cit.*, p. 188.

50. *Hearken, O Ye People: Discourses on the Doctrine and Covenants*, Sperry Symposium 1984, Randall Book Co., Sandy, Utah, p. 3.

51. *Answers: Straightforward Answers to Tough Gospel Questions, op. cit.*, p. 43.

52. *Ibid.*, p. 53.

53. *Ibid.*, pp. 56, & 57.

54. *Ibid.*, p. 203.

55. Widtsoe, *Discourses of Brigham Young*, Edition 1925, pp. 165, 700, 703, & 705.

56. Brigham Young, *Journal of Discourses*, 15:138-139, August 24, 1872.

57. *The Key to Theology*, 1938 edition, pp. 80-82.

58. *Deseret Weekly*, August 30, 1890, p. 306.

59. *Gospel Doctrine*, 5th ed., 1939, *op. cit.*, p. 484.

60. Text: William W. Phelps; first published in *Times and Seasons* in August 1844 just one month after Joseph Smith was martyred.

61. *A Comprehensive History of the Church of Jesus Christ of Latter-day Saints*, Volume 1, *op. cit.*, pp. 344, 351, & 355.

62. B. H. Roberts, "Joseph Smith: An Appreciation," *Improvement Era*, 36, Dec. 1932, p. 81.

Chapter 7:

1. Carter E. Grant, *The Kingdom of God Restored*, Deseret Book Company, Salt Lake City, Utah, 1957, p. 328.

2. Drew Williams, *The Complete Idiot's Guide to Understanding Mormonism, op. cit.*, p. 102.

3. *The Pearl of Great Price, Joseph Smith* 2:18-20.

4. *A Sure Foundation: Answers to Difficult Gospel Questions*, Deseret Book Company, Salt Lake City, Utah, 1988, p. 212.

5. Terryl and Fiona Givens, *The Crucible of Doubt, op. cit.*, p. 85.

6. *The Restored Church*, Deseret Book, Salt Lake City, Utah, 1973, p. 180.

7. *The Story of the Latter-day Saints, op. cit.*, p. 71.

8. *The Mormon Hierarchy: Origins of Power*, Signature Books, Salt Lake City, Utah, 1994, p. 80.

9. *Ibid.*, p. 91.

10. *What of the Mormons? Including A Short History of The Church of Jesus Christ of Latter-day Saints*, published by the Church of Jesus Christ of Latter-day Saints, 1954, p. 102.

11. *American Massacre, op. cit.*, p. 12.

12. *Ibid.*, p. 15.

13. *Ibid.*, p. 16; see also Hallwas and Launius, *Cultures in Conflict*, p. 139.

14. *Ibid.*, p. 60.

15. *Doctrines of Salvation* Vol. III, Bookcraft, Salt Lake City, Utah, 1956, p. 287.

16. *A Comprehensive History of The Church of Jesus Christ of Latter-day Saints*, Century I, Vol. 1, *op. cit.*, pp. 322-323.

17. *The Mormon Experience, op. cit.*, p. 55.

18. *This is My Doctrine: The Development of Mormon Theology, op. cit.*, p. 503.

19. *Doctrine and Covenants Commentary*, p. 359.

20. "Celebration of July Fourth," *Deseret News*, July 9, 1856, 140/3.

21. *Joseph Smith: Rough Stone Rolling, op. cit.*, p. 379.

22. *Doctrines of Salvation* Vol. III, *op. cit.*, p. 268; italics in original.

23. *Ibid.*, p. 283.

24. *Ibid.*, p. 188.

25. *Doctrines of Salvation*, Vol. II, Bookcraft, Salt Lake City, Utah, 1955, pp. 303, & 311.

26. *Doctrines of Salvation*, Vol. III, *op. cit.*, p. 300.

27. *Ibid.*, p. 255.

28. Gerrit de Jong, Jr., *Greater Dividends from Religion: A Discussion of the Practicality of some Religious Teachings of a Peculiar People,* Deseret Book Company, Salt Lake City, Utah, 1950, p. 97.

29. *Teachings of the Prophet Joseph Smith, op. cit.,* p. 139.

30. *Gospel Standards: Selections from the Sermons and Writings of Heber J. Grant,* Deseret Book Company, Salt Lake City, Utah, 1976, pp. 3, & 24.

31. *The Doctrine and the Covenants Speaks Vol. I, op. cit.,* p. 155.

32. *The Millennial Messiah, op. cit.,* pp. 594-595.

33. *Mormon Doctrine, op. cit.,* p. 811.

34. *Teachings of Presidents of the Church: George Albert Smith, op. cit.,* p. 3.

35. *A Comprehensive History of The Church of Jesus Christ of Latter-day Saints,* Century I, Vol. I, *op. cit.,* p. 393.

36. *The Doctrine and Covenants Speaks Vol. I, op. cit.,* p. 98.

37. *For Righteousness Sake, op. cit.,* pp. 131, & 148.

38. *Deseret News,* September 26, 1860, p. 234.

39. *Teachings of Ezra Taft Benson,* pp. 164-165.

40. "Absolute Truth," *Ensign,* September 1978, p. 8; italics in original.

41. Ronald Barney, citing the report of a long-time colleague in Public Affairs, private correspondence to Philip Barlow; see the article in *Faith Matters,* "The Only True and Living Church?" by Philip Barlow, April 12, 2020.

42. Carl Moser, Francis J. Beckwith, and Paul Owen, *New Mormon Challenge: Responding to the Latest Defenses of a Fast-Growing Movement,* HarperCollins, New York, NY, 2002, p. 75.

43. *Ibid.*, p. 66.

44. Benjamin E. Park, "Build, Therefore, Your Own World": Ralph Waldo Emerson, Joseph Smith, and American Antebellum Thought, p. 60.

45. *Hearken, O Ye People, op. cit.*, p. 246; emphasis added.

46. *The Story of the Latter-day Saints, op. cit.*, pp. 167, & 168.

47. *The Mormon Experience, op. cit.*, pp. 66, & 36.

48. *Greater Dividends from Religion, op. cit.*, p. 38.

49. *The Mormon Experience, op. cit.*, p. 46.

50. *Teachings of the Prophet Joseph Smith, op. cit.*, p. 112.

51. *Ibid.*, p. 320.

52. *Documentary History of the Church*, Vol. V, p. 402, May 21, 1843.

Chapter 8:

1. Bruce R. McConkie, *Mormon Doctrine*, Salt Lake City, Utah, Bookcraft, 1966, pp. 43, & 44.

2. Hugh Nibley, "The Passing of the Church." *When the Lights Went Out: Three Studies on the Ancient Apostasy*, Salt Lake City: Deseret Book Co. 1970, p. 13.

3. *New Mormon Challenge, op. cit.*, p. 57.

4. "The Great Apostasy: Did the Church Disappear?", *op. cit.*; italics in original.

5. *Matthew 28:19-20 KJV*; emphasis added.

6. *Apologeticus*, Chapter 50.

7. *Documentary History of the Church, op. cit.*, 5:212.

8. *Times and Seasons* 5:744.

9. *Ibid.*, 5:744.

10. John MacArthur, *The Truth War, op. cit.*, p. 49.

11. Charles Spurgeon, *The Metropolitan Tabernacle Pulpit*, vol. 5, London: Passmore & Alabaster, 1879, p. 41.

12. *The Journal of Joseph*, compiled by Leland R. Nelson, *op. cit.*, p. 170.

13. *Joseph Smith: Rough Stone Rolling, op. cit.*, p. 156.

14. *Ibid.*, pp. 156-157.

15. *Deseret News: Semi Weekly*, March 31, 1868, p. 2.

16. John MacArthur, *Hard to Believe*, Thomas Nelson, Nashville, Tennessee, 2003, pp. 22-23.

17. The Spurgeon Archives, The New Park Street Pulpit, "Christ Lifted Up," A Sermon No. 139—Delivered on Sabbath Morning, July 5, 1857 at the Music Hall, Royal Surrey Gardens.

18. *Pulpit Commentary Homiletics* "A Great Work Needs Great Help" 1 Chronicles 12:22.

19. "Christ Our Peace" (No. 3386) A Sermon published on Thursday, December 25, 1913 at the Metropolitan Tabernacle, "On the Lord's-Day Evening," January 19, 1868.

20. John MacArthur, *The Truth War, op. cit.*, p. 50; italics in original.

21. Alexander B. Morrison, *Turning from Truth: A New Look at the Great Apostasy*, Salt Lake City, Deseret Book 2005, p. 2.

22. *Ellicot's Commentary for English Readers* (*Luke 10:19*).

23. Brigham Young to Charles S. Kimball, 31 December 1864, Letterbook 7:414-16.

24. Charles R. Harrell, *This Is My Doctrine: The Development of Mormon Theology,* Greg Kofford Books, Salt Lake City, Utah 2011, Ch. 2.

25. Tomas D. Ice, in an article published in Liberty University's *Scholar's Crossing*, May 2009, titled: "The Rapture in 2 Thessalonians 2:3."

26. H. Wayne House, "Apostasia in 2 Thessalonians 2:3: Apostasy or Rapture?" in Thomas Ice and Timothy Demy, eds., When the Trumpet Sounds: Today's Foremost

Authorities Speak Out on End-Time Controversies (Eugene, OR: Harvest House, 1995), pp. 275-76.

27. Daniel K. Davey, "The 'Apostasia' of II Thessalonians 2:3," Th.M. thesis, Detroit Baptist Theological Seminary, May 1982, p. 27.

28. *Ibid.*, p. 47.

29. Kenneth S. Wuest, *Prophetic Light in the Present Darkness*, Grand Rapids: Eerdmans 1956, p. 40.

30. Wuest, "The Rapture—Precisely When?" *Midnight Call*, October 2005, p. 6.

31. *The Popular Handbook on the Rapture: Experts Speak Out on End-Times Prophecy*, General Editors: Tim LaHaye, Thomas Ice, and Ed Hindson, Harvest House 2011, p. 160.

32. See *Blue Letter Bible* under "Chuck Smith: Verse by Verse Study" on *2 Thessalonians* (c2000).

33. Chuck Smith, *The Final Curtain*, Harvest House 1991, Eugene Oregon.

34. Back to Basics with Brian Brodersen Devotional—Falling Away, March 2, 2020.

35. In an article published in *Faith Pulpit* titled "The Rapture: A Hope or a Hoax?" April 1986, Faith Baptist Theological Seminary.

Chapter 9:

1. John Greenleaf Whittier, *Howitt's Journal*, as quoted in *Millennial Star*, X (October 1, 1848), pp. 302-303.

2. Jon Krakauer, *Under the Banner of Heaven*, Anchor Books, New York, 2003, p. 55.

3. Josiah Quincy, *Figures of the Past from the Leaves of Old Journals,* 3rd edition, Boston, 1883, p. 381.

4. *Doctrines of Salvation* Vol. III, *op. cit.*, p. 212.

5. *Joseph Smith and the Restoration*, *op. cit.*, p. 54.

6. Paul C. Gutjahr, *The Book of Mormon: A Biography*, Princeton University Press, Princeton and Oxford 2012, p. 61.

7. *Documentary History of the Church*, VI, pp. 477-478.

8. *History of the Church*, 4:425-26.

9. *Hearken, O Ye People, op. cit.* p. 153.

10. Robert L. Millet and Joseph Fielding McConkie, *The Life Beyond*, Bookcraft, Salt Lake City, Utah, 1986, p. 30.

11. *Teachings of the Prophet Joseph Smith, op. cit.*, p. 270.

12. *Mormon Doctrine, op. cit.*, pp. 246, & 554.

13. Devotional Address titled "Our Relationship with the Lord," delivered at Brigham Young University, Provo, Utah, on March 2, 1982; see also Bill McKeever and Eric Johnson, *Mormonism 101,* Baker books, Ada, MI, 2000, p. 24.

14. *The Millennial Messiah, op. cit.*, p. 706.

15. *Ibid.*

16. *Ibid.*

17. Stephen R. Covey, *The Divine Center: Why We Need a Life Centered on God and Christ and How We Attain It*, published by Bookcraft in Salt Lake City, Utah, 1982; also published by Deseret Book Company, Salt Lake City, 2004, pp. 67-68, & 83.

18. *The Complete Idiot's Guide to Understanding Mormonism, op. cit.* p. 15.

19. *Demonstratio Evangelica*, 5.1.20; 4.3.7.

20. *How Wide the Divide?, op. cit.*, p. 117; italics in original.

21. *Ibid.*, pp. 117-118.

22. *Ibid.*, p. 121.

23. *The Millennial Messiah, op. cit.*, p. 679; italics added.

24. "The Bible, a Sealed Book," in *Teaching Seminary: Preservice Readings*, Church Educational System manual, 2004, p. 127; emphasis added.

25. *The Millennial Messiah, op. cit.*, p. 685.

26. Bruce R. McConkie, "The Mystery of Mormonism," italics added.

27. *Journal of Discourses*, 15:364; italics added.

28. *Mormon Claims Answered, op. cit.*, p. 26.

29. "The Song of Solomon" by Harry Reeder, *Tabletalk Magazine*, February 1st, 2007.

30. *Teachings of the Prophet Joseph* Smith, *op. cit.*, p. 267.

31. *A Joseph Smith Chronology*, by J. Christopher Conkling, Deseret Book Company, Salt Lake City, Utah, 1979, p. 204; italics in original.

32. Joseph Smith, Jr., *Times and Seasons*, October 1, 1842, Vol. 3, No. 23, p. 927.

33. *The Mountain Meadows Massacre*, University of Oklahoma Press, 1950, p. xxvi.

34. *Journal of Discourses*, 18:117.

35. J. Reuben Clark, as recorded by D. Michael Quinn, *J. Reuben Clark: The Church Years*, Provo, Utah: Brigham Young University Press, 1983, p. 24.

36. John Stuart Mill, *On Liberty*, ed. Currin V. Shields, Indianapolis: Bobbs-Merrill Co., Inc., 1956, p. 21.

37. *The Seer*, 1853, p. 15.

38. *Journal of Discourses*, Vol. 13, p. 271.

39. *Deseret News: Semi-Weekly*, July 6, 1880, p. 1.

40. *History of the Church* 2:460; *Messenger and Advocate*, August 1836, p. 368.

41. *Teachings of the Prophet Joseph Smith, op. cit.*, p. 327.

42. *Documentary History of the Church*, Vol. III, p. 385; italics in original.

43. *The Millennial Messiah, op. cit.*, pp. 271, & 272.

Chapter 10:

1. Brigham Young, *Journal of Discourses*, Volume 7, p. 139.

2. Joseph F. Smith, *Juvenile Instructor* 41:178.

3. Gordon B. Hinckley in *Conference Report*, October 1998, pp. 90-91.

4. "Unknown God," *A Scrapbook of Mormon Literature* published by Ben E. Rich (a spokesman for the LDS Church in the early 20th-century) 1911, p. 536; *The Millennial Messiah, op. cit.*, p. 430.

5. coldcasechristianity.com; italics in original.

6. Charles Colson, *Against the Night: Living in the New Dark Ages*, Servant Publications, Ann Arbor Michigan 1999, pp. 153-154.

7. *A Joseph Smith Chronology, op. cit.*, p. 178.

8. *Ibid.*, p. 180.

9. *Answers: Straightforward Answers to Tough Gospel Questions, op. cit.*, p. 217.

10. *Are Mormons Christians?, op. cit.*, pp. 73 & 38; italics in original.

11. *Joseph Smith: Rough Stone Rolling, op. cit.*, p. 172.

12. *What Do Mormons Believe, op. cit.*, p. 83.

13. Rev. Martin VanderWal in an article titled "The H-Word (2)" in *Not All Pious and Ecclesiastical*, May 29, 2020, pp. 67-69.

14. *For Us and for Our Salvation: The Doctrine of Christ in the Early Church*, Crossway; Wheaton, Illinois, 2007, p. 20.

15. *Are Mormons Christian?, op. cit.*, p. 60.

16. *Ibid.*, p. 70.

17. *Joseph Smith: Rough Stone Rolling, op. cit.,* p. 153.

18. *The Essential Nibley, op. cit.,* p. 31.

19. https://rsc.byu.edu/archived/let-us-reason-together/mormonism-and-heresies.

20. Dale Williams, *The Complete Idiot's Guide to Understanding Mormonism, op. cit.,* pp. 1, & 11.

21. *If Thou Endure It Well,* Bookcraft, Salt Lake City, Utah, 4th printing, 1999, p. 79.

22. The *Palmyra Reflector,* January 6, 1831; see also Francis W. Kirkham, LL.B., PH.D., *A New Witness For Christ in America; The Book of Mormon,* 1959, p. 285; italics in original.

23. *Joseph Smith: Rough Stone Rolling, op. cit.,* p. 171.

24. "In The Name of the Prophet—Smith," published in *Household Words: A Weekly Journal Conducted By Charles Dickens* No. 69, Saturday, July 19, 1851, Vol. III, p. 385.

25. Richard J. Dunn, "Dickens and the Mormons," *BYU Studies,* copyright 1968.

26. Leland A. Fetzer "Tolstoy and Mormonism," Brigham Young University Studies, Vol. VI, No. 1, Spring 1971, p. 21.

27. *Heresy Hunters: Character Assassination in the Church,* Huntington House Publishers, Lafayette, Louisiana, 1993, p. 50.

28. https://rsc.byu.edu/archived/let-us-reason-together/mormonism-and-heresies.

29. *Barnes' Notes on the Bible, 1 Timothy 1:4.*

30. *New Mormon Challenge, op. cit.,* pp. 67, & 68.

31. *Joseph Smith: Rough Stone Rolling, op. cit.,* p. 113.

32. *Brigham Young: Pioneer Prophet, op. cit.,* p. 233.

33. Benjamin Franklin Morris, *The Home Missionary and Pastor's Journal*, Volumes 13-14, p. 150.

34. *Mormon America: The Power and the Promise*, published by HarperSanFrancisco, 1999, p. 218.

35. *The Mormon Experience, op. cit.*, p. 29.

36. *Eyewitness Accounts of the Restoration*, Deseret Book Company, Salt Lake City, Utah, 1986, p. 134.

37. "The Mormons" published in *The Atlantic*, February 1900 issue.

38. *Teachings of the Prophet Joseph Smith, op. cit.*, p. 203.

39. *Documentary History of the Church*, Vol. VI, pp. 313-314, April 7, 1844; See also *Ibid.*, p. 304.

40. *Ibid.*, p. 205.

41. *Millennial Star* 19:197, November 2, 1856.

42. *Doctrine and Covenants* 50:3-4.

43. *Journal of Discourses*, 11:7.

44. *Joseph Smith and the Restoration, op. cit.*, pp. 171, & 341.

45. *The Refiner's Fire*, Deseret Book Company, Salt Lake City, Utah, 1980, p. 293.

46. *The Journal of Joseph*, compiled by Leland R. Nelson, *op. cit.*, p. 99.

47. *Ibid.*, p. 119.

48. *Ibid.*, p. 219.

49. *Documentary History of the Church*, Vol. III, pp. 391-392, and Vol. IV, p. 581 in a sermon delivered on April 1, 1842; also found in *Teachings of the Prophet Joseph Smith, op. cit.*, p. 214.

50. *Ibid.*, p. 213.

51. *Teachings of the Prophet Joseph Smith, op. cit.*, p. 238.

52. *A Brief History of the Church of Christ of Latter Day Saints*, Manuscript circa 1838-1839, p. 16.

53. *Ibid.*, pp. 17-18.

54. *Joseph Smith: Rough Stone Rolling, op. cit.*, p. 151.

55. "A Warning Voice," *Improvement Era*, Volume 16, September 1913, p. 1148.

56. In *Messages of the First Presidency*, 4:285.

57. *The Doctrine and Covenants Speaks Vol. I, op. cit.*, p. 365.

58. *Ibid.*, pp. 365- 368; *Conference Report*, April 1946, pp. 119-121.

59. *Teachings of the Prophet Joseph Smith, op. cit.*, p. 130.

60. "Reading Church History," speech delivered at the Ninth Annual Church Educators' Symposium at BYU, Provo, Utah on August 16, 1985.

61. *Gospel Doctrine*, 5th ed., 1939, *op. cit.*, pp. 376-377.

62. *Improvement Era* 45:761.

63. *Documentary History of the Church*, Vol. III, p. 392.

64. *Reflections on Mormonism: Judaeo-Christian Parallels, op. cit.*, p. 41.

65. *Teachings of Presidents of the Church, Spencer W. Kimball, op. cit.*, pp. 104-105.

66. *Deseret Weekly*, November 7, 1896, p. 643.

67. Brigham Young, *Journal of Discourses*, 3:43-44, October 6, 1855.

68. *Teachings of the Prophet Joseph Smith, op. cit.*, pp. 179, & 205.

69. *Juvenile Instructor* 37:562, September, 1902.

70. Joseph Fielding McConkie, *Prophets & Prophecy*, Bookcraft, Salt Lake City, Utah 1988, p. 155.

71. *Ensign*, November 1989, p. 14.

72. *Answers: Straightforward Answers to Tough Gospel Questions*, *op. cit.*, p. 87.

73. Excerpt from *Man, the Dwelling Place of God*, A.W. Tozer, WingSpread Publishers, Camp Hill, PA, 1966, pp. 125, & 126.

74. *Millennial Star* 57:339-340.

75. *Journal of Discourses*, 3:229-230.

76. John MacArthur, *The Truth War: Fighting for Certainty in an Age of Deception*, Thomas Nelson, Nashville, Tennessee, 2007, pp. 181-182; italics in original.